WHAT PEOPLE ARE SAYING
ABOUT THE BOOK

"Every single day we hear about what is happening to children. And the question is always what do we do? What do we do? Here's the answer. *Raising Safe Kids in an Unsafe World* is an easy solution to a very difficult topic."

> — Major Calvin Jackson, USAF (Ret.)
> Forensic & Child Abuse Expert, Charlotte, NC

"I have been soaking up all the information like a sponge! Finally, everything I should know in one place. My children thank you. I thank you."

> — Susan Bodulow, mother, Petaluma, CA

"Without question, parents who educate themselves and their children with the basic safety knowledge are empowered to act responsively rather than react helplessly to child abuse and abduction. The knowledge in *Raising Safe Kids* should be in every parent's hands."

> — Dr. George Jones, Lynchburg, VA

"My daughter now asks question about Tricky People and we are able to discuss the whole concept in a non-threatening way. In other words, neither one of us is scared when we have our disucsssion so she is getting information she can use and I am assured that she is learning how to stay safe."

> — Roger Wade, Sr. Deputy Sheriff, Community
> Service Office for Travis County, Austin, TX

"*Raising Safe Kids* is sensitively and carefully compiled with compassionate parental and expert input. It doesn't pander to fear, which can only exacerbate the problem of denial by children and parents. This book comes from a parent's heart through an author's pen and accomplishes its goal, which is to better equip parents in keeping their loved ones safer."

> — Melody C. Gibson, grandparent, Everett, WA

Raising Safe Kids in an Unsafe World
IS A PARENT/TEACHER HANDBOOK
FOR SURVIVING THE DANGERS
OF MODERN CHILDHOOD

IT IS THE FOUNDATION OF
THE YELLO DYNO METHOD™

RAISING SAFE KIDS

IN AN

UNSAFE WORLD

30 PROVEN WAYS

TO PROTECT YOUR CHILD FROM BECOMING LOST, ABDUCTED, ABUSED, OR VICTIMIZED

JAN WAGNER

FEATURING A NEW FORWARD BY
GAVIN DE BECKER

Raising Safe Kids in an Unsafe World

30 Proven Ways
to Protect Your Child from
Becoming Lost, Abducted, Abused, or Victimized

By Jan Wagner

Layout and Typesetting: Ryan Blum-Kryzstal
Cover Design & Art Direction: Dennis Wagner
Yello Dyno Illustrations: Barry Geller
Content Editors: Jenica Renay, Lia Austin & Jane Stewart
Researchers: Karen Jonson & Betty L. Skur

First Printing September 27, 1994
Original Library of Congress Catalog Card Number: 94-061259
New Edition (6th Printing) October 1, 2002

ISBN 0-9641842-8-1

Yello Dyno Publishing
203 Barsana Avenue
Austin, Texas 78737
Phone (512) 288-2882
info@yellodyno.com
www.yellodyno.com

Yello Dyno Publishing is a child advocacy publishing organization that specializes in personal safety education through a variety of communication methods including books, printed material, music, video, online resources, and other electronic media. Yello Dyno products are available wholesale to the trade, and at special discounts for bulk purchases for sales promotions, premiums, fund raising, or educational use. Special books, workbooks, book excerpts, songs, and other products can be created to fit specific needs. Yello Dyno also offers other child security and identification products.

Disclaimer

This book contains information obtained from authentic and highly regarded sources. A wide variety of references are listed. Great care has been taken to publish reliable data and information, but neither the author nor the publisher assumes responsibility for the validity of all materials or the consequences of their use.

To My Children
Meera and Micah

Yello Dyno with his creators, actors and future teachers at a Yello Dyno Teacher Training convention in San Antonio, TX.

SPECIAL ACKNOWLEDGEMENTS

To *Dennis*, Yello Dyno's creator, my husband and life partner, who's been through it all trying to help me save the children of the world.

To *David Ham,* our creative partner, whose 9 Clio nominations for music pale in comparison to the love and safety he has brought children in the *Can't Fool Me!* album.

To *Gavin de Becker*, whose Introduction to this book has validated my life's work.

To *Melody & Mike Gibson*, who have brought so many missing children home that only the angels know the score.

To *Seth Goldstein, Esq.*, who believed in me long before child safety was politically correct, and whose ground-breaking book is the bible to prosecute and convict "The Bad Guys."

To my *Yello Dyno Program Directors*, standing and fallen, who have fought a hard but imperative battle for many years on behalf of all children.

To *Michael De Luca*, my most special *Yello Dyno Program Director*, for his unbelievably persistent efforts in making *Yello Dyno* a reality for the children of New York. And to his lovely wife, Juliet, who has supported him all these challenging years. Thank God for you, Michael, for there are enough doctors and lawyers in the world.

To *Bruce Perry, M.D., Ph.D.*, whose stunning research on the effects of child abuse has given our society the understanding we need to protect and heal the hearts and minds of our children.

To *John Walsh*, whose "tears of rage" moved the mountain.

To *Maureen Kanka*, whose personal sacrifice provided the awareness to create Megan's Law.

To *Greg Sarnow*, who flies under the radar, and is forever our quiet ally.

And to my crew here at the U.S.S. Yello Dyno: Barbara Worden, the ultimate giver and multi-tasker, for keeping me and the submarine glued together; Mary Joyce Wyatt for making sure my passion doesn't get too far ahead of my means and who has never failed to dot an "i" or cross a "t"; Jane Stewart, our heroic helper who's willing to put out any fires (as long as it doesn't interfere with time with her grandkids!); and Rich Love who keeps my love-hate relationship with technology on the love side.

TABLE OF CONTENTS

FOREWORD

Gavin de Becker

A mong all the possible risks to our children, from the freak accident to the predictable accident, from the chemical under the sink to the chemical sold on the street corner, nothing is more frightening to us than the danger posed by people, the danger that is by design, the danger that is conscious.

The danger that is conscious may reside within the sixteen-year-old neighborhood boy who makes us uncomfortable, or the babysitter we do not trust, or our daughter's new boyfriend, or the mall security guard who stares at our daughter. Though many people act as if it's invisible, the danger that is conscious is usually in plain view, disguised perhaps, but in plain view nonetheless. Some of the behaviors that precede this kind of danger are designed to distract, confuse, or reassure us, but those behaviors are themselves signals. There is a universal code of violence, and like every parent, you already know that code.

Imagine you've just been blessed with a newborn baby girl. She is the latest model of human being, the proud result of ages of R & D that makes the most fantastic computer seem like an abacus. She has more brain cells than you and me combined, more in fact, than there are grains of sand on your favorite beach. She can learn, teach, design, build. She has within her the cleverness and dexterity to catch an ant or a whale. She can fly – literally. She can travel to another planet, and many of her contemporaries will.

Can you believe, even for a moment, that this astonishing being was designed without a defense system? Nature's investment in this child is far too great for such an oversight. Parents are the defense system designed to spot danger at the earliest possible moment, and qualified to avoid it, evade it, escape it, or destroy it. By protecting our children, we accept life's clearest responsibility.

As the years go on, whose responsibility that is becomes less clear. Does it still belong to the parents, or is it now the daycare center, or the parents of your child's friend, or the school, or the mall, or the police, or the university, or the government? And when do our children themselves take over? Is it the first time they are allowed to be alone in the house or the first time they walk to school on their own? Or is it that afternoon when they first back the car down the driveway (and over the sidewalk) into the street?

Of course, all parents worry about their children, even though one of the ironies of worry is that it can actually enhance risk. That's because as you worry about some imagined danger, you are distracted from what is actually happening. Perception and not worry is what serves safety. Perception focuses our attention; worry blurs it. And most ironically, the things we worry about are often chosen specifically because they are not likely.

Here's an example: It is easier for the worrier to wring his hands about the possible risk posed by an unknown molester who might wander into the neighborhood, than to accept the intuition that someone who was invited into the house is sexually abusing a child. Before you banish that thought, understand that nearly 90 percent of sexual abuse is committed by someone the children know, not by strangers.

Sexual abuse is far from the only abuse children might suffer. We are also challenged to protect and empower them against abduction, date-rape, emotional abuse, bullying, and outright violence. Sexual abuse is merely the most denied, for hard as it is to accept the idea that some well-liked neighbor or friend of the family might be sexually abusing a child, imagine the idea that it's someone in your own family. The denier doesn't have to consider this because it's so easy to replace that unwelcome thought with a warmer one like, "Not in this family." Yet, one in three girls and one in six boys will have sexual contact with an adult, so somebody must be responsible.

You can be certain that wherever abuse is happening, a denier is sitting in a box seat watching the performance that precedes the crime, watching a predator snake his way into a position of advantage, watching an adult persuade a child to trust him. During the beginning of sexual abuse, deniers are unconscious co-conspirators. And after sexual abuse, deniers will volunteer for the job of designing theories to explain the onset of a child's sleep disturbances or eating problems or sudden fear of that same adult she liked so much just a week ago.

If a discussion requires exploration of some hard reality, the denier will first try to wriggle away: "Talking about those things, you just bring them on yourself." Some deniers will give in and seem to acknowledge risk: "You're so right," they might say, "sexual abuse is an enormous problem, particularly for young teens. Thank God mine aren't there yet."

No, sorry, says reality, one of the most common ages at which sexual abuse begins is three.

"Well, sure, if you have homosexuals around small children, there's a risk."

No, sorry, says reality, nearly 100 percent of sexual abuse is committed by heterosexual males.

"Yeah, but that kind of pervert isn't living in our neighborhood."

Sorry, says reality, but that kind of pervert is living in your neighborhood. The U.S. Department of Justice has estimated that on average, there is one child molester per square mile.

"Well, at least the police know who these people are."

Not likely, says reality, since the average child molester victimizes between thirty and sixty children before he is ever arrested. (And anyway, when he is arrested, there's always a denier vouching for him with the familiar mantras: "But he's like such a nice man," or "You can't believe everything a child says.")

When all the defenses against reality are taken away, the denier switches to resignation (literally resigning from responsibility): "Well, there's nothing you can do about it anyway." Jan Wagner doesn't agree that there's nothing to be done about it. Her visionary work with developing and teaching *The Yello Dyno Method*™ takes issue when deniers sing the ever-popular hit-single: "How Could I Have Known?"

Deniers, more than any other people, have it in their hands to protect our children and change our nation. Why? Because the solution to sexual abuse and other victimization in America is not more laws, more guns, more police, or more prisons. The solution to child victimization is acceptance of reality.

If you are still reading by this point, and if you are giving children the gift of *Yello Dyno*, you are not a denier. Your acceptance of reality is, all by itself, the greatest asset you bring to protecting children.

Yello Dyno encourages and even enhances Nature's stunning protective resource: Intuition.

Intuition is knowing without knowing why, knowing even when you can't see the evidence. Denial is choosing not to know something even when the evidence is obvious. It's easy to see which of these two human abilities is more likely to protect children from violence.

If you do not accept that you are a creature of nature, fully endowed with powerful defenses, how can you nurture the defenses in your child? If you cannot make a safe place for yourself in the world, can you make one for your child? If you cannot conquer your own unwarranted fears, can you soothe those of your child?

The Yello Dyno Method helps answer these questions. As important, since *Yello Dyno* is entertaining, I've found that children remember the vital lessons, and that is not the case with many of the traditional approaches to teaching about safety.

Children, who could be our best source of information about abuse and abusers, are rarely empowered to spot inappropriate behavior, to tell, or to resist.

Yello Dyno has changed that for millions of children, and hopefully will for millions more.

There comes a day when the people initially responsible for a child's safety welcome a new member to the team: the child. Parents may agonize over whether he or she is ready; they may even delay the day, but the day will come. Though it's at the end of a gradual process, your son or daughter will make that walk to school, or to a friend's house, or to the market. The eyes that used to casually take in the sights will have to detect, assess, perhaps even deter danger.

To be fully capable on their own, your children will eventually need lots of information, and they can learn much it from *Yello Dyno* – without being frightened or bored.

Only parents know what their children are ready to learn and how to best inform them. I can offer a test of what children would ideally know before they are ever alone in public. (I am noting just those points relevant to violence and sexual predation, and I am leaving out obvious requirements such as knowing one's home address, important phone numbers, and other basics.)

THE TEST OF TWELVE
TO BE AS SAFE AS POSSIBLE YOUR CHILDREN WILL NEED TO KNOW...

1. How to honor their feelings – if someone makes them feel uncomfortable, that's an important signal;

2. That you (the parents) are strong enough to hear about any experience they've had, no matter how unpleasant;

3. It's okay to rebuff and defy adults;

4. It's okay to be assertive;

5. How to ask for assistance or help;

6. How to choose who to ask;

7. How to describe their peril;

8. It's okay to strike, even to injure, in self-defense if they believe they are in danger, and that you'll support an action they take as a result of feeling uncomfortable or afraid;

9. It's okay to make noise, to scream, to yell, to run;

10. If someone ever tries to force them to go somewhere, they should scream, "This is not my father" (because onlookers seeing a child scream or even struggle are likely to assume the adult is their parent);

11. If someone says "Don't yell," the thing to do is yell (and the corollary: If someone says "Don't tell," the thing to do is tell);

12. To fully resist ever going anywhere out of public view with someone they don't know, and particularly to resist going with someone who tries to persuade them.

Plenty of adults themselves, could not pass the Test of Twelve. For example, many people have never even considered that if a predator says "Don't yell," he is actually saying that yelling would serve you and silence would serve him. Too many people feel compelled to cooperate in their own victimization, in part because they assume they'll be hurt if they don't. When an intimidating criminal gives us an order, our intellect begins to analyze based on incorrect assumptions: "If I do as I'm told, he won't hurt me."

On TV shows, when the tough guy says, "Keep your mouth shut and come with me," actors do just that. But in real life, when a predator says, "Don't yell," he is telling you what cards you hold, literally informing you of the way to mess up his plans. "Don't yell" should be heard by a child as "YELL." (It's probably obvious what a fun role-playing game can be used to teach this skill. It's called "Don't Yell/Yell!")

The corollary guideline is if someone says, "Don't tell," your child should hear "TELL."

Item number 12 can take the most courage to apply. To resist fully is not easy, but if a predator orders you to go somewhere with him, he is really telling you that staying put is to your advantage and to his disadvantage. He wants to take you to a place where he'll be able to do whatever it is he can't do there. Since people often cooperate out of fear of being injured, it is essential for children to learn that initial injury is far from the worst consequence of a violent crime.

It's true that in some armed robberies, safety can be best served by simply giving over what the robber demands, but I'm not discussing robberies here. My observations focus on crimes where the predator must take his victim elsewhere.

In America, we protect children brilliantly when they are very young (we have one of the lowest infant mortality rates in the world) and then less well each year as they grow. Indeed, it takes a village to protect a child, but that's tough to accomplish when the village itself is not a safe place. While journalists are half a world away covering some buildup of troops, an unreported civil war is being waged against too many of our children right here. We have drive-by shootings instead of missles, and drug addiction instead of starvation and disease, sexual abuse instead of torture, but it's war nonetheless, with all the predictable fear, suffering, and bitterness. Quite unlike almost every other conflict in the world, however, this one is not being negotiated. America has surrendered. Big as we are, we just take the casualties as if we can afford them.

There are plenty of things we could do instead, and the book you are reading is among them. Though it's clear we cannot prevent all child abuse, what we can always do is take the best steps toward protecting our own children. You and your children then become models that teach others. Since some of the children now being mistreated will grow up angry and violent, and our kids will live in the same society with them, we cannot afford to do less.

In the most literal sense, anyone abusing any child might as well be abusing ours. Bless you, Jan for offering one of the best resources to help kids who need never become victims at all.

Gavin De Becker

PREFACE

Seth Goldstein, Esq.

There are a few, essential, classic, parenting books that every parent shoud have. Among them is *Raising Safe Kids in an Unsafe World*. It stands alone as the one parenting book addressing something you may never think you need to teach your child: SURVIVAL.

If there were ever a need to protect our children, the need is even greater today. With each passing day, media reports of missing, murdered and molested children have placed this issue on the national agenda.

Compounding the problem are the shrinking budgets and other educational mandates of public institutions that compete for the time that child assault prevention lessons take among other equally important educational objectives. Unfortunately, due to these competing priorities, schools have to make child safety education programs short, mostly one-time events in a child's life. However, moving in the right direction, the state of New York has made child abduction prevention a mandate. Other states have made anti-victimization a higher priority. Yet, there needs to be a greater alliance between the schools and the home, with parents taking a more active part in educating children about their own protection.

Proper safety education requires a well thought-out supportive framework that allows parents to educate their children in a non-threatening, pro-active fashion. The New York Police Department once published a prevention guide for children and parents that suggested that parents *enlighten*, not frighten their children about personal safety. This is important, because we need children to have the ability to act logically, rather than be paralyzed by fear in a dangerous situation. Similarly, we do not want to create or instill in children a fear of the things they don't yet understand, such as their own or another person's sexuality. Through gradual and matter-of-fact discussions and lessons between parents and children, our children will be empowered with knowledge and confidence. Research has found that when learning is fun, it sticks.

A short twenty years ago, children were given simplistic messages such as "Look out for strangers with candy" and "If someone bothers you in the movie theater tell the usher." Yesterday's lure of candy has become trips to McDonald's and lost kittens. Even the once considered sacrosanct zone at home has been violated. In fact, children are kidnapped, molested, and murdered in virtually every place they play, pray, go to school, and live. In some cases, children have even been molested right in front of their own parents without anyone realizing what was happening. Of the hundreds of child sexual abuse cases on which I have worked, one fact repeatedly comes to the surface: children need personal safety survival tools and self-esteem to prevent abduction and molestation from happening in the first place. The front line for developing these tools is the school. Educational programs can make a difference, but they need to be emphasized and reinforced in the home to be truly effective. This book helps form a partnership, building a bridge between home and school.

Parental involvement in children's safety education is even more important because children learn through repetition and reinforcement – the two things that school safety programs rarely afford. In the home, the lessons that you, as a parent, think are important and need emphasis, may be repeated and reinforced with your child. How then does a parent begin?

Through rhyme and music we have learned our lessons of the ages - "A Stitch in Time, Saves Nine," "Doe a deer, a female deer..." *The Yello Dyno Method* uses this successful concept in a musical, fun, memory-enhancing program.

When the issue of missing children first entered the national spotlight, photographs of missing children appeared on milk cartons as a means of trying to find those children. Today, the TV screen has become the prime time reminder and message machine for Amber Alerts. One morning during the milk carton era, a twelve-year-old son of a friend of mine was looking at a milk carton and asked his dad, "What does 'abducted' mean?" His father, a seasoned police veteran of twenty plus years, simply asked, "What do you think it means?" The boy said that he thought it meant that someone had taken a child. His father replied, "Yes, there are people who sometimes do bad things to children and you must be aware of it wherever you are." The boy said, Oh, and that was the end of the conversation. The father had used neither fear nor hyperbole to answer his son's impromptu question. *The Yello Dyno Method* takes this lesson to the next level. When I asked my then ten-year-old daughter what she would do if threatened by a dangerous person, she said that she would yell what her friend had told her to yell, "bloody murder". We used that opportunity to discuss with her how people would respond if she did yell that phrase and we gave her some other options.

What a shame my colleague and I didn't have Jan Wagner's parent/educator handbook, *Raising Safe Kids in an Unsafe World*. The book's simple and non-fearful guidelines to child security could have helped us take these important lessons even further with our own children. The personal safety lessons contained in *Raising Safe Kids* can be a lifesaver for your child. Jan's dream is to prevent "every parent's nightmare." To help make this dream a reality, she has spent countless hours researching, planning, and applying these child safety principles through *The Yello Dyno Method* for over 16 years. The lessons and preventative guidelines described in *Raising Safe Kids* are unique. Moreover, they directly involve parents in protecting their children from being victimized.

Parents will have less stress when their children leave their presence. They will have the confidence that, when used as directed, *Raising Safe Kids* will provide their children with the tools they need to avoid or respond to any potential threat. These lessons afford parents and educators the opportunity, through direct interaction with their children, to enlighten the spirit, body, and mind.

Seth Goldstein, Esq.
Former Police and District Attorney Investigator
Founder, Child Abuse Forensic Institute
Author, *The Sexual Exploitation of Children*
Pacific Grove, California, September 2002

INTRODUCTION
HOPE FOR THE FUTURE
Jan Wagner

Response to abduction, abuse and violence in our society is predictable: it has continued to be primarily "reactive" (let's fix it after it's broken), rather than proactive (let's make sure it doesn't happen). While this modus operandi has enormous social costs, there is a bright ray of hope for the children in your life, and that's a good place to start, isn't it?

Like the diet change after the heart attack, or the Volvo purchase after the car accident, most of us do not engage in prevention, or do so begrudgingly after the fact.

Unfortunately, however, this includes not preventing the victimization of our own children. What is it about humans that we wait to act until *after* a tragic event comes home to roost to do something? Already, most people have fallen back asleep after the summer's round of child abductions and the melt-down in the Catholic Church. It's the "Not My Child" syndrome and, except for people like you, the events have passed and the majority of parents and educators have returned to the reactive mode.

The mysteriously motivated media just chose the summer of 2002 to put child safety in lights on the marquee. But nothing has changed. Children are lost, abused, neglected, molested, bullied, raped, abducted and murdered every day. And while it's a wildly exciting world, it is increasingly dangerous for children – your children – especially if you go to sleep or abdicate responsibility to others. Fortunately, you have this book in your hands, so YOU are not sleeping – YOU are not abdicating. And that means there is hope for the children in your life, because you will soon learn that not only is the victimization of children preventable, you'll have the tools to do it. And even more amazingly, *Yello Dyno* will make it relatively simple, fun, and memorable!

When child safety experts believe 80% to 85% of all child abuse and victimization can be avoided, why do we put off preventative actions? I believe there are two main reasons – lack of hope and not knowing what to do.

Firstly, other than the outstanding efforts of Oprah Winfrey and a few other pioneers, the media in general paints a picture of little hope for protecting our children. They give tremendous air-time to sensational and tragic stories about abducted children and violent children. We are left repeatedly with a sense of helplessness as we are shown scenario after scenario of children making the wrong choices, and the people who harm children being painted as freaks whose actions follow no pattern. I believe this mass *mis*information creates a quiet desperation in those who love and teach children – leading them to believe that there is really no way to protect them. *Nothing could be farther from the truth.*

Secondly, parents and educators often do not respond to the issue because they honestly do not know what to do. Rarely are parents and educators handed useful information. For example, with last summer's heightened awareness of stranger abductions, the prevention method favored by the media was electronic devices. This saddens those of us who know the truth. Not only is the focus on recovery rather than prevention, it once again divests parents and communities of responsibility, thinking somehow, magically, this little device will bring their children home. Do they think it will help with sexual abuse? Bullies? Date rape? Violent kids? Further, don't you think "The Bad Guys" know how to deal with an electronic device? How can our society abdicate the safety of our children to an alarm or tracking device? What ever happened to teaching children about the changing world? When personal survival is the basis of the continuation of our species, whatever happened to personal safety education?

Parents and educators are left to sort through various types of advice from a variety of so-called experts. These "experts" include just about anyone who is willing to talk on the subject of prevention regardless of their experience in the field. For instance, most of what we heard with the latest round of media activity (which is mostly misdirected and hyperbolic on top of that) is adults talking to adults about the problem of raising safer kids. This includes various sensational cases, hand-wringing, and speculating about what to teach our children. But it's talking about teaching, not teaching itself. Sadly, there are very few good tools for the children themselves and most adults don't know these tools are even available.

Lots of information is offered, but little education. During last summer's publicized round of abductions, I heard one "expert" on a well-known national talk show give the "final word" on protecting your children. It went something like this: "Make sure to tell your child every week to avoid strangers."

My jaw actually dropped when I heard it. Now bear in mind this was the "final word." This "advice" was what was left in the minds of millions of parents and educators. I don't know of any diplomatic way to say it – it's about the most dangerous advice imaginable. Let's analyze the statement.

First, you can't "tell" kids anything. It's "talking heads" and left brain. They don't learn like we do (it's much more multi-sensory). Further, you can't talk to children as if they are adults. Research indicates that most children aren't fully cognitively developed with full reasoning powers until their early 20s.

Second, it's what I call "scary talk". It does not help children. It does not make them safer. Rather, it makes them more anxious about the world they live in. It does, however, move them closer to misdiagnosed Ritalin prescriptions.

Third, no parent in the world is going to tell any child anything once a week (except something like "clean up your room"). Not only could the parent not remember (or have the time for) drumming this mantra every week, but the child would become so numb from hearing it, that it would become meaningless if not downright harmful, with the child rejecting the so-called training.

Fourth, telling a child to "avoid strangers" is terrible advice. I thought this "stranger danger" thing was dead and buried years ago, but I am continually amazed at how entrenched it is in the national consciousness. It's not strangers most children have to fear. Even for the few strangers that are dangerous, it only takes minutes for "The Bad Guy" to change the child's perception of "stranger." Also, what if the child is lost and needs to go to a "stranger" for help? The list goes on.

Finally, what's with the abduction angle? Every expert knows that abduction is a small part of the problem, but the media insist on making it big. It's sensationalized because its every parent's nightmare. The misery created by child victimization in its various forms is the real problem. This includes emotional and physical abuse, sexual abuse, neglect, molestation, bullying, date rape, internet porn, internet stalking, violent kids and school violence. It is like cancer, quietly destroying our society. As former Attorney General, Janet Reno, realized in her years as a prosecutor, there is a strong link between a miserable child and a violent teen or adult. Our society is creating more and more miserable children who will, of course, generally become miserable or violent teens and/or adults. You will meet these children again and again, and when you do, you best be prepared.

What's the key to keeping the children in your life safe? Even though it misses the heart of the issue, (which we'll get to in a minute) part of the key is relevant laws. Since John Walsh first pioneered child safety legislation after the loss of his son, Adam, parents of slain and damaged children have driven successful legislation, improving both general awareness and the recovery process. However, programs to date, while a significant step forward, have been reactive in nature. Further, they don't deal with the real issue (the various forms of child victimization), but rather focus on predatorial violence. With those caveats, two of these important tools are the Amber Alert and Megan's Law.

The Amber Alert

The Amber Alert is a "recovery tool." Once a witness reports an incident to law enforcement the plan is activated. The media interrupts programming on radio and television to alert the local community to the possible kidnapping of a child. Communication between police jurisdictions is also heightened, and messages are activated on roadside digital signs (where available). This program was first initiated in Dallas/Fort Worth, Texas, after Amber Hagerman was forcibly taken off her bike and carried into a black truck. A neighbor saw her taken and alerted police. Amber was killed and the case was never solved. If the community had had access to the Amber Alert, she might still be with us today. Born from this tragedy, the Amber Alert has proven successful in many cases, so it is being adopted in almost every state. Legislation at the national level, which includes following abductions that cross state lines, is before Congress. The Amber Alert is an excellent recovery tool because it heightens the community's awareness and involves everyone in the safe recovery of a child. But it does not prevent the abduction.

Megan's Law

Megan's Law is an "awareness tool." It is named after seven-year-old Megan Kanka, a New Jersey girl who was raped and killed by a known child molester who had moved in across the street from the family without their knowledge. In the wake of the tragedy, the Kanka family sought to have local communities warned about sex offenders in the area, believing that if the local families had known the criminal background of their neighbor, Megan and Amber might be pen-pals today.

While Megan's Law is somewhat preventative, the problem is that only a small percentage of child victimization cases ever go to court. Most are plea-bargained, dismissed ("He's a fine, upstanding citizen"), or otherwise "resolved." None of the other predators at large (and by far the greater percentage) will be required to register their whereabouts. Therefore, these predators will not be on your radar. Further, even if you do know where a registered offender is living, you still have to educate your child about personal safety, teaching them to navigate safely through a challenging world, and "scary talk" won't work.

This ground swell of attention and enactment of important laws has been created by families who have paid the ultimate sacrifice. While making our children safer, these efforts to identify predators or recover abducted children are still a reflection of a reactive society. Once again, they deal only with abduction and predatorial violence, which is just the tip of the iceberg.

Additionally, these efforts do little to persuade predators to stop in the first place. However, *we* have the power to be safe and to not become victims. Gavin de Becker, a nationally recognized expert on predicting and managing violent behavior, tells us that no one is dangerous to everyone all the time. Those that are most dangerous usually slip up and make their way into the prison system. However, the others walk among us, but thankfully, they are "not dangerous to everyone all the time." Gavin would go on to teach you how not to become their victim. I would add, if you can't get rid of the predators, remove the prey. Yes, these people need to be stopped, but this will not break the cycle of violence. Putting them in prison is another reactive (and temporary) solution; necessary because of our past failure as a society, but wholly inadequate against a danger that is growing rapidly. While I am honored that this best selling author of *The Gift of Fear* and *Protecting the Gift* has written the introduction to this book, I am even more thrilled about the knowledge contained in his Forward.

Resources like Gavin are much more than writers. They are, in fact, social prophets. They are telling us that if we don't do something about it, the system will break. Another such resource is Andrew Vachss, author, children's attorney, and child advocate extraordinaire:

> "We know the root cause of our societal ills and evil –
> the trans-generational maltreatment of children. We
> know today's victim can become tomorrow's predator.
> We know that while many heroic survivors refuse to
> imitate the oppressor, the chains remain unbroken as
> abused children turn the trauma inward and lose their
> souls to self-inflicted wounds...from drug and alcohol
> abuse to depression and suicide. Their lives are never
> what they could have...<u>should</u> have been.
> — Andrew Vachss, in a Postioning Statement for
> *CIVITAS* Child Trauma Programs

So where do we go from here? *Prevention.* It will be far easier to help assure a safer childhood by being proactive than by fixing our broken children. My life's mission is to this end, and *Yello Dyno* is an important part of the solution, as well as offering hope for children and the people who love them.

Right Knowledge

While these legislative efforts and the corresponding community enactments are a step in the right direction, I believe the solution to child safety is being largely overlooked. When there are no more victims, predators will be stopped. It takes two to tangle. To remove our children from becoming potential victims there is but one solution: *right knowledge,* and there are four fundamentals to learn *involving both you and your children,* the "how to" of which will follow throughout the book. They are:

1. Recognizing Situations & Behavior: Learning to both identify and understand the situations and the behavior (generally deceptive) that makes your child vulnerable.

2. Trusting Your Instincts: Acknowledging, reawakening and/or developing powerful old friends in both of you – your feelings and instincts.

3. Building Self-Confidence: Recognizing the value of self-confidence is vital, because a child with little self-worth will not feel worth being safe. Lack of self-worth can make teaching difficult, because it is coming up against "hidden programming."

4. Acting: Teaching the Action Steps to your children will arm them with the tools they need to avoid becoming a victim. And you'll be more at ease. At the end of the day, doing something about it is the only thing that makes the difference.

You are holding the tool to do this in your hands. And it doesn't matter if the victimizer is a child molester with access to the 1st grade, a bully in the 5th, a Classroom Avenger in the 9th, or an abductor, date rapist or any other kind of predator at any age; your application of this knowledge will keep your child safer for a lifetime.

When I began working in this field sixteen years ago I focused on parents. What I have found is that about 20% of parents were very active in prevention (that's you), 30% react for a few days or weeks when there is a tragedy and then they go back to sleep, and 50% (the true abdicators) never become involved unless it comes through their child from an outside program, such as school programs or one given by law enforcement or other community service groups. Over the years I have learned that to reach all children, these programs must have a component that includes education through the schools or these other service groups. The educational system is now coming on strong because they not only realize the need to keep children safe, but also the need to recognize and deal with violent children for their own safety.

One of the states in the forefront of anti-victimization education for children is New York State. They are to be commended on their ground-breaking legislation and follow-through. While it initially focused on abduction, it has broadened over the years to include the deeper problem of child abuse in all its forms. Amazingly, New York's foresight went back to 1994 with Bill 803A. It even includes a parent education component because they recognize the importance of an educational partnership.

Yello Dyno, with our NY State Director Michael De Luca leading the charge, has worked closely with thousands of schools thoughout New York to implement various personal safety programs and curricula. New York is clearly the flagship of prevention education, and their example should be followed, just as the Amber Alert and Megan's Law have been adopted outside the school environment. A key component to New York's success is that funding was attached to the bill, not just political rhetoric. While it's possible for parents to provide child safety education at home, it works better in a partnership between parent, child and educator; whether that takes place in school, or in community venues with groups like non-profits, community service and law enforcement (some using the school's facilities for their presentations).

Even when schools come on board, we have an unfortunate situation - there is too much fear and anxiety in the learning environment.

Fear in Schools

When there is so much emphasis on improving the education of our children it is time to take note of how anxiety and fear play a role today in our schools.

> "When considering the learning experiences of the traumatized child – sitting in a classroom in a persisting state of arousal and anxiety – or dissociated...the child is essentially unavailable to process efficiently the complex cognitive information being conveyed by the teacher."
>
> – Bruce D. Perry, M.D., Ph. D., "Memories of Fear," Baylor College of Medicine, *CIVITAS* Child Trauma Programs

Perry's use of the term "arousal" means being abnormally alert – generally at some level of the "flight or fight response," even if quietly persisting in the background (like worrying about the next attack from a bully). Bullying, just one aspect of child victimization, is an example of how fear inhibits the educational process. The National School Safety Center calls it "The most enduring and underrated problem in American schools...Bullying leaves its mark on the 1 in 4 kids who say he/she is a victim." Then you have memories of Columbine and many other school shootings. We wait quietly for the next one which we all *KNOW* is coming. How much easier might the educating of students be without this underlying current of anxiety and fear? And what about children who are experiencing victimization outside the school setting? Abuse and neglect at home is one of the many challenges. And finally, fear is generated because we now live under a level 3 or 4 terror alert most of the time. At the very least, anxiety and fear damage the learning process, if not cut it off entirely in many cases. If you want to reduce the danger and fear in schools, let's look at how we spend the money.

At the same time New York was implementing its new law a few years back, I was speaking before the Connecticut Women's Legislature. As we were entering the extremely impressive state building, State Representative, Ann Dandrow, commented that it had recently been remodeled for a cost of $50,000,000. I commented that it was interesting (translation: a tragedy) that not even $1,000,000 of the remodeling costs was diverted to bring abduction and abuse prevention education to the children of Connecticut. She responded with a series of heartfelt comments reflecting her frustration on this topic. Then we discussed how it takes $1 for prevention but $9 "after-the-fact" – money spent by governments on recovery or prisons to hold these abused children. Pretty buildings but damaged kids. Talk about poor fiscal planning.

In addition to parent/child safety education in the home, the next step is for other states to follow the example set by New York and implement laws that bring anti-victimization programs into every school and community. Like New York, school and community-based solutions must also include a component for parent education and the appropriate funding. Again, personal safety education is best served by a partnership of parent, educator and child, but without community involvement and funding, the task is made more difficult.

This book is in your hands for a purpose. There are children in your life who need your help. Myself, I accidentally stepped into the arena of missing children in 1987 when I lost my young son at an amusement park. I hope you never have to go through that experience because its not the "friendly little village" anymore. While my story had a happy ending, many do not, and I woke up. We all realized how totally unprepared our entire family was for the challenges of modern times. That one simple event was enough to transform me from a reactor to a protector, which subsequently became my life's work, as well as that of my husband, Dennis. Our children, who are almost grown-up now (and with whom I'm still reviewing an occasional Safety Rule), have willingly shared their lives in this cause. The result is *Yello Dyno's Anti-Victimization Programs for Children*, which I believe is the very best there is, providing hope for the future with a genuine solution for personal safety education. The foundation of these programs is this parent/educator handbook, created to help you and your children survive the dangers of modern childhood. While *Raising Safe Kids in an Unsafe World* is as relevant today as it was when first published in 1994, this New Edition has over 110 pages of important new education, and the entire content has been updated and refocused. From our family to you, your family, your schools and communities, we share this gift of personal safety. As *Yello Dyno* says, "Safety Rules!"

Yours for a safe and beautiful childhood,

Jan Wagner, Yello Dyno Founder
Austin, TX, September, 2002

Raising
Safe Kids
in an
Unsafe World

All *Safety Rules* apply to both boys and girls.
He/she and *him/her* are used interchangeably.

PART ONE

PROTECTING CHILDREN
IN THE
21ˢᵗ CENTURY

I

THE NON-FEARFUL APPROACH

"'Telling a child that some bad people exist is very different from telling him that the world is a bad place, full of bad people' [says author Grace Heehinger]."
— "Missing Children," *American Baby*

"All parents may sometimes be reluctant to teach their young ones about strangers, concerned that the information will make the kids fearful. But remember that information empowers children. 'What terrifies a child is ignorance,' says John Walsh, founder of the Adam Walsh Child Resource Center ....'You owe it to your child to give him appropriate, intelligent information,' he asserts. And you owe it to yourself, for your own peace of mind."
— "Careful, Not Fearful,"
Sesame Street Parents' Guide

As the founder of Yello Dyno, I have found that parents feel fearful about children's personal safety. Not just fearful of losing a child, but of even discussing this topic with their children. Even when I have approached friends with safety knowledge, a few have said, "You're not going to scare my children, are you?" My response is, "They are probably already scared." Even the most protective parents and guardians can't shield their children from the information that comes at them through television and in school.

Children are egocentric. They think that the things they hear about will happen to them. During the extensive media attention on twelve-year-old Polly Klaas's abduction and murder in Petaluma, California, in late 1993, a *Time* magazine article reported that "the number-one topic among third-graders was abduction." Amidst all of the sensationalism about kidnapping and abuse, very little attention is usually paid to proactive solutions. No wonder children often feel afraid and helpless. Also, children become afraid when they sense that their parents are afraid.

Why should it be scary to teach kids how to stay safe, to say "no" if they don't like being touched in a certain way, to run or yell if they feel threatened, and to always ask for their parent's permission before going anywhere?

Taking the non-fearful approach to child safety reminds me of a story I once read in *Reader's Digest* about a little girl who asked her father about a troubling issue of our modern times. The father, who was on his way to work, told his daughter he would answer her question, but first he wanted her to carry his briefcase to his car. She agreed. But as she attempted to pick up the briefcase she found that it was too heavy. She told her father that she couldn't lift it. He knelt down and explained to her that some things in the world are like his briefcase, too heavy for her to carry right now. When she was a little older she would be able to pick up his briefcase, and when she was a little older he could answer her question, because then she'd be able to handle it. Sharing safety information with our children is similar: you tell your children only as much as they can handle for their particular age. For example, you cannot explain to a three-year-old the concept that some people use "tricks" to lure children away (instead, parents must take the responsibility to watch children who are five or younger at all times). But by the time a child is four you can start introducing many of the lessons in this book plus the concept of Tricky People and describe some of the simple lines they use. Then you can build on this knowledge as the child grows up.

As parents, it is our job to educate our children about topics that are important to their welfare. However, when we have to share knowledge about scary issues we do not have to make the information itself fearful. My concept of safety education does not involve telling our children that there is a man on every street corner waiting to steal them. Just as we do not describe the consequences of being hit by a car when we tell children to look both ways before crossing the street, we do not have to scare them about personal safety. I prefer presenting safety education in a non-fearful, empowering format.

I've seen first-hand the benefit of safety education with my own children. One night my son and daughter and a couple of their friends (ages eight to fourteen) were together. I asked them to watch two videos. First, I showed them an evening news report on the abduction and subsequent murder of a child. Their feelings of fear and helplessness filled the room. Could this happen to them? They all felt that yes, it could.

I put in the second video. It was an educational program that described how children can protect themselves from ever being abducted. While we watched the program, each child's expression changed from fear to confidence. We discussed the information and how they personally would respond in a variety of situations. As I praised their correct answers and guided them to a clearer understanding of what they can do to stay safe, I could literally feel them becoming stronger and more confident. This was such a dramatic example of the power of non-fearful education for me. There are no two ways about it, knowledge empowers children. If we give children the right knowledge and training, they will generally be able to pull themselves out of a crisis. In fact, experts tell us that with the right knowledge, 85 percent of the dangerous situations children might face can be avoided.

The *30 Proven Ways* presented in this book are valuable tools for parents. There is also another educational tool that charms children and makes it possible for them to understand difficult concepts. It is music. The Yello Dyno Program has been offering safety education through music for many years. The songs on our *Can't Fool Me!* Album (CD or cassette) are powerful, fun, non-threatening, and easy for children to remember. Parents are always surprised when they find that their children want to play and sing the safety songs over and over again. Countless parents have expressed their joy – and relief – with the music's success. Without question, music gives parents an invaluable aid in this challenging area of parenting. Teaching through music is therefore one of the cornerstones of "the non-fearful approach."

The success of non-fearful safety education will be realized when your children feel strong and confident as they grow up safer in our increasingly challenging world. How wonderful for parents to have this peace of mind!

2

GETTING THROUGH THE DENIAL RESPONSE

"The country's in denial. Kidnapping by strangers is a terrifying thing."

> — David Collins (of the Kevin Collins Foundation, whose son Kevin was kidnapped in 1984), "Father Dedicates His Life to Searching for Missing Kids," Prime News, *CNN*

"To bury your head in the sand and say my child could not be victimized, in light of all the things that have happened in this country and what continues to happen, is doing your child a disservice. It's tough stuff. But you've got to remember your child is the potential victim. You won't be the victim."

> — John Walsh, "How To Raise a Street Smart Kid," *HBO*

Denial surrounding the topic of child abduction and abuse is rampant. It takes many forms. For example, some people like to remind us that "*only*" one to three hundred children a year are taken by strangers. Then there are the adults who see children hanging around the house of a man down the street day after day, but ignore their gut feeling that something isn't right.

Admittedly, it is easy to understand why parents want to believe that if they don't think about it, it will go away and never happen to them. And why so many others hope, wish, and pray that this will never happen to their children. Sometimes I too turn away from the facts and say, "This is just too much for me to think about right now." But how can a parent honestly ignore this topic? How can we deny that it exists when the facts tell us that it is all too real?

While offering child security education over the years, I have sometimes had to resort to the frightening facts to get parents' attention. I am not trying to scare anyone. I am trying to awaken them. If the facts are the only thing that will wake parents up, then I will call on the facts every time. Here are some common forms of parental denial, along with "real-world" perspectives.

Parent's Denial Response:

"My children are too young."

Fact: "Child molesters never think that your kids are too young." (Major Calvin Jackson, USAF, Ret., Forensic Expert and former child abuse investigator.)

Parent's Denial Response:

"It won't happen in my small town."

Fact: Listen to the words of one convicted child molester: "I went through her window. My plan was just to do it while they were asleep and they'd never know about it. I committed the perfect crimes...Sure you like to think of small towns as being safe. Small towns [are] easy." (Now, NBC)

Parent's Denial Response:

"It only occurs in the inner city."

Fact: "One of the important things about this case is that we are an ordinary middle-class family, not rich, not poor. We weren't living in the 'wrong part of town.' My husband and I both have good professions, and we were two immigrants who made good. We always put our kids first. We taught Allison to be careful, and she was a child who obeyed the rules. If this can happen to us, it can happen to anybody." (Mother of an eleven-year-old girl abducted and murdered by a man who wanted to "photograph" her. (Paulette Cooper and Paul Noble, *Reward*)

Clearly, burying your head in the sand will not change the reality. Unfortunately, it often takes highly publicized abductions to break through many parents' denial. For example, I saw so many parents and children who were frightened by Polly Klaas's abduction and subsequent murder in late 1993. That abduction occurred in a small town and Polly was taken out of her own home, from her own bedroom, with her mother asleep just down the hall. Once again in the summer of 2002 the media has focused on the abduction and murder of our children. Case after case parades before us on our TV screens. In Salt Lake City, fourteen year old Elizabeth Smart was taken from her bedroom at gunpoint in front of her nine year old sister. Five year old Samantha Runnion was dragged, kicking and screaming, from the driveway of her apartment building where she was playing the board game Clue with a friend. Although the number of abducted and murdered children has decreased from nearly 300 a year in the 1980s to around 100 cases in 2002, the invasion of places that we consider "safe" for our children has brought our attention back to the fact that victimization of our children is not acceptable and solutions must be found. These tragic events are among the handful in our history that truly awaken parents to the possibility that this could happen to their children. During such times parents reach out for help and take the time to learn more on how to protect their children. Due to media coverage they are often misdirected into thinking their primary focus should be protecting their child from stranger abduction. In truth, at least 90% of the victimization of children, whatever form it might take, is not by a stranger but by someone the child knows and most likely trusts. These tragic and heartbreaking stories need to awaken all of us to the reality that we must take a proactive approach, instead of a reactive one, to keeping our children safe. If abduction or molestation occurs, it is a violation of a child's life that can never be fully repaired. I would rather that parents and children get a little scared and deal with this issue, than risk letting another child get hurt deeply for the rest of his or her life.

I believe that when parents grasp the true need for safety education they will not avoid the responsibility. Parents often deny tough subjects because they feel, deep down, that they can't do anything to change the problem and hope it will never enter their front door. Denial is a form of fear, and fear is removed by knowledge.

This book will give you the knowledge as well as the specific Action Steps you need to release yourself from fear and be proactive about your children's safety — more easily and effectively than you can imagine. This is one of the few areas of parenting where you can accomplish so much with the correct knowledge. With only a little time, you can make an important difference in your child's life.

3
PARENTS'
RESPONSIBILITY

"...parents have the primary responsibility for keeping their children safe."

> – "Missing Children:
> The Ultimate Nightmare," *Parents*

"You need to understand that you can reduce the odds. You can empower your children to stay safe. You can't make them absolutely safe, but you can make them safer."

> – Rosie Gordon's father (ten-year-old Rosie was
> abducted and murdered), "How to be Safe in
> America," Prime Time Live, *ABC News*

Just as parents take the responsibility to teach their children about good hygiene, proper nutrition, and correct moral behavior, they must take the responsibility to teach children about how to keep themselves safe. Why is it parents' responsibility to educate their children about personal safety? One main reason: nobody else knows or loves your children as you do.

However, parents do have an ally – their child's school. Together they should make the commitment to safeguard and educate their children in personal safety. Lessons taught in school should have parent components so parents know what and how to reinforce the knowledge. As a parent you have the opportunity to make sure your child has truly learned all of the important safety rules. What if he or she were sick one day and missed an important lesson? Or, in a class of twenty children, is there time to ask every child his response to a practical scenario and then wait to see if some other thoughts bubble up? Encourage your school to not limit this vital knowledge to a one or two day class event over the year, but to make personal safety education an ongoing integral part of education in the 21st century.

Still, parents must be the primary source for educating their children about personal safety and reinforcing that knowledge. Because parents know their children better than anyone else, they are the only ones who can ensure that their children truly comprehend what they have learned. Moreover, the most natural environment for reinforcing children's knowledge as they grow is in the parent-child relationship.

The advantages of parents educating their children about personal safety include the following:

Review and repeat.

If a dangerous situation occurs, children must react spontaneously, as there is little time to review options. To do this there must be a "well grooved" pattern of action. Repetition is important with children because they have short memories. When you work with them, you have the opportunity to regularly review the information you teach them and the information they may have learned in school. You can test them through role-playing and what-if games to make sure they fully understand how to keep themselves safe. Also, when you instruct them, your children receive the added value of one-on-one learning. This can help strengthen your parent-child bond.

Make the information age-appropriate.

Children require different safety rules and different levels of information depending on their age. As a parent you have the unique advantage of being able to update their safety knowledge as they mature. For example, as previously mentioned, you cannot expect a three-year-old to understand the concept of strangers, so you must make sure that they know not to run away from you in a public place. By age four, they can begin to recognize behavior that means danger and start to participate in their own personal safety.

Tailor the information.

You can tailor the information to match your child's unique personality, and to fit your child's natural strengths and weaknesses. For example, some children are outgoing and will not flinch when you tell them to say "no" to an adult if they feel unsafe or tricked. Another child may be shy and, therefore, need more encouragement to assert himself around adults. A third child will be very compassionate and friendly and have a more difficult time not talking to people she does not know. A fourth child might be curious and, therefore, easily drawn in by the influence of others.

Create an emergency plan with your family members.

Together, you and your children can create a plan for your family, before an emergency arises, which includes the rules that your family members will follow to stay safe. For example, you can decide together who can pick up your children from school in case of a family emergency, where exactly your children would run to if they were scared while walking home, and what to say to a caller when you are not at home. Parents can only adequately fulfill their responsibility to educate their children about safety when they themselves are educated. The *30 Action Steps,* (that correspond to the *30 Proven Ways*) will provide parents with the knowledge they need to bring safety education into the regular day-to-day routine of raising their children.

4
WHO ARE
"THE BAD GUYS"?

"They called him the Big Brother."

"I trusted him."

"His friends say he loved children. Police say he hunted them."

> — Child Hunter, "Comments about a Convicted Child Killer," 48 Hours, *CBS*

"I don't know why, I just have to do this every so often. It helps to relieve the tension."

> — Comment by a man after he killed a young girl, America's Most Wanted, *FOX*

"There is no (psychological) profile to help parents identify a molester."

> —Ian Russ, Ph.D., The Home Show, *ABC*

With dismay in their voices, parents often ask, "Who would do this type of thing to children?" If only there were an easy answer. Unfortunately, there is not. In this section, I have tried to give parents useful information without dwelling on the deeply disturbing nature of the "The Bad Guys." My hope is that more child abductors and molesters will be recognized and stopped sooner with the help of this information.

The problem of who are "The Bad Guys" starts with one fundamental fact: it is hard to pick them out from the people who live and work within our everyday lives. According to author and child abuse investigator Seth Goldstein, Esq., in *The Sexual Molestation of Children*, "Not all child molesters are the same. Not all molesters are pedophiles. Not all child molesters are passive, non-aggressive people. Child molesters come in all shapes, sizes, races, sexes, and ages and are motivated by a wide variety of influences. There is no single investigative or interview technique to deal with all of them." One psychologist, who worked with convicted child molesters, says that among the group in one child sexual abuse therapy session were a doctor, a teacher, a lawyer, and only one person whom anyone could describe as a stereotypical "dirty old man."

One of the reasons that we cannot easily pick child molesters out is that they work hard at being viewed as "normal" so that their behavior will not be suspected. To let you know how deceptive some of these people are, here are a few of the descriptions of convicted child abductors and molesters from people who knew them:

"He was a good boy, he liked to help people. He went to preachers' school, he was a gentleman, intelligent, quiet, a good Samaritan."

"He was a good kid, a favorite with children. He was president of the local Kiwanis Club."

"He bought the kids bicycles and toys, and he was so helpful."

Who would guess that these types of people abduct, molest, and even kill children? No one, and that's the problem. But while we cannot identify them, molesters, in general, share some similar characteristics.

- They often lack social competence with adults.
- They usually seek legitimate access to children through jobs and volunteer work.

- They spend unusual amounts of time with children.
- They often, though not in every case, were abused children. Because they are hurt from abuse and didn't receive treatment, they rarely acknowledge the hurt they inflict on children.
- They seem to have two sides to their personalities. They are, in effect, modern-day Dr. Jekylls and Mr. Hydes.
- Normally they are not correctable; studies have shown that people who are attracted to children cannot be changed. It is important to remember that if you know someone who was convicted of child molestation, you should not be lulled into thinking he won't do it again.

Here are a few statistics that I find shocking. (This information was compiled by Kenneth V. Lanning, former Supervisory Special Agent with the F.B.I.'s Behavioral Science Unit.) In a study of 561 sex offenders, Dr. Gene Abel, in Atlanta, Ga, substantiated what seems almost unbelievable. He found pedophiles who targeted young boys outside the home committed the greatest number of crimes: an average of 282 acts, with an average of 150 partners. Molesters who targeted girls within the family committed an average of 81 acts with an average of 2 partners. He also found that 23 percent of the 561 subjects, offended against both family and non-family targets. The typical offender is male, begins molesting by age 15, engages in a variety of deviant behavior, and molests an average of 117 youngsters, most of whom do not report the offense.

Hard to believe, isn't it? Clearly, this is not a small problem. We need to know who they are. The U.S. Department of Justice estimates that there are 4 million offenders in the U.S. Like rape, child molestation is one of the most underreported crimes: only 1-10% are ever disclosed, states the FBI. What we don't want to believe is that these people live and work in our communities. But they do.

Where do molesters come from? When we look around us, the signs are there. One is the breakdown of the family unit. Our society has created an environment where children can be raised into dangerous adults. The security and strength of a strong family unit that provides the loving environment for raising children is non-existent for many children. We live in a mobile society. Family members are rarely found in the same town, let alone the same state. Mothers have joined the work force in increasing numbers. This has been brought about by the economic pressures requiring two parents to work to meet basic living needs. Now, over 60 percent of mothers work due to necessity and another 20 percent choose to work. This places additional strain on the collapsing family unit.

There is another growing dilemma: single parenting. Over 50 percent of households are run by single parents, who can't be everywhere at once. How can one person realistically attend to all the needs of a child that were once handled by grandparents, aunts, uncles, husbands, wives, cousins, and siblings? It is simply impossible. When you take a hard look at our society, is it really any surprise that our children are so vulnerable to the friendship offered by a child molester or other predators who look for children hungry for attention and acceptance? The disintegration and problems of the family are recounted over and over again in our media. Here are just a few quotes:

> "In her years as a prosecutor, Attorney General Janet Reno saw first hand the link between a miserable child and a vicious adult."
>
> — "Trust, Justice and the Reno Way", *Time*

"The current system has already pulled the family apart...Nothing could be more harmful than that."

> — Robert Rector, a senior policy
> analyst with the Heritage Foundation,
> "The Vicious Cycle," *Time*

"I firmly believe that the biggest danger to us is the disintegration of the American family."

> — President George Bush
> "The Grandfather in Chief," *Time*

If you want to build a building, the foundation is critical. If it is weak, the whole building will suffer. If it is too weak, it will collapse. We ask, "Who are these people who become predators?" They are the ones who could not survive a weak foundation and they have "collapsed." These people were once children. Many were victims. Now many of our children will become their victims. Research shows that child abductors and molesters themselves were often molested as children. In their attempt to fulfill their distorted needs, they as adults, draw in children — just as they were drawn in. We must realize that there are hundreds of thousands of abused children who might grow up and continue this cycle. Among the many studies conducted on the sexual abuse of children, it has been found that, depending on the focus of the research, 10 to 40 percent of all children today will encounter some form of molestation before they are eighteen years old. (These statistics do not include the activities of children who are naturally curious about their bodies.) This problem is not limited to the inner cities, to one economic class, or to one race. There are, in fact, no limitations on where and when child abuse can occur. This problem has existed for generations and, so far, has been handled poorly. It can no longer be swept under the carpet.

Another important fact is that many abductors and most molesters are actually seeking love and affection, but in a distorted way. Because garnering love from children requires an indirect approach, abusers have developed "patterns" for entangling children. One of these approaches is to "stalk" a child over a few hours, days, or months. Molesters may even take as long as a year to build a relationship with a child before they actually begin the sexual abuse. They even have a name for this approach — they call it "grooming" the child. Clearly, the abuser is often far from being a stranger to the child by the time the actual abuse takes place. Here are the chilling words of one child molester from the HBO video, *How to Raise a Street Smart Kid*.

> "It's this sixth sense most molesters have, they know [when] the child won't put up much resistance. I gave [kids] this feeling. I gave them the feeling of affection, of belonging, of being wanted. And it was like spinning a spider web and before you know it, they're caught...Most of my victims were easy targets. If you're really into it, and you want to pick up kids off the streets, you pick one that's always alone. You can tell by the look on their faces. That sad puppy-dog-eyed look...I'll do this for you, I'll take you somewhere if you do something for me. Most cases they trusted me; 80 percent of the time my victims would do whatever I asked them to do."

In extensive research conducted by former Supervisory Special Agent Kenneth V. Lanning of the F.B.I.'s Behavioral Science Unit, child abductors have been shown to fall into five general categories and child molesters into two general categories.

Child Abductors

1. Non-traditional. These abductors include women who kidnap babies from hospitals. Most often they steal the babies to fill an emotional need, to preserve a relationship with a man, or fulfill a need to mother if they cannot have children.

2. Profiteers. These abductors steal children because they know the child has a monetary value, usually in an underground network.

3. Kidnappers. These abductors take the child to sell back to his parents for ransom.

4. Sexual offenders. These abductors take a child to have sex. Once they accomplish their goal, they either keep, return (the majority), discard, or kill the child.

5. Child killers. These abductors take children with the primary motivation of killing them. They may also have sex with them, but not necessarily.

In addition, there is the miscellaneous criminal. This catch-all category includes all other forms of child abduction, for example, if someone takes a child as a hostage.

Child Molesters

1. Situational. Situational abusers are not specifically attracted to children, but take advantage of an opportunity to have sex with a child due to a personality regression, a lack of morals, a desire to "try anything," or mental deficiencies.

2. Preferential (pedophile). Pedophiles interact with children primarily for sexual gratification; in fact, many are addicted to children. Pedophilia is a way of life for this group. Some groups even have newsletters to communicate with each other, including "tips of the month" for seducing children. They spend much of their time trying to convince themselves that they are giving love to and receiving love from children. They usually seduce children with attention, affection, and gifts.

Because those who prey on children have the habit of picking up and moving when adults become suspicious (or after they have plea-bargained down an abuse charge), it is important to have a background check on all people you do not know who will have access to (or be working with) your child or the children in your community. I recommend a federal background check rather than one at the state level because these Tricky People move from state to state, leaving their records, if any, behind. It is relatively easy and inexpensive to run a background check. The people whose background you should check include all school employees, coaches, church youth leaders and volunteers...literally anyone involved in group activities for children.

Much of this review process of the people in your child's life just comes down to being alert, to really seeing and understanding what is already in front of you. Oprah Winfrey's television show on recognizing child molesters offered the following valuable tips on what to look for:

- When your child attends youth groups, camps, sports leagues and the like, watch for adults whose behavior is unusual, and don't forget to ask your child and their friends what they think of the person.
- Adults who seem preoccupied with children.
- Adults who spend time volunteering with youth groups who do not have their own children in those groups.
- Adults who work with children and frequently spend their free time doing "special" things with kids.
- Adults who act like children with children or who allow children to do questionable or inappropriate things.
- Adults who seem to know too much about the current fads or music popular with children.
- Adults who seem able to infiltrate family and social functions.

Speaking of adults who are able to easily "infiltrate" our lives, there is one key quality that is almost always operating, either overtly or covertly. That quality is called *charm*. In fact, *charm* is such a prevalent factor in all aspects of personal safety at all ages, that the Bad Guy throughout *Yello Dyno's* videos, *Tricky People!* and *Can't Fool Me!* is Reginald Charming III, a charming twenties-something record producer for kid's bands. While it's rather like a David Copperfield name (Scrooge, et al), it's right on target, being designed to alert children on how to recognize dangerous behavior. It bears repeating: charm in its various forms is constantly used to victimize children (and adults, for that matter).

In his bestselling book, *The Gift of Fear,* Gavin de Becker provides this profound insight and instruction about charm and niceness:

> "Charm is another overrated ability. Note that I called it an ability, not an inherent feature of one's personality. Charm is almost always a directed instrument which, like rapport building, has motive. To charm is to compel, to control by allure or attraction. Think of charm as a verb, not a trait. If you consciously tell yourself, 'This person is trying to charm me,' as opposed to, 'This person is charm-ing,' you'll be able to see around it. Most often, when you see what's behind charm, it won't be sinsiter, but other times you'll be glad you looked... 'He was so nice' is a comment I often hear from people describing the man who, moments or months after his niceness, attacked them. We must learn and then teach our children that niceness does not equal goodness. Niceness is a decision, a strategy of social interaction; it is not a character trait. People seeking to control others almost always present the image of a nice person in the beginning. Like rapport building, charm, and the deceptive smile, unsolicited niceness often has a discoverable motive."

On that note, you can certainly see that *charm* moves quietly through much inappropriate behavior. Just think how you've been conned (charmed) in your own life, then imagine how easy it is to *charm* children. So, to help you recognize some of the signs of inappropriate behavior, I have created *8 Red Flags for Identifying Child Molesters*. But first here's Kathleen's story, a true story of how one mother used these "red flags" to help her see the obvious, a Mr. Charming in her own child's life. Take heart, the story has a happy ending.

"The Yello Dyno Program saved my son's life. When I first received my Yello Dyno package, I was too busy to read it, so I put it aside. Some weeks later, I had a feeling of urgency telling me to read the material. I sat down with my highlighter pen and began to read, thinking that I would be teaching this to other people who needed it. As I read the 8 Warning Signs of an inappropriate relationship, a man's face appeared in my mind. This face belonged to a very dear friend of 13 years and a member of my own church! Oh, No, No, No! The feelings were overwhelming as I rushed upstairs and asked my son, who was six at the time, if this person had ever done anything to hurt him or that he didn't like. His face crumbled and he couldn't tell me fast enough about being touched and tickled inappropriately and being spanked with a belt to keep quiet. My heart was broken. I was so shocked and hurt, I couldn't breathe. I felt guilt for not being able to protect my son and could not comprehend how a friend could hurt him so, someone I had trusted. I called the pastor of our church and the authorities immediately. Without Yello Dyno, I would not have caught this situation until it was too late, if at all. As it is, my son is not permanently harmed and others will be protected from this person. When people tell me that they don't need Yello Dyno because they watch their kids closely, I can share this story and maybe save more childhoods. I hope this story can help someone else." (To protect the family's privacy, full names are withheld.)

While it is difficult to make a list of definitive identifiers of a child molester because they conceal their behavior very well, here are some helpful guidelines.

It is *very important* to understand that one red flag is generally not enough to identify a potential problem. However, if you find that two or more red flags apply, you may have a situation that you need to look into. The idea here is to identify inappropriate behavior and remove the prey (your child)

8 RED FLAGS FOR IDENTIFYING CHILD MOLESTERS

1. An adult enjoys being with your child more than you do.

2. A much older child or adult spends excessive amounts of time with your child.

3. Your child has new toys or gifts that you did not purchase.

4. Your child speaks knowledgeably of places and/or activities that you did not introduce to him or her.

5. A person continually offers to care for your child so as to give you a breather or time to yourself. (Often he does not want any payment for watching your child.)

6. A person comes to your house regularly to spend time with or transport your child to activities.

7. A person engages in activities that involve only your child and him that do not require others to be present.

8. A person is preoccupied with and/or often stares at your child.

from a possible predator. You should not attack the predator. Be very, very careful. This knowledge is not a "call to arms," but rather a means of recognizing and avoiding problems. Be extremely careful not to make accusations. Get help from law enforcement, social services, or professionals trained to deal with these problems. If you suspect something, you shouldn't be afraid to report it. If you do not report it, or try to do something on your own, you can, at the very least, hurt the case.

Reading through all of this appalling information on the people who hurt children, we must keep a healthy, balanced perspective. We have to remember that the majority of the people in the world do not abuse children. It will not do us or our children any good to distort the natural – and healthy – affectionate interactions between children and adults. However, it's an increasingly weird world and we need to be vigilant. We simply need the knowledge and the awareness to spot truly inappropriate behavior. Parents and children must understand this or the natural, loving, appropriate interactions of family members and friends with our children may be unnecessarily harmed. Loving physical interaction is crucial for children. After all, who couldn't use a big hug!

5

STRANGER DANGER: MYTH AND REALITY

"It isn't strangers [we have to fear], it's us. If you keep drilling 'beware of strangers,' you're missing 90 percent of what happens to kids. Ninety percent of what happens is done by non-strangers – parents, stepparents, extended family, neighbors, friends ....people the kids know."

— "Missing Children," Charles Sutherland, publisher of The Missing Persons Report, Search, Inc., *American Baby*

"Many unanswered questions still bother Mrs. Przybylak [Mandy's mother]. 'Was Mandy taken from our house or did she go into someone's truck earlier? I believe she wouldn't have gone with a stranger. If somebody tried to make Mandy do what she didn't want, she would scream or run like hell. So she probably knew the person she went off with,' she speculates."

— Paulette Cooper and Paul Noble, "Mysteries for a Mother," *Reward*

I am thankful that the majority of adults who work with children are good, caring professionals. Over the years I have met and talked to many people who have gained my respect because of their dedication to helping children. These caring adults have dedicated their lives to protecting, recovering, and helping to heal children who were not able to protect themselves. One of these people is a psychologist who specializes in child abuse at the National Institute of Mental Health in Maryland. Jim Breiling's years of work in this area have given him clear insight into the matter of child sexual abuse. When we asked him what information would be the most valuable to parents who want to keep their children safe, his answer was, "Tell parents to check out their friends and family members first." This may not be what we all would like to hear.

Of course, through the media we always hear about and fear most the dramatic cases of *stranger* abduction and molestation. To protect their children, parents buy personal alarms, enroll their children in self-defense courses, and set up teams of parents to walk children home from school. But the fact remains: the circle of adults and caregivers around a child is the first ring that needs to be secure. The statistics vary from 70 to 90 percent, but every source says the same thing — children are sexually abused by people known to the child's family. Often it is a family member or close family friend. Sometimes it is someone the child or family sees in the regular course of their lives such as a worker at school, a checkout clerk at the neighborhood grocery store, or a person who lives down the street. That is why, despite media reports that often focus on stranger danger, parents need to know that strangers are not the most probable source of harm to their children.

Regarding sexual abuse within families, Major Calvin Jackson (USAF, Ret.), who is a leading forensic expert and former child abuse investigator in the U.S. military, found that abuse is woven throughout the entire structure of a family. The abuse often has deep roots, and to try and cut those roots often means breaking apart the family — an option often too difficult for the family members to face. So families may have great difficulty dealing with the abuse at all. In many of the child sexual abuse cases Major Jackson investigated, the child would talk in confidence to a close friend, then that friend would tell his parents, and those parents would contact officials. If the case reached the courts, a key witness in the family often backed out before the trial date, usually to avoid further conflict within the family. Once that happened, Major Jackson's hands were tied. Tragically, he had no avenue for helping the harmed child.

Convicted abusers are perhaps our best source of advice on this issue. They say that parents are too quick to trust people with their children. One man said, "The parents let me baby-sit their children after knowing me for only one week. They felt that I was safe because I worked with children in my profession."

To understand how abusers' minds work, let's take a simple example. If you really want to learn how to play golf, you spend time at the golf course. You put yourself in situations that will help you to get what you want. Child abductors and molesters do just that. In fact, studies show that child molesters will choose jobs or volunteer activities that put them in direct contact with children, becoming teachers, coaches, and troop leaders. Also, is it not uncommon for child molesters who were discovered abusing children in one state to simply move to another state, get another job working with children, and start all over again. An example of this occurred in Plano, Texas. During the investigation of a young girl's abduction at a soccer field, officials conducted background checks on the town's soccer coaches and found that the head of the soccer league was a convicted child molester from another state, although he did not turn out to be involved in the case in question. Further investigation showed that he had been forced to move from his previous home town because of incidents of abuse that occurred there. The man who did abduct and kill the seven-year-old was a convicted child molester out on parole.

In one case of child abuse, the parents immediately befriended their son's new scout leader, and invited him to dinner. The mother of the abused child says, "He brought four children with him who I thought were his. Later I found out that he was abusing them, as well...[Molesters] want you to feel secure with them. They draw you in."

One point to consider: if a person likes to be with your child more than you do there may be something wrong. Who loves your child more than you? Here are a few points parents and teachers can use as guidelines to observe adult's behavior around their children:

- Find out why an adult wants to spend unsupervised time with your child.

- Find out what attraction there is for your child to spend a lot of time at an adult's home.

- Be watchful of adults who shower your child with gifts or invite him or her on outings.

- Watch out for adults who use games that are really lures and tricks that will become a means to entrap a child into a physical relationship. An adult may use a few simple toys or games, or he might go to the extreme and turn his home into a virtual playland for children.

- No one does something for nothing; if they look too good to be true, they just might be.

- Ask for several references, including job and volunteer work, from adults in positions of authority, such as troop leaders, and follow up with phone calls to the references. When talking to the references be sure to ask how long they have known the person who will be spending time with your child. If the adult is new to your town, find out why he or she left their previous home. Don't take the person's word for it; do the best you can to talk to a variety of references.

- Make sure your children know that they need to tell you if any adult touches them in any way that doesn't feel right to them.

When the myth of "Stranger Danger" is realized, parents will be able to offer their children a safer and more secure environment in which to grow up.

6

EDUCATION IS THE FIRST SAFETY RULE

"Education is a child's best self-defense because 75 percent of self-defense is mental. Only 20 percent is physical and 5 percent is luck. Therefore, there is absolutely no excuse for any child to be without the right personal safety and security knowledge."

> — Sensei David Ham, Matial Arts Instructor,
> *Member of Aikikai Foundation*, Tokyo, Japan

"The best defense against abduction and the general fear surrounding the subject is education. If we can give children accurate guidelines appropriate to their ages and teach them to be on the lookout for certain kinds of individuals and situations, we can help them to become careful and confident, rather than overly cautious and fearful, as they grow up in a world that is less than perfect."

> — "Every Mother's Fear: Abduction,"
> *Family Circle*

"The real lesson to be learned from cases like Cassidy Senter's and Polly Klaas's, advocates say, is how valuable awareness and education can be. No neighborhood watch or electronic device can replace solid safety rules and emergency strategies for children."

— "Awareness, Education Help Fight Abduction,"
Austin American-Statesman

Safety education is an ongoing part of parenting. The sooner the process begins, the easier it is to keep the dialogue open as your children grow. My own children certainly receive ongoing information about keeping themselves safe, so I've seen firsthand the value it has brought to their lives. While educating your children about personal safety, don't try to cover everything in one "learning" session or even in a few nights. Instead, using small, easy steps, make it a part of their whole lives. Modify and expand on safety concepts according to their age — so that your children, in effect, grow up with safety.

Role-playing, teaching by example, and music are among the important steps in educating your children to stay safe. Here is how they can help.

Role-Playing

Children have an easier time learning safety concepts through things that they say or do, as compared to what they see and hear. That is why "what-if" games and role-playing are such valuable teaching methods. Because these games are interactive, they instill the safety skills into children's bodies and minds. Also, through role-playing, parents can find children's weak spots and work on them, and they can regularly reinforce the safety rules with their children. Remember, it is much better to play out a potentially scary situation with a child ahead of time than to have them experience one without being prepared.

In "what-if" games, children's fears often bubble to the surface, so they must be in an environment where they can safely express their feelings or fears. Your own parent-child relationship is the most important, supportive, and secure place for these games to occur. It provides a loving environment for sensitive and critical learning. In a classroom, children may feel that they have to look good in front of classmates and so they cannot be entirely honest about what they are feeling and may not ask the questions they need answered.

When appropriate, the *Action Steps* in this book include role-playing suggestions. To play these educational games, you ask your children a variety of questions about hypothetical situations to see how they would react and what actions they would take. As you wait for their answers, don't be tempted to answer for them. It doesn't matter if children give the wrong answers; it's much safer if they make mistakes with you than in the real world. Praise them when they are right. When they are wrong, gently guide them to the correct answer.

Because of the wonderful imaginations of children, "what-if" games can even be fun. A story with my own son when he was eight years old reflects this. One day while he helped me with the dishes, I asked him, "What if a man approached you and had a weapon?"

"I'd take a baseball bat and hit him," he said as he whipped the dish towel through the air.

"But there's no baseball bat around."

"Then I'd punch him in the gut," he said as he did a karate kick in the middle of the kitchen.

"But he's bigger than you. Why not just run away?"

"Because it's more fun to fight," he said, with a bold stance.

I explained that, while it may look fun when kids beat up adults in the movies, in reality big people are much stronger than children, so it would be best to run away.

A thoughtful expression crept over his face and he stopped jumping around. Looking up at me with a furrow across his brow, he said, "But an adult can run faster than me."

That's a natural concern for a child. So I explained that people who kidnap children prefer children to go with them without a struggle, and that when a child yells and starts running away, the person will generally leave them alone so as not to draw attention to themselves. My son found this very reassuring. He gave me a big hug and went dashing out the door to get in some last-minute basketball before nightfall. Whew! Another lesson slipped into the midst of a busy schedule. Just one of these lessons a night, and reviewed as they grow older, can be the foundation for your family safety program. Time has passed and now my son is in high school and my daughter is going off to college. I am still reviewing several of these fundamental safety lessons with them. They are truly lessons that can apply for a lifetime.

Remember that when playing "what-if" games, it's important not to stop too soon. If your child gives the right answers you may relax and think he understands. But this story from the *Sesame Street Parents' Guide* shows that what your child understands may not be enough:

"A mother asked her child, 'If somebody came up to you and said that he'd lost his puppy, would you go and help him find the puppy?' The child said, 'No.' Then the mother asked, 'What if he lost his kitten? Would you help him find the kitten?' The child said, 'Yes,' and the mother asked, 'Why would you do that?' The child replied, 'Because kittens need more help than puppies do.'"

Another story, from another mother, Trish Charron-Holt, also illustrates the value of not settling for the first answer your child gives. By pushing a little, you may reveal a clearer view of your child's actual perceptions of safety.

"A while ago I saw a TV program about the lures people use to abduct children. I got a transcript of the show and when it arrived my daughter flipped through it. I decided to discuss it with her and we did a role-play using the 'photographer at the mall' lure. I asked her what she would do if someone approached her and said that she could be a model and offered to take her picture. Right away, she said she wouldn't go, that she would know better. But I kept pressing for her reactions to different approaches. I said, but what if the person told you that he was giving out $100 bills to each person who agreed to be screen-tested and you would get paid no matter what. The person also told you that he had already paid four people today and all you had to do was come out to the van parked outside and smile. She thought for a few seconds and looked up at me with concern in her eyes. "I would go," she admitted. We both looked at each other and realized at that moment that we had a lot more work to do in the area of personal safety."

Guideline for Role-Play with Your Children

- As you ask questions, don't answer for your children; give them time to respond.

- If they make a mistake, gently guide them to the correct understanding and answers. Praise them when they give the correct response.

- Try role-playing in a natural setting, such as a park.

- When role-playing the various safety scenarios, make it a fun, special, and non-fearful experience for your child.

- Instruct your children never to play role-playing games with people they do not know.

- Play the games to their natural conclusions, giving your children time to look at a problem from many angles, so that you can discover and fill in any gaps in their logic.

- Once they know the safety rules, continue playing what-if games occasionally to reinforce and remind your children about important safety rules. One father recommended video taping children while role-playing so that they can see themselves in action later.

Teach By Example

Children model their parents' behavior. That's why you should demonstrate safety skills, especially when you are with your children. By being safety conscious yourself, you set a pattern for safety in your children's lives. To be truly effective, it is important that personal safety rules are part of the overall rules that your family lives by. You can blend them into your day-to-day teaching just as you do the importance of brushing one's teeth every night and turning off the burner on the stove.

To emphasize that safety rules are to be taken seriously, you must honor them as well. For example, we teach children that they are in charge of setting the boundaries for physical attention with their body; so we must respect their wishes ourselves and stop hugging them when they pull away, and stop tickling them when they say to stop. The following guidelines will help parents as they "teach by example" the important safety rules to their children.

1. Children naturally need and enjoy affection, but let them set the limits. With your child or other children, be aware of the child's level of comfort when you show him or her physical affection and respond accordingly.

2. Do not force them to give or accept other people's physical attention. Many adults love to hug and kiss children. However, a child may not actually enjoy it. You may have a hard time adjusting if they do not want to accept grandpa's kiss or Aunt Sue's hug, but you must give your child the right to decide what level of physical attention is comfortable for her.

3. Always tell your children where you are going and when you will be back. If you want your children to keep you posted on their comings and goings, parents can set a good example and extend the same courtesy. It helps set a pattern for communication in your family.

4. Do not ask children who are alone for directions or assistance. Adults should not ask children for help. Also, if a child you don't know starts to chat with you, ask the child's parent if it is okay to talk to the child; and always ask a child's parent before giving the child anything such as food or a toy.

5. If you find a lost child, act responsibly. Keep the child with you in plain sight and seek assistance from others to help find the child's parent. Reassure the child that people are helping find his or her parent.

Music: The Fun Way to Learn Safety Rules

"Music creates a low anxiety and high interest environment."

> – Kristin Lems, "For a Song: Music across the ESL Curriculum," *Languages and Linguistics*

"Music is a more potent instrument for education than any other."

> – Plato

While the safety education in this book is vital, safety education embedded in music makes it even more attractive and powerful for the child. Music is an amazing tool for teaching children safety rules, though from what I've observed, its value has been largely underestimated. I have always been puzzled by this because for years I have seen the powerful results of using music to teach children about personal safety. There is also a substantial amount of scientific research supporting the effectiveness of music in education (although that is beyond the scope of this book). There are 5 main reasons why music is so effective as a teaching tool.

1. Music is fun.

2. Music takes less time to teach and takes much of the "educational pressure" off parents and teachers.

3. Music is from a "third party" authority and is therefore often more credible in the child's mind than those they are familiar with on a daily basis. ("A prophet is never accepted in his own country," so to speak.)

4. Song lyrics are a non-fearful way to instruct children about a serious and difficult topic.

5. Children remember concepts they learn through songs and music, even under stress. Further, because children will play the songs over and over again, music is also great for reinforcing information.

To understand the power of music, think about how you recall the lyrics to songs that you heard years ago. Yello Dyno has been involved in creating music to broaden and further reinforce important safety concepts for years. This safety education music is based on the latest research on how children can keep themselves safe. For example, some of the songs on the *Can't Fool Me!* album are: "Tricky People," which teaches children how to identify some of the "lures" adults use to abduct children; "My Body's Mine" teaches children that they are in control of their bodies and can set limits for physical affection; and "Help Me Operator" teaches children how to remember their telephone numbers, and when and how to call emergency numbers for help. The full song lyrics and a commentary on each song in the *Can't Fool Me!* album can be found in Appendix D.

For years we have heard from grateful parents who have used our music to help them educate their children about personal safety. However, while music helps to create a non-fearful environment for learning and helps children retain information, remember that it is not a complete solution in and of itself. Musical education should be supplemented with other learning, including (but not limited to) the knowledge in this book. *The combination of music, role-playing and teaching by example are the strongest tools parents can use to keep their children safe.*

7

YOUR CHILD MUST BE ABLE TO PROTECT HIMSELF

"Children who have been taught to think for themselves are the safest children of all."

> — Sherryll Kerns Kraiser,
> *The Safe Child Book*

"Don't wait for your children to be hurt. Make sure that they know everything they need to know and that they are going to be safe. Because you're not going to be there when this happens. They're going to be alone."

> — "Child Hunters," 48 Hours, *CBS*

"'Hundreds and hundreds of children are not abducted because they are equipped with knowledge,' says Anne Cohn Donnelly, former executive director of the National Committee to Prevent Child Abuse."

> — "Child Abductions: What a Mom Must Know,"
> *McCall's*

The fact is that when faced with a dangerous or uncomfortable situation, your child will almost always be on his or her own. The bottom line is that your child must have the knowledge, the skills, and the confidence to use his or her own judgment to keep himself or herself safe.

It is hard to express how deeply encouraging it is to me that thousands of children each year get away from adults who attempt to harm them by using simple safety skills. Here are a few of their heartening stories.

"Twelve-year-old Rebecca Savarese says she wasn't afraid when a scruffy-looking man pointed a gun at her as she walked to school. But when he told her to get in a truck parked nearby, she thought, 'I have to get away'...When the man grabbed her backpack, Rebecca raced down the hill, screaming to a janitor, 'I almost got kidnapped!' "
— "Student Newsline," *The Boston Globe*

"One day last fall, eleven-year-old Amy Fraser and a friend went fishing at Willow Pond, a small park surrounded by big houses with broad lawns, a block from her home in suburban Willowbrook, IL. A stranger drove up, watched the girls bait their hooks and cast their lines, then got out of his car and walked to the water's edge. That was all it took. 'We were scared and we just ran,' recalls Amy."
— "Never Talk to Strangers—And Watch Out for Nice Guys, Too," *Newsweek*

"The girl was walking to a Girl Scout meeting when she passed a Jeep...A man in the vehicle asked the girl to accompany him, but she turned and ran home. The man got out of the Jeep, followed the child to her house, and knocked at the front door. He left when no one answered."
— Wilmington, DE, "Stranger in Black Jeep tries to Kidnap Seven-year-old Girl," *News Journal*

"...a man driving a burgundy van like the one the molester sometimes uses called out to a seventh grader a block from (her school). She ran to some friends and reported the incident when she got to school."

— "Stalking the Children," *Newsweek*

"An old, beat-up pickup truck passed as she walked along, stopped and backed up, the father said his daughter told him. The driver said something like, 'Hey little girl, are you cold? Would you like a ride?' The girl started walking faster, and the truck followed. She ran to a nearby house. No one was home, so she hid behind a tree at the side of the house, she told her father. The truck disappeared."

— "Attempted Abductions Make Twin Tiers
Children Fearful," *Star-Gazette*

As you can see, safety education works. Because it's a different world than when we grew up, it should be part of modern parenting and in-school education. In summary, children's best overall defense against all forms of victimization include:

- Having the ability to identify behavior that means danger.
- Trusting their feelings and instincts.
- Having a healthy self-confidence.
- Knowing that children have rights and hurting a child is against the law.
- Having the ability to accurately assess and handle a wide variety of situations.
- Knowing where and how to get help.
- Knowing they will be believed.

Part One of this book is designed to help parents and educators understand a difficult topic, and to help them realize why they must be involved in educating their children about important – even lifesaving – Safety Rules.

Part Two will introduce you to *The Yello Dyno Method*™, a unique educational philosophy that lays the groundwork for the Safety Rules. Once learned, these skills will last your child a lifetime.

It bears repeating: the same 5 year old girl who can say "no," to an unwanted touch will be the same teen who can say "no," to an unwelcome advance is the same woman who can say "no," to a relationship that becomes abusive.

PART TWO

THE
YELLO DYNO
METHOD™

"So in *The Yello Dyno Method*™, your child learns simple lyrics. They are attached to memorable songs. Under stress they readily come to mind. And we never have to explain bio-mechanics, or bad guys, or anything frightening or negative. In the *Tricky People!* song, for instance, the child is left with a joyous image of running like the wind, a memory evoking one of the common pleasures of innocent childhood and, in winsome moments, a longing in every adult's heart."

    — Sensei David Ham,
      Songwriter and Producer of *Can't Fool Me!*
      San Antonio, TX

44

THE YELLO DYNO METHOD™

A house is on fire in Alexandria, Virgina. A leading expert on fire safety is stunned. After a lifetime of service in the fire industry, he sees smoke pouring from his own home. It has finally happened to him! It's a real fire, not a pan burning on the stove. His two grandkids run screaming through the smoke. He rushes to the phone and picks it up to dial for help. While staring at the keypad, his mind goes blank. He looks to his terrified daughter and says, "Honey, what do I do?"

At the same moment this national expert on fire safety flunked his "fire drill," Sam is sitting in class ready for his vocabulary test. Even though he has prepared well, he feels anxious. Sam turns over his test paper, reads the first question, and proceeds to forget almost everything he's learned. Disaster strikes. He fails the test. Self-esteem crumbles. "I'll have to face mom and dad." "My friends will think I'm stupid." What happened? Where did his learned information go?

Some find the fire story hard to believe, but it really happened. Even though you, personally, may perform well in a crisis or stressful situation, many do not. Like Sam, his story occurs every day to countless children. The apparent loss of important learned information is an unfortunate reality for millions of people every day in big ways and small – from 911 emergency calls to tests in school. What do these two events have in common? Why do we often forget much of what we have learned, whether it's an emergency phone number or a simple vocabulary word? It's surprisingly simple, yet has profound implications for personal safety education for children. The reason? *Because the information that was needed to manage the event was stored in a part of the brain that was not accessible in an anxious or fearful state of mind.*

Cognitive learning (traditionally learned information) is often hard to access during times of pressure, anxiety and fear: fear of failure, injury, and humiliation top the list. Now, if you think a test in school produces anxiety, imagine what the anxiety or fear can be like for a child confronted with a dangerous situation of personal safety or abuse. Remember the fire expert? After a lifetime of education, he "forgot" everything he had learned in a crisis situation. In other words, what he needed was not accessible.

> "If a child has information stored in cortical areas but in the specific moment is very fearful, this information is inaccessible. In this regard, cognitively-stored information does little good in the life-threatening moment."

> — Bruce D. Perry, M.D., Ph.D., "Violence and Childhood Trama: Understanding and Responding to the Effects of Violence on Young Children," *CIVITAS Child Trauma Programs*

So, how do you store information so it's accessible in times of challenge or crisis? Dr. Perry goes on to say:

> "...information learned in song, rhyme or rap is more easily recalled when in a state of high arousal (anxiety). This is due, of course, to the fact that this

information is stored in a different fashion than traditional verbal cognitive information."

This is why I place such great importance on music. I have seen it work miracles for many years. Having said that, however, and while music is the best method for delivering safety education, there are fundamentals that lie beneath music and these must be in place or it doesn't matter how good an educational song may be. It needs a foundation.

That foundation begins with the child's *right to be safe*. Rights for children are a relatively new social phenomenon. In fact, many people today would not agree that children have this right (or they would pay lip service to the concept but not support it in their actions), but it's not to them I am speaking. If you accept the fact that a child has a right to a safe childhood, then there are 3 core fundamentals that complete the foundation of Yello Dyno's safety education method. We might say this is the pre-training for the *30 Proven Ways*.

1. Trusting Instincts

A child's natural instints are an extremely powerful tool. Unfortunately, due to social conditioning, many of our children have either hidden, buried, or forgotten their "personal powers." Yello Dyno helps to re-open the door and provide a healthy framework for the expression of these vital fundamentals so necessary to personal safety.

2. Recognizing Deceptive Behavior

This teaching helps children recognize the deceptive behavior of Tricky People, a phrase we coined that is so effective with children that it's the key "handle" of our safety instruction. Children learn that it's not what people look like, but what they do that matters: how they act, their behavior. Whether a person appears happy or grumpy, handsome or ugly, smart or stupid doesn't matter. What matters is their actions. Most "attacks" on children are based on various lures:

behaviors that, in fact, are deceptive in nature. Once deceptive behavior is recognized (including the fundamental lures), this knowledge will apply to relationships throughout a person's life, not just in childhood. The little girl who can say "no" to an unwanted touch will be the same teen who can say "no" to an unwelcome advance who will be the same woman who can say "no" to a relationship that becomes abusive. Teaching through the broader and more accurate concept of Tricky People embraces and clarifies the outdated (*and* amazingly pervasive *and* persistent *and* dangerous) concept of "Stranger Danger."

3. Building Self-Confidence

It is very important to understand that children who do not have at least some self-esteem or confidence will not believe they are worth keeping safe. As a result, they will just go through the motions of personal safety education (either to please the adults in their world or because they have no other choice), while quietly believing they are not worthy. Obviously, teaching personal safety to such a child becomes difficult, if not impossible. Unfortunately, this reality is a common and heart-breaking aspect of modern childhood. It is my heart's desire that Yello Dyno can find and help as many of these children as possible.

You are probably already thinking, "How does one help build confidence in a child who has none?" Every parent and educator knows what a difficult problem this is. However, there is hope, and for an excellent start we can begin with the previous two "developments," *trusting instincts* and *recognizing deceptive behavior*. In fact, these actually help build self-confidence in and of themselves. Why? Because when instincts have been reawakened, when children believe they can trust their instincts because the adults in their lives have supported them, when they have rediscovered their "gut" and "inner voice," these feelings are very empowering for children.

They have been heard. They have been believed. It means a great deal to children to have the adults in their lives validate their thoughts and feelings. And even in very good environments, this can often be overlooked or marginalized with statements such as, "Sure, I listen to my child."

Next, when they begin to understand the deceptive behavior of Tricky People, confidence continues to grow, because many things "fall into place" in the child's mind. They already feel something is amiss in certain relationships with others, they just don't have the framework to deal with it, *unless you give it to them by listening and believing them.* All children have intuitions and quiet feelings and doubts about certain people in their lives...but now they become clear and something they can act on (because you are validating them). For instance (and with respect to just child abuse alone), did you know that when children report child abuse that 95% of the time they are telling the truth? Unfortunately, however, the adults in their lives validate the child's truth only a fraction of the time. Is it any wonder, then, that children don't trust their instincts? Is it any wonder, then, that children lack self-confidence? When we say that it's okay for children to trust their feelings and that it's okay to question suspicious behavior, even a damaged child will start to open up. It's like a fresh rain that sooths and clarifies their agitated and confused minds.

With adult permission granted (that's it's okay to question behavior and they will be heard) and their perceptions validated ("I believe you."), the child's understanding of the deceptive, self-serving actions of Tricky People often becomes an "Ah-Ha!" experience – a small enlightenment, if you will. "Mom! I just knew something was weird about so-and so!" "I just knew" comes from intuition. Gavin de Becker makes the point in his books that the word intuition means to "protect" or "guard." A child's intuition will start to blossom if you set it free, protecting the child like a guardian angel.

Children who are in families that encourage an environment of domestic violence, neglect or abuse, or who are bullied in school, are especially prone to low self-esteem. This is obvious. But what is not so obvious is that they can be helped by just one person who cares. These are children that are constantly reminded that their experience and feelings have no value, that this abuse is acceptable behavior and that they must live with it. Here is an opportunity for you to "step up" and change the lives of these children forever.

For those of you who are thinking your child is, thankfully, not one of the above, but one who already has a healthy dose of self-confidence in a loving environment, that's great. You are a big step ahead. Now build on it, and let Yello Dyno help you and your child identify bravura (fake confidence) and replace it with the real thing.

Now, with a foundation of self-confidence either being started, being restored, or being improved upon, each Safety Rule that follows will continue to encourage and further build self-confidence in the child.

Once these three core fundamentals have developed, the child can then do something amazing: *the child can sense, recognize, understand, accept and trust warning signs*. A child must learn to recognize these warning signs in order to identify potential and/or escalating problems so he can navigate safely through the waters of the early 21st century. If warning signs can be recognized, the dangerous situations they are predicting can usually be diffused or avoided entirely. Gavin de Becker calls warning signs "pre-incident indicators," indicators a child can act on because they believe in their perceptions and they believe they can improve their situation. It's called hope. Violence expressed in its various forms is often the lack of hope. Yello Dyno offers hope and therefore provides healthy alternatives to violence in all its forms.

With these core fundamentals being understood and accepted, it's time for the next step: embedding the safety rules in music, games, and dramatic stories. The safety rules are translated into "mnemonically crafted phrases" that are then role-played and practiced to the music, games and stories. This simple yet powerful technique helps children recall the right action in a challenging situation. If one occurs, chances are very good that the correct response comes back to the child and they act on it. It's not unlike training in the military, although the method is entirely different (it's fun, for instance). In a challenging situation, the training takes over. The child doesn't have to sit there, running through so-called "safety lists" in the left brain, trying to remember what to do: it's too little, too late.

The scientific validation of the use of music in *The Yello Dyno Method* is something our creative partner and songwriter, David Ham, has known intuitively all his life. To give you some idea of just how deep the rabbit hole goes, how carefully we have thought through the various Safety Rules, David offers an example of how Safety Rule 9 (*Take Three Steps Back*) and Safety Rule 10 (*Run Like The Wind*) were woven into one of the songs, *Tricky People!*.

> "*Three steps back and run like the wind* is a very simple, memorable, and lyrical phrase. But from a bio-mechanical perspective, it works through some basic human limitations for the bad guy and some obvious advantages for the child.
>
> All walking is a controlled fall. Example: A person has the intention of walking forward. The head and eyes target the path. The shoulders shift balance forward over the hips and the leg glides out, shifting the balance between the legs. Then you repeat the process using the opposite leg. We learn this as toddlers. It's so automatic we don't realize we are doing it. Try and get out of a chair without leaning forward.

We also learn as toddlers that falling down hurts. As adults we avoid falling like the plague. In older people with weakened bones it can be fatal: fractured hips, lots of rehab or worse.

Let's imagine an adult Tricky Person. The last thing a Tricky Person wants to do is draw attention to himself by falling or causing any memorable scene for future witnesses.

We assume the Tricky Person is taller than his target. He may approach the child. If he does, he will either pull the child to him mentally (lures and grooming) or physically (grabbing). As he engages the child, he usually bends over or at least puts his head in a downward position. This shifts his shoulders over his hips which locks the knees (the body doesn't want any loss of balance and a fall so it automatically locks the knees to get more stability, a compensation for the balance being positioned forward). When knees lock, motion is inhibited. Being caught 'flat footed' is an old fighters' term meaning the person got hit when his body was not on the balls of his feet with knees relaxed. It is also known as being 'knocked out.'

If a child senses danger by their instincts (*we trust our feelings all the time*), he *takes 3 steps back*. To grab a child who is outside of arm's length, an adult must pull his shoulders upward back over his hips to prepare to move his body forward to cover this new distance. His locked knees prevent him from lunging/grabbing downward at the lower target. So he is faced with a choice: bend over for a grab, over balance forward and fall, or straighten up, shoulders over hips for a forward motion lunge.

This 'righting motion' to regain balance is necessary to unlock the knees. Unlocked knees are necessary to step forward to grab his target that is now past arms length. So bio-mechanically, to grab the child he must move back away from the child!

The lowered height of the child, the arms length distance from the child who has *taken 3 steps back*, and the necessary backwards righting movement the Tricky Person must make to unlock his knees, puts the child at an advantage in both time and space.

The child being way more flexible and lower to the ground, *takes 3 steps back* (implying a backward motion, facing the Tricky Person), and *runs like the wind*. The simple instruction, *run like the wind*, implies a turn and run command, as well as visually running as fast as you can with your head in the direction of where you are running.

A child running like the wind is a totally joyful experience and given a threat, humans will go toward pleasure and away from pain. Especially in children who have melodies with those instructions ready to recall. Remember being called on in class for your A-B-C's? Dollars to donuts, under stress, you sang the *Alphabet Song*.

So in *The Yello Dyno Method*™, your child learns simple lyrics. They are attached to memorable songs. Under stress they readily come to mind. And we never have to explain bio-mechanics, or bad guys, or anything frightening or negative. In the *Tricky People!* song, for instance, the child is left with a joyous image of running like the wind, a memory evoking one of the common pleasures of innocent childhood and, in winsome moments, a longing in every adult's heart."

> — Sensei David Ham,
> Songwriter and Producer of *Can't Fool Me!*
> San Antonio, TX

You are about to enter the door to *30 Proven Ways*, the "no spin zone" of personal safety for children. I have placed the three most important *Safety Rules for Children* at the beginning, as they are directly related to the foundation of *The Yello Dyno Method*:

- Trusting instincts (Ch. 1: Trust Your Instincts);
- Recognizing deceptive behavior (Ch. 2: Beware of Tricky People);
- Building self-confidence (Ch. 3: My Body's Mine!).

However, I have placed the three most important *Safety Rules for Parents and Teachers* at the end, because I want them to be fresh in your mind when you are finished reading the *30 Proven Ways*:

- For without Safety Rule 28, *Knowing the People in Your Child's Life,* your children will be severely handicapped by being overly exposed to difficult situations;
- For without Safety Rule 29, *Promoting Your Child's Self-Esteem*, they will not believe they are worth keeping safe and peer pressure will then rule their lives in their teen years;
- And for without Safety Rule 30, *Listen To Your Child,* you can forget personal safety education altogether and just let them learn what they can from "the street" and hope for the best (while preparing for the worst).

The Yello Dyno Method has been developed over 16 years of direct field experience with how children learn and react under stress and anxiety. Thankfully, the solution is not only fun, but also complimentary and supplemental to traditional safety education. If it works for child sexual abuse, the most difficult area of parenting and child safety education (and the one most denied), believe me, it will work for any type of personal safety education, whether it's child abuse (physical and emotional), bullying, date rape, internet stalking, violent kids or other forms of victimization. In fact, many teachers have told me that they wished all subjects were taught with this method. I have received hundreds of testimonials from parents, educators, law enforcement and other professionals who are amazed at the personal growth, safety and happiness that has come to children they know from using *The Yello Dyno Method* as prescribed. I hope the children in your life are next.

> *"Children have fought wars.*
> *They've built nations.*
> *They are strong and they have courage.*
> *Don't treat them any less than that*
> *because they are young."*
>
> — Indian Chief (*Poltergeist 2*)

Dear Jan,

Thank you and Yello Dyno for such wonderful and non-threatening materials to teach children about personal safety.

I became a school counselor eight years ago and the materials that I had to use were "scary" and the topic was difficult to approach in the classroom setting. I inherited a copy of *Tricky People!* when I transferred to a new school and was sold!

I have used the *Tricky People!* video to introduce my personal safety unit in fourth grade for the past two years and it has paid off. Thanks to the information in the video, two of my students were able to react appropriately when approached in our local mall by a stranger. As a result of their knowledge, the man was arrested. Later, it was discovered that he had a prior arrest for lewd acts to a minor.

We also had a man in our community trying to lure children to his car. My students immediately reported this and an investigation was begun.

I am excited this year about teaching personal safety and using the new materials I purchased. Now all of the children in my school will be able to benefit from Yello Dyno and his fun and non-threatening message. I am also going to conduct the parent meeting using your materials. I will let you know how it goes. Again, thank you for helping me protect my kids, your program has paid off!

Sincerely,

Mandy S. Crosland

Mandy S. Crosland
Waccamaw Elementary

Founder Jan Wagner and Yello Dyno

Yello Dyno Defines & Exposes

TRICKY PEOPLE

And Corrects the Outdated Concept of Stranger Danger

WHY MUSIC?

"...if a child has information stored in cortical areas but in the specific moment is very fearful, this information is inaccessible. In this regard, cognitively-stored information does little good in the life-threatening moment..."

On the other hand,

"...information learned in song, rhyme, or rap is more easily recalled when in a state of high arousal (anxiety). This is due, of course, to the fact that this information is stored in a different fashion than traditional verbal cognitive information."

- Bruce D. Perry, M.D., Ph.D, CIVITAS Violence and Childhood Trama: Understanding and Responding to the Effects of Violence on Young Children

THE YELLO DYNO METHOD™

Non-Fearful · Musically-Driven · Memory-Enhancing · Award-Winning

Yello Dyno Starts with the Child's
RIGHT TO BE SAFE
3 Core Fundamentals...

...underlie all types of personal safety, whether it's abuse, sexual abuse, molestation, abduction, bullies, date rape, internet stalking, or violent kids.

1 **2** **3**

IDENTIFYING
Deceptive Behavior

It's not what people look like, their age, or if you know them – it's what they ask you TO DO that matters.

Song: Tricky People!

RESTORING
Instincts & Feelings

These innate abilities have been buried in many children due to social conditioning.

Song: We Trust Our Feelings

BUILDING
Self-Confidence

If children do not feel valuable, they won't feel worth being safe, thus making teaching difficult.

Song: My Body's Mine!

Child then *senses, recognizes, understands, accepts* and *trusts* warning signs.

Powerful, Scientific
MUSICALLY-DELIVERED KNOWLEDGE

Knowledge is power. Knowledge removes fear.
Music is the best way to learn and REMEMBER safety knowledge.

▲ The Above Foundation Underlies All Yello Dyno Safety Rules ▲

Most other systems start here, with "the rules".

Yello Dyno builds a foundation *before* "the rules".

SAFETY RULES!
Brought to you by that Purveyor of Protection, that Paleozoic Personality, that foot-stompin', tail-thumpin' Safety Maven O' Soul,

YELLO DYNO!

IT'S FUN!

PART THREE

30
PROVEN
WAYS

TO PROTECT
YOUR CHILD FROM
BECOMING LOST, ABDUCTED,
ABUSED, OR VICTIMIZED

So when your light says something's wrong
You should act - not wait too long
When you're feeling all alone
You have the power to be strong

~ Lyrics from *"We Trust Our Feelings"*
   Can't Fool Me!
   Yello Dyno Records

I
TRUST YOUR INSTINCTS

"The most important thing we come across when we talk about staying strong and free — if it feels bad on the inside...then something's not right and we need to get help."

— "Kids and Strangers,"
Cincinnati, *WKRC-TV 12*

> *Well wouldn't you know*
> *I saw this stranger in the mall*
> *He looked real nice*
> *But I thought twice*
> *And you know that I said "NO!"*
> *And then I moved*
> *At least three steps back*
> *In my heart was a bell*
> *So I ran to tell*
> *And I sang my song like that*

> ~ Lyrics from *"My Body's Mine"*
> *Can't Fool Me!*
> Yello Dyno Records

Among the reported cases of attempted child abuse and abductions are countless children who listened to their instincts and steered clear of danger. Instinct is that deep, nagging, and often uncomfortable feeling that we get in our stomachs telling us that danger might lie ahead. Instinct conjures up our natural "fight or flight" response, and can enable children to avoid danger and avert personal harm. For example, a child may get a funny feeling if a man in a car seems to be following him or if a coach seems to be touching him a little too often.

Children are by nature's design open to their survival instincts as each day contains new uncharted experiences. This natural alarm is gradually silenced as they turn to their parents and teachers to evaluate what is the appropriate response to a person or situation. As we grow older, socialization often overrides our more primative but vital instincts with educated logic justifying why we need not be concerned. It would do many a parent good to take a look at why their child is uncomfortable with a babysitter or finds an older child in the neighborhood creepy. Your pre-teen may avoid a classmate because he knows that child is troubled and "feels" he will harm someone. In fact, children often sense that something is wrong before abuse or violence actually occurs.

There are many hours in the day when most children are not with their parents, even at a young age. Parents and teachers too must take the time to listen to children's concerns so they may be alerted to danger. By listening, your children learn that you value what they experience, and to speak up if they feel unsafe or uncomfotable with a person. Responding to their inner bell and making a decision to step out of a questionable situation or turn to you for help is easier than the decisions that are so painful after a tragedy occurs. In fact, a child's natural instinct deserves respect — it is one of the most important tools for protecting your child.

You touch the light down in your heart
It's so easy—just a thought
It's the same around the world
For every guy and every girl

~ Lyrics from *"We Trust Our Feelings"*
Can't Fool Me!
Yello Dyno Records

Children will appreciate knowing that when they get that funny feeling inside it is a power – like a friend – that can help them stay safe. So even if they are smaller than the person who is bothering them, they still possess a strong power to avoid or stop the situation.

ACTION STEPS

1. Teach your children to trust their instincts and "little voice."

Children usually experience instinct in their stomachs or "gut," and the "little voice" in their heads or hearts. Explain that these are not imaginary feelings, but real feelings that they might get when something scares them or doesn't feel right. If someone makes your child feel uncomfortable or funny inside, he should not ignore that feeling but act on it. Tell him that even if he feels 50/50 that trouble is about to occur, it's always smart to make a move if he feels scared or unsure. For example, if a car is getting too close or he feels that he is being followed, he should immediately turn and run in the opposite direction.

2. Tell your child that you will back him up if his inner alarm system (instinct) ever goes off.

Encourage your child to do immediately whatever he has to do to keep safe. Reaffirm that you will respect his feelings. After all, if you don't trust your child's feelings, how can you expect your child to do so?

2

BEWARE OF TRICKY PEOPLE

"The tactic used by abductors is to become a good person in the child's eyes...The abductor poses as a trustworthy person – someone working for a church, a policeman, a fireman, or a Santa-like figure giving a present."

> – "A Terrified Generation?"
> *Parents*

"*20/20*'s investigation of childhood abductions has shown that the lures used by criminals can be put into categories. Among them: assistance – request for directions, carrying packages, helping to find a lost dog – the variations are limitless, the criminals are cunning. Bribery – the age-old lure of candy has been joined by those involving drugs, alcohol, toys and motorcycle rides. Authority – posing as truant officers, clergymen, and even police officers. Emergency – 'your mommy is very sick, come with me to the hospital.' Again, the variations are endless."

> – "The Lures of Death,"
> 20/20, *ABC News*

To keep your children safe from the adults who prey on them, you must teach them more than just, "Don't take candy from strangers." These days that simple lesson doesn't even begin to instruct children about all of the many "come-ons" adults use to engage them, to entice them, and to frighten them. As the child's guardian, you must first learn the lures these Tricky People use, and then you should instruct your children how to never be "tricked." The reality of this topic may be overwhelming for many parents. But this section is designed to be supportive, as well as instructive for you and your children.

(For a deeper understanding please review Part 2 of *The Yello Dyno Method*, Point 2: Recognizing Deceptive Behavior.)

The fact is, people who want to lure children have amazingly creative and effective ways to do so. Most often abductors and molesters do not use physical force. They don't have to. Lures work. Nearly all abductors and molesters use them to attract children. These lures are cleverly designed to confuse children's natural instincts. Many children who have been hurt by those who prey on children were drawn into a trap that began with seemingly harmless requests.

Former police officer and child abuse investigator, Seth Goldstein, Esq., wrote the definitive book on child sexual abuse for child abuse investigators across the country. In his book, *The Sexual Exploitation of Children*, he describes the "methods of seduction" used by child abusers. He classifies them into 11 basic methods. According to Goldstein, the abusers are typically not well organized; they simply use whatever lure works. Some of these tricks are: affection, assistance, authority, rewards, bribery, fame, emergency, fun and games, heroes, name recognition, pornography, threats and fear, drugs and alcohol. (Appendix A has in-depth explanations of the methods and styles of seduction as cited by Goldstein.)

Over the years, "acted-out" scenes of a reporter or so-called safety expert disguising themselves as an abductor and luring a child off a playground have been shown in many variations. It's dramatic and horrifying for parents, but it is not realistic. Even a child who is fairly well trained is not going to "sense" danger, because no real danger is present. The parents of the children being tested often say their child is well trained. Of course they are going to say that, as anything less woud implicate them as bad parents, and they probably have done their best. As they watch their child go with a stranger, tears fill their eyes, and every parent watching now believes there is no way to protect their child. Nothing could be farther from the truth. Just because a child has been taught, it doesn't mean he or she has been taught properly. "Talking heads" education is not very effective with children, especially when they need to recall the knowledge under duress.

Experts say that abductors' "scripts" take advantage of children's natural innocence, kindness, and friendliness. For example, children like to be helpful. That's why John Wayne Gacy was able to lure 33 boys, whom he then molested and killed. He simply asked them for help and offered them money to carry items to his vehicle; then he forced them inside.

If adults can be caught off guard by predators, is it surprising that children, even those who have been educated by their parents or in safety classes to recognize these tricks, have been caught off guard too? To protect our children we can start by reawakening the intuition of how to protect ourselves. In *The Gift Of Fear*, chapter 4, Survival Signals, Gavin de Becker teaches you in adult language how to recognize behavior that means you are in trouble. As you go through the chapter and review the Survival Signals discussed, don't be surprised to have memories of past events flash before your eyes. In most cases the results were maybe embasassing, but not life threatening. You will be able to see how such strategies can be applied to overpower and harm a child of less experience. So take heart – if these lessons are woven into a child's life as they grow, the pattern of personal safety will be deeply ingrained in their minds and the odds will be in their favor. Then, understanding the catagories of tricks makes sense. Examples of some common tricks are:

"I can make you famous".

"But no one ever warned her about 'photographers.' Someone should have because, according to Detective Stephen Irwin of the Metropolitan Toronto Police Force Sexual Assault Squad, a phony photographer act 'is something that is used with all age groups, even by serial offenders. Holding a camera is a way to get people's attention and get their guard down. It helps start a conversation and personalizes it. Often there's not even any film in the camera.'"

> — Paulette Cooper and Paul Noble
> "Three Canadian Children," *Reward*

"Can you help, me find my puppy?"

"Why didn't you run away?"

"Because he wanted me to find Shorty."

> — Exchange between five-year-old and her
> mother, after the daughter went with a man
> claiming to have a lost puppy.
> "How to be Safe in America,"
> Prime Time Live, *ABC*

"Come with me I know your parents."

"Seven-year-old Steven Stayner was abducted in Merced, California, by a man who lured him into a car by saying he was working for a church and was driving to Steven's house to ask his mother for a donation. After driving awhile, the abductor left the car pretending to phone Mrs. Stayner for permission to have Steven spend the night with him. Later, he told Steven that his parents didn't want him."

> — "A Terrified Generation?"
> *Parents*

"I'm a police officer, and you have to come with me."

"I seen these two kids, getting in and out, in and out of parked cars. One of these kids had smashed out one of the headlights with his foot – just literally kicked it right out. I stopped and I got out of the car. And [my] car looked like a police car. I mean, it righteously looked like a police car. It had a Bearcat scanner, a 40-channel digital readout CB, CB antennas and scanner antennas. I told them: I said, 'I'm going to take you to the police station.'"

"Did you have a badge?"

"Yeah, I had a badge all the way back to, you know, 18, I guess."

> – Exchange between convicted child abductor and
> a reporter, "The Lures of Death,"
> 20/20, *ABC News*

"Let's go to my house and have some fun."

"All the kids on the block knew him...in fact, he bought bikes for them to ride. But they could never take them home." Police said that was part of Allen's tactic to gain children's trust. He would befriend children by buying them clothes, toys, food and arcade tokens and tickets, police allege.

One of the most interesting examples of how this knowledge is fundamental to all forms of personal safety is how children have applied the concept of Tricky People to all situations where anyone is not telling them the truth.

Because *Beware of Tricky People* is such an important lesson for children, I have included a section from our *Yello Dyno Pro Curriculum* for parents and teachers to show how we make the information age-appropriate, and present it in a format that removes fear and empowers children.

YELLO DYNO PRO
Teacher Friendly Lesson Plan
Excerpt from:

CAN'T FOOL ME!
Grades 2–4
An Anti-Victimization Curriculum

YELLO DYNO'S SAFETY RULE #3:

TRICKY PEOPLE: IT'S WHAT THEY ASK YOU TO DO THAT MATTERS.

Teacher: Tigers are hunters, aren't they?

Kids:

Teacher: If a tiger is hiding in the grass and watching a herd of zebras, what is he waiting for?

Kids:

Teacher: That's right, a chance to catch a zebra and get away. A tiger picks a zebra that he thinks he can beat, right?

Kids:

Teacher: He's not going to go after the biggest and strongest, is he?

Kids:

Teacher: He's going to pick the one that is smaller.

Kids:

Teacher: What about a zebra that doesn't have any friends around to help him?

Kids:

Teacher: Did you know that there are people who are like the tiger?

Kids:

Teacher: They don't pick on someone their own size. They pick on someone they think they can beat or trick: like a kid who is off by himself, or a kid who is littler than he is, or a kid who is lonely and who needs a friend. These are Tricky People aren't they?

Kids:

Teacher: We all know how our bodies can be hurt – but how can a Tricky Person hurt our heart and our mind?

Kids:

Teacher: One way a Tricky Person might do this is by asking you to keep a secret – one that may make you feel uncomfortable or unsafe. All these Tricky People have one thing in common – they are not what they appear to be. And what they do that hurts you is wrong. Tigers can't go to jail, but Tricky People can go to jail for hurting you. Did you know that?

Kids:

Teacher: Why would anyone want to hurt a kid?

Kids:

Teacher: That's hard to understand, isn't it?

Kids:

Teacher: These are people who have lots of pain in their hearts.

Kids:

Teacher: Most people are good but some people have lots of pain inside. They can be a stranger or someone you know – like a family member, a baby sitter, a coach, someone who lives near your home. They can be older kids or adults. They can be boys or girls, or men or women. In the animal kingdom, all the animals know that the tiger is a hunter and to watch out for him. He has big teeth and claws. They all know he is dangerous. But what about people? How do you know someone is a Tricky Person?

Kids:

Teacher: They're not as easy to spot, are they? Why not?

Kids:

Teacher: Because they can look nice on the outside but not be nice on the inside. They can have teeth and claws on the inside.

Teacher Prop: Draw two pictures of an apple on the blackboard. First draw a nice looking apple and then draw an apple with a worm.

 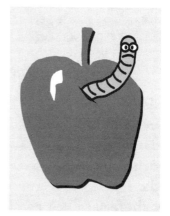

Teacher: Most apples are good and can look delicious, but when you take a bite you might find a worm inside. Yuk!

Today you're going to learn how to spot Tricky People, the ones with the worm inside. Yello Dyno is going to help you learn how to protect yourself from Tricky People.

Tricky People rarely attack or use force like a tiger. What do they do instead? They use tricks. They are tricky. They use tricks to make you do things you don't really want to do. Have you ever watched a magician pull a rabbit out of his hat?

Kids:

Teacher: You know the rabbit is not in the hat but it looks like it, doesn't it? Tricky People use tricks to get you to do things you don't really want to do.

Have you ever been fishing?

Kids:

Teacher: Tricky People go fishing for kids. They cast out a lure or trick and wait to see which kid will take the bait. Then they reel them in. We're learning that it doesn't matter what someone looks like or even how well you know him. What's important is what he asks you to do. If it doesn't look or seem right, or you don't feel safe, trust your feelings. Don't do it and always be sure you go tell an adult you trust.

We have a video called *Can't Fool Me!* with Yello Dyno and The Band. I'm going to show you some scenes from the video with Mr. Charming. You'll see how Tricky People work their schemes. You'll see how they try to trick you. Then we will discuss what we saw and how to stay safe.

ACTION STEPS

1. **Discuss with your child the kinds of "lures" used by Tricky People.**

   Your child should not accept anything, such as candy or money from a person he does not know. Also, he should not go anywhere with a person he does not know, especially to help find a lost puppy or other animal. By the time your child is four or five years old, you can start introducing him to the variety of approaches used by Tricky People, such as the ones listed here and in Appendix A. It's not necessary to go over every trick in one sitting. You can gradually work the tricks into your children's safety lessons over a period of a month or more. Along with a description of the tricks, explain to your child that if any adult approaches him in any of these ways, he must cut the conversation and get away from that person immediately. Add that he should always tell you or an adult he trusts about the incident.

2. **Play "what–if" games thoroughly.**

   Ask your child what he would do if a person came up to him and asked for directions, asked for help to find a lost pet, or asked him if he wanted to play video games, etc. Play these "what–if" games thoroughly to be sure that your child truly understands the concept of tricks. Remember the little girl mentioned in Part One,

Chapter 6, "Education is the First Safety Rule," whose mother discovered that she would not help a man find a lost puppy, but would help him find a lost kitten? If the mother had been satisfied with her daughter's first response, she would not have uncovered her daughter's weakness for kittens.

3. Warn your child about authority figures.

Because the use of authority to gain control of children is so pervasive (most child abductors in prison confess to owning fake law enforcement badges and official-looking uniforms or clothing), be sure to explain to your child how he should respond if a person representing himself as a law enforcement officer, security guard, park ranger, or other authority figure approaches him. Your child should politely tell the person that he has been instructed to ask someone who works behind a counter if he works there, and then call his parents, 911 or the local police station to verify the person's credentials before he goes anywhere with him. Legitimate officers will not be offended by this request.

3

MY BODY'S MINE!

"One father said, 'I love kissing my darling three-year-old daughter good night, but sometimes she just looks up at me with a naughty little face and says, 'No kisses.' It can be really hard to respect her wishes when I love her so much, especially if I'm about to go out of town. But I know this is the best thing to do.'"

— Irene van der Zande, "Boundaries With People We Know," *KIDPOWER Guide*

My body's mine
Mine, mine
My body's mine
Mine, mine
I'm no fool
I play by the rules
'Cause I know my body's mine

~ Lyrics from *"My Body's Mine"*
Can't Fool Me!
Yello Dyno Records

Of all the lessons I have seen children respond to, this is their favorite. Children in a healthy family are extentions first of their mother, then their father, then their extended families. Their sense of individuality gradually develops as they grow, until the day comes when they are ready to build a life and a family of their own. But in today's world children are often on their own at a very young age. This creates an internal angst that undermines their sense of security. As I watched a three-year-old child tell a playmate who pushed him down, "Stop, my body's mine!" and a fourth grader in an assembly of 300, respond with joy to the song and lesson on *My Body's Mine*, I marveled at the power such a simple lesson could have.

Most children, as is natural, have not thought about their body being their own. In a more biologically natural environment, children are surrounded with a barrier of protection from their mother, father, extended family, and the small village they live in. But today, children live in a neighborhood where neighbors know little about each other. By the age of two or three they often spend 8 to 10 hours a day in a day-care setting, followed by an elementary school with 300 to 500 students, and by high school they are with 1000 to 3000 students. Modern society mandates that children learn from a very young age the boundaries that are theirs.

My Body's Mine enlightens, so to speak, in a positve and upbeat way that they are often on their own, but that they are in charge of their body. Learning that it is against the law to hurt them reinforces that adults support and wish to protect them. They, not anyone else, have the right to choose the level of physical contact that feels comfortable to them, particularly in regards to affection. With this knowledge, you can literally see the posture of children change to one of confidence. That self-confidence presents an air of security that replaces their stance as a potential victim. Once they understand this rule, they will be better able to resist if they are ever approached by people intending to harm them.

Children have a natural sense of appropriate and inappropriate touching. For example, they readily accept hugs and kisses from family members, but not from people they do not know. Sometimes parents may worry that addressing the issue of physical abuse will affect their children's natural friendliness or affection. Too often, molestation starts with an adult who touches a child in a seemingly innocent way, such as by playing games that involve touching. But there is a great difference between affection and abuse. When touching crosses over from one to the other, a child senses the difference. In some instances, the sexual abuse can have some physically pleasant sensations but the child instinctively feels uncomfortable. Too often, parents unwittingly create mixed messages in children when they force them to kiss grandpa or put up with tickling from a sitter. Children have to know that touching for the sake of teasing, playing, or affection is always a choice. They must be allowed to set the limits on physical affection and on touching such as being kissed, hugged, or tickled.

> *Just the other day*
> *A lady came up to me*
> *She said, "This is the cutest little guy*
> *That I have ever seen"*
> *And then she hugged*
> *So tight my air was gone*
> *So I said, "No! That hurts me so"*
> *And sang my body song*
>
> ~ Lyrics from *"My Body's Mine"*
> *Can't Fool Me!*
> Yello Dyno Records

The important thing is to make it clear that children have the right to stop unwanted touching or teasing. If children can set boundaries about minor intrusions, such as being hugged too tightly or being tickled, they can use that same skill to set boundaries before sexual abuse ever occurs. It's our responsibility to give them information and direction so that they can keep themselves free from inappropriate touching.

This lesson will continue to apply to your child's life as he grows. His ability to sense and protect his boundaries, and his ability to stop teasing or other inappropriate behaviors will be skills that help him stop the attack of a playground bully. A bully, like any other predator, wants a victim and is not interested in picking on someone who will stand up to him. And as your daughter enters the teen years, she will know she is worth keeping safe. Her response to inappropriate advances will be a firm, "No!" (*My Body's Mine!*)

ACTION STEPS

1.   Tell your child that her body is hers.

Discuss with your child that she has rights with respect to her body. A child has the right to say who touches her and how; this includes Grandma's cheek pinches, Uncle Fred's hugs, and even your kisses. It can be frightening and confusing for a child to deal with setting boundaries with people she loves. One way to help her understand appropriate boundaries is to tell her explicitly that it is not okay for someone to play with her private parts; in fact, it is against the law.

2.   Teach your child the difference between appropriate and inappropriate touch.

Tell your child that the body parts covered by underwear and bathing suits are private. It is not okay for someone older to touch or ask to touch these private parts. Your child can touch himself there but, in general, other people should not. With your child, discuss the natural situations where an adult may have to touch his private parts. Let your child help you name some examples of touches that are okay, such as when a parent has to help him clean himself, to check him for any medical reason, or to help answer any questions he may have. A baby-sitter or relative may have to take him to the bathroom or help him clean himself Also, a doctor or nurse may need to touch his private parts for medical reasons.

3. **Help your children overcome their natural embarrassment.**

Often children won't say anything when they don't like physical attention because they are too embarrassed, especially if it involves people they know. As a parent you have to help them understand that their safety and comfort are more important than their own, or anyone else's, embarrassment. Also, discuss that they should not feel bad if an adult acts like the child is hurting their feelings by not allowing forced physical affection. Reassure your child that you will deal with the consequences if the adult gets angry.

4. **Tell your children that it's okay to change their mind.**

If they liked Grandma's hugs yesterday, but not today, that is okay.

5. **Teach your children how to stop uncomfortable touching.**

When they don't like the way they are being touched, your children should be able to say, "No," along with phrases such as, "I don't like that," "Leave me alone," or "Would you please stop touching me like that?" Children can be instructed to add emphasis to their words with body language, such as moving away from the person.

6. Instruct your child to "tell" when an adult will not stop touching him.

Your child should know that people who don't respect his wishes not to have his body touched are breaking the safety rules. If your child gets in a particularly difficult situation he can say, "Stop or I'll tell." Then your child should definitely tell you or someone he trusts. If he has no other option, he could call "911" or "0" to get help right away. To help your child get used to telling people to stop touching him, you could have family members or friends pat your child's head, pinch his cheek, or pull him on to their laps. Let your child get comfortable with stopping the physical contact.

7. Reinforce that your child's body is his own.

Reinforce that his body is his own by making a game: both of you touch the tips of your toes, put your hands over your heart, then on the top of your head while saying, "My body's mine, mine, mine!"

What if you see a guy in town
Who wants his puppy found
What do you do when he asks for help
And no one is around ?

Tricky people
Tricky, tricky people
Have pain down in their heart
Tricky people
You can't fool me
'Cause I'm too smart!

~ Lyrics from **"Tricky People"**
 Can't Fool Me!
 Yello Dyno Records

4

IDENTIFY STRANGERS

"Up until at least age 10, children may feel that someone is no longer a stranger even after a few seconds."

— "Missing Children: The Ultimate Nightmare,"
Parents

Telling children to "stay away from strangers" doesn't work. Children's concept of strangers does not include a nice looking and friendly person. Having asked thousands of children what a stranger looks like, these are responses that show how a child's mind works:

"A stranger looks mean and has a beard."

"A stranger wears a black mask, like Darth Vader."

"A stranger is missing a lot of teeth and he sits around in a vacant lot all day."

"Creepy looking."

"Dirty."

"Bigger than most people."

These descriptions show that children's concepts of strangers are not accurate, which means that they are vulnerable to the persuasive dialogues of the truly dangerous people who look "nice" or "fatherly." Dangerous strangers often look like fathers, uncles, aunts, teachers, and doctors — because that's exactly what they are. The fact is, predators don't label themselves for us, and worse, they purposely work at being nice, helpful, and likable so that they can throw everyone off guard. This works because typically children do not perceive an engaging adult as a stranger. Since most children are naturally friendly, they have to clearly understand these three guidelines:

1. A stranger is any person they do not know, including people they may see regularly, such as a store clerk or a neighbor.

2. A person's looks do not matter.

3. They must pay attention to an adult's behavior, and recognize when that behavior is wrong.

Parents should be encouraged by the fact that there are many cases of attempted abductions where the children stayed safe and free from abuse because they stayed away from people they didn't know.

While we need to teach children an accurate concept of strangers, we do not have to scare them. One way to present this information in a non-fearful way is to explain to your children that most people are nice, but every so often there is a person who is not nice. Parents can explain this to children in a way that children can understand such as this: "There are people who are hurting on the inside, but we can't see their hurt. Because a person is hurting, he hurts others. Since we cannot tell on the outside if a person is hurting or not, we need to stay away from any person who makes us feel uncomfortable or unsafe."

For a more in-depth discussion of strangers and how to teach children about Tricky People, please review the lesson *Beware of Tricky People,* (Chapter Two in this section).

1. Discuss who is and who is not a stranger.

Explain to your child that a stranger is any person he does not know. To help integrate this concept, run down a list of people with your child whom he considers strangers: include people such as a neighbor down the street or one of your co-workers. One way to further help your child integrate this concept is to take a pile of pictures, including your family members and friends, mixed up with clips of people from magazine pictures. One by one, hold up a picture and ask your child if that person is a stranger. Discuss your child's responses and correct him when necessary. Be sure your child fully understands that anyone he does not know, no matter how attractive or friendly looking, is a stranger. Also, be sure your child understands that even if someone he doesn't know approaches him in a familiar surrounding, such as a school or church, it doesn't mean that he should be alone or go with the person he doesn't know. Abductors and abusers often hang out in places where kids feel comfortable.

2. Gauge the concept of strangers to your child's age.

Since children under five have more trouble telling the difference between good and bad strangers, you must teach them not to run away from you in public. By age three, experts say that children can begin to distinguish between people with whom they can be friendly and those with whom they cannot. By age four, parents can discuss with their children the difference between someone being friendly and someone making suspicious overtures. Through the age of six, instruct your children to ask for your approval before they talk to, or go with a person they do not know. From age seven to ten, they can respond with polite hellos to people they do not know, but they should not engage in conversation. By age eleven, they can engage in light conversation with adults they do not know, but should not allow the conversation to become too personal.

3. **Explain that you cannot know a person from the outside.**

Your child should understand that a person may look nice on the outside, but not be nice on the inside. To explain this concept describe how most apples look good and taste good, but occasionally one has a worm inside. Explain to your child that whether he has on his good school clothes or a scary Halloween costume, he is still the same good person on the inside. Just as with a costume, any person can change their appearance and hide what they are really like inside.

4. **Instruct your children to keep their distance from strangers in vehicles.**

When there are stranger abductions it is almost always a man and it involves a car (a get-away vehicle), so a very simple but powerful lesson for your children is to never go near or talk to adults in vehicles.

5. Let your child talk to strangers when you are together.

This will allow you to observe your child's behavior with people she doesn't know. You'll have the opportunity to see if she is overly open to people she doesn't know or if she is shy. A simple way to figure out the tricks that would work on your child is to think what tricks or rewards you use to get your child to do what you want her to do.

5

GO TO THE RIGHT STRANGERS FOR HELP

I can find a mom with kids
I'll be glad if I did
Ah! a security guard
That wasn't very hard
Dad's probably just runnin' behind
He'll do better next time

~ Lyrics from *"If Your Parents Get Lost"*
Can't Fool Me!
Yello Dyno Records

"Teaching children to avoid all strangers isn't useful...If children develop a fear of strangers, you're setting up a dangerous situation...If they're ever alone and in trouble, they're isolated from help."

— "Careful, Not Fearful,"
Sesame Street Parents' Guide

Telling your child never to talk to strangers without qualification sets your child up for trouble. If she ever becomes lost, she may not know what to do. Remember that a child approaching a stranger for help and a stranger approaching a child are two very different things.

Parents should explain to their children that there are times when they do have to approach strangers. For example, if they are lost, it is smart to go to a stranger for help – it just has to be the right kind of stranger. The right strangers might include a mother with children, a grandmother, a store clerk, a security officer, a policeman, etc. The following true story from Debi Fuller, a Dolton, Illinois mother, shows that going to the right person, in this case a security guard, can help.

"On a family outing to the ballpark, our eight-year-old daughter became separated from us as we were trying to exit the stadium. Our first reaction was to panic. How were we going to find her in a crowd of 47,000 people? A security guard saw the frightened look on our faces and asked if he could help. We explained the situation and showed him our daughter's Yello Dyno I.D. card. He smiled and told us that he had just seen a very scared child that looked just like her standing at the bottom of the exit ramp with another security officer – they were looking for her family. Within seconds we were reunited with our daughter."

This little girl went to the right "stranger" for help.

1. Prepare your children to go to the "right" strangers for help.

While we want children to understand that they cannot be sure of the motives of people they do not know, we have to explain that there is a big difference between a person they do not know approaching them, and they themselves going up to a person they do not know for help. If your child is ever lost, one of the best things he can do is go to a stranger for help. Often the safest person to approach is a woman or a mother with children. They will be the most sympathetic to your child's plight and the least likely to be dangerous. A lost child could approach employees who are supposed to be there, for example people behind a check-out counter. To make asking for help easier for your child, next time you eat out let your child go up to the cashier by himself to pay for the meal.

2. Instruct your children never to leave a public area with a stranger they have approached for help.

If the person says, "Come with me to the office," instruct your child to tell them, "My parents told me to stay in a public place."

6

AVOID PRIVACY
AND CONTROL

"If a man who intends sexual assault or rape has Privacy and Control, he can victimize someone. If he does not have PC, he is not dangerous, period. Accordingly, just the presence of those two features in a situation can trigger a young woman's heightened awareness and readiness. The presence of Privacy does not mean a man is sinister, but it does mean a girl is vulnerable. At that point, she'll benefit from carefully evaluating how the man got Privacy; was it by circumstance or by his design?"
   – Gavin de Becker, *Protecting the Gift*

Key to avoiding becoming a victim is recognizing that predators of children and teens *need privacy to have control*. PC was created by Gavin de Becker and is, in fact, one of those lessons that applies to all ages: young and old, boys and girls, men and women. In this chapter I will use "she" for the potential victim, but remember that it could just as easily be a boy.

In an attempted stranger abduction, your child is most likely to remain unharmed if she does not go with the stranger, thus removing his abilitiy to have Privacy and Control. Also needing PC is an abuser who is known to the child. He will avoid exhibiting unacceptable behavior if he can be seen by others, particularly adults whose testimony will hold up in court. Again, with PC, a teen or adult predator who is well respected in the commmunity can override the voice of his victim if the victim is the only witness. Tragically, date rape is on an increase in our high schools and colleges. For date rape to occur it takes privacy. In virtually every instance where the predator is setting up the move to a private location, there will be pre-incident indicators (warning signs) that, with proper training, cannot only be perceived, but should awaken a person's intuition – that there is need for concern. In date rape situations it has been found that girls sensed trouble up to a half hour before the event.

Begin this lesson with your 5-year-old and you will find yourself reminding her not to forget about PC as she goes off to college. Most victimization occurs in familiar places, such as your own home, a friend's home or apartment, a car, at school, a dark movie theater, a park or a remote parking lot. A room that provides privacy where those nearby will not hear your child resist can be all the privacy that is needed. So if someone acts in a way that sets off your child's internal alarm (or just makes her uneasy), she should be aware of PC. She has nothing to lose by stepping out of a situation or redirecting an encounter to a location where others are present. She can also gain control of the situation by not going along with his suggestions. For example stating that , "I would rather stay downstairs," shows that she will not be easily persuaded, thus limiting his options to force or create fear. Most predators prefer charm and persuasion and will move on to the next victim if the opportunity is too risky. If she finds herself in a PC situation, remind her to stay calm and look for a way out. I wonder how many adults who are learning about PC are now remembering events in their lives where an understanding of PC could have helped them.

1.   Define Privacy and Control.

First, define **Privacy** as isolation or concealment. A private place is where no one is likely to show up or be able to assist you if you call for help. Second, define **Control** as a relationship between two people, in this case between a victimizer (the Tricky Person), and his target, a child or teen. Control exists when one person is persuaded or forced by the other. Have your child name places where she thinks she could be alone with someone. Places you could suggest if your child misses them are: a car, an apartment, a house, a room in a house that is away from everyone else, a closed business, a locker room, a park, or a remote parking lot. After your child brings up examples, ask her how she would step out of the situation if she felt uncomfortable being alone with someone; or, where she could go to have other people around. Be alert to places she might suggest that you wouldn't think of.

2.   Leave or firmly redirect the encounter to a location with others present.

Practice phrases she might say that would help her avoid PC, or regain control. For example, when your child knows the person, she might say, "I would like to see that movie, but why don't you bring it over to my house to watch?" or "I would like to ride in your new car, so Katie and I can go for a ride with you in a few minutes." This gives her time to evaluate the situation, leave if necessary, and when she is not in danger discuss her concerns with a trusted adult.

3. Review with your child that if she feels uncomfortable or unsafe she should not stay for the wrong reasons, such as:

1. She fears being injured if she resists.
2. She doesn't want to hurt his feelings.
3. She wants to avoid rejection.
4. She doesn't want him to tell others or hurt her reputation.

4. Strangers need PC, too.

Reinforce with your child that a stranger is unlikely to hurt her if he does not have PC. Even if he has a gun or knife, she is better off running away than going with him. But if it is a robbery, the situation may need to be handled differently because the motivation is different.

5. Tell your child that without Privacy and Control, Tricky People are not likely to be dangerous.

If a Tricky Person has privacy and control he could hurt her. Without PC, he is not likely to be dangerous. If she finds herself with someone who makes her uncomfortable, do not let him have PC. If she finds herself in a PC situation, remind her to stay calm and look for a way out and be sure to tell an adult she trusts.

7

YOU CAN SAY "NO!"

"All Adam's small life we taught him not to take candy from strangers, all the things that we thought were appropriate. But we also taught him to respect authority figures unequivocally: that he should be a little gentleman. I think if we had put more emphasis on the fact that he had the right to say 'no,' maybe the outcome of his case might have been different... he might have been alive today if he wasn't such a little gentleman."

— John Walsh,
"How to Raise a Street Smart Kid," *HBO*

"...he tricked his victims into going with him willingly. If a child just said "NO" and made some noise, he left him or her alone."

— "Child Abductions: What a Mom Must Know,"
McCall's

Children should understand that there are times when they do not have to be perfect little gentlemen and ladies. A child who can say "no" to an adult when he is uncomfortable or scared will be the child who has a chance to keep himself safe. Most parents like to think that they are raising polite children, but when a child's personal safety is threatened a child should not have to worry about whether or not he or she is going to offend an adult or hurt an adult's

97

feelings. What he should be able to focus on is, "Am I going to be safe if I do what this adult is telling me to do?"

Predators often approach children with "lines" that are designed to short-circuit the child's instincts. These lines could include a stranger asking, "Can you help me find my puppy, Sammie?" or a neighbor saying, "You could be a model. Can I take your picture?" or a camp couselor who is beginning the grooming process of breaking down the zone of privacy by asking, "Can I help you tuck in your shirt?" If an adult approaches a child with a "line," the child's natural instincts or "gut" may be shouting "no." But the child's belief that adults and older children, such as babysitters, must be obeyed can interfere with his ability to listen to his instincts. Because the child was raised to be respectful of adults, and to be kind and helpful, he may comply with the adult's request. He may not even stop to think that he can refuse.

In our society "no" doesn't always mean "no." How often have you said "no" to your child in a store and he kept asking and eventually you bought him something? Other meanings for "no" have become "Maybe," "I'm not sure," "Not yet," or "Give me time." If a child or young lady is kind-hearted or not forceful in response to unwanted advances this may be how her response is viewed. The ability to say "no" and have your request respected has broken down. Movies repeatedly show a girl saying "no" to the advances of a boy. He responds by ignoring what she has said and continues to press his wishes on her, until eventually she says "yes" and they live happily everafter. Such inappropriate images in movies and music videos have made it necessary to counter the effect by teaching "gender respect" to junior high and high school boys. Part of what the boys are surprised to learn is that if a girl says "no" it's not part of a game and it's rape if you don't stop.

As parents, we have to make certain our children have our approval to say "no" when anyone attempts to do anything that does not feel right to the child. We should make sure our children know that their personal safety is more important than being kind, obedient or respectful.

ACTION STEPS

1. Teach your children that it's better to be safe than polite.

By the age of two children have already discovered the power of the word "no." Give a positive direction to this natural instinct by teaching your children that they have the right to say "no" to adults who make them feel uncomfortable with their requests or touches. Teach your children that if someone gets too close they should say "no." If someone asks them to do something they don't usually do or that doesn't feel right they should say "no." Then they should get away and tell a trustworthy adult as quickly as possible.

2. In our society "no" doesn't always mean "no."

Set an example of being clearer with your children by only using "no" when you mean it. Don't just override a child's "no" – work it out with them. Respecting their feelings is the foundation not only for helping to keep them safe but for keeing the doors of communication open when they become teens.

3. Give your children supporting statements beyond "no."

Besides "no," teach children expressions that they can use when any person's actions make them feel uncomfortable. For example, they can say, "Please stop, I don't like that," or "That's not fun anymore. I don't want you to do that." To help them get comfortable with asserting themselves, you can role-play together. For example, you, a family member, or family friend can hug them tightly or tickle them; they can use these new phrases when they've had enough.

4. Test your childrens' ability to say "no."

To ensure that your children are comfortable saying "no," play what–if games. Ask them, for example, what they would say if your neighbor came over and started tickling them and they didn't like it. Keep asking what–if questions like this until you are sure that your children feel comfortable expressing their feelings to adults. They should practice saying "no" in a clear, forceful voice. To help them further integrate the concept, you can even make a fun game of saying "no" in a variety of ways, such as saying "no" like a mouse or saying "no" like a lion.

5. Reassure your child that you are on her side.

Assure your child that you will never be angry at her if she refuses a request for physical attention or appears to be rude to an adult, older teen or classmate in the process of keeping herself safe. Let her know that you will handle the consequences if that person is annoyed or angry, or if their feelings are hurt.

You don't touch me there
Cause I will run and tell
It's against the law
And I'll tell what I saw
And sing my body song

~ Lyrics from *"My Body's Mine"*
Can't Fool Me!
Yello Dyno Records

8

CUT THE CONVERSATION!

"Do not get into a conversation with them. As soon as they start to talk to you, get out of there...bam, you're out of there...Get your knees in the breeze."

— Detective J.J. Bittenbinder,
"Street Smarts: Straight Talk for Kids,"
Teens & Parents, *PBS*

"You must be prepared to handle inappropriate behaviors immediately to let the abuser know that you will not tolerate abuse."

— Denise Martin,
founder of SAVVY!, Portland, Oregon

One of the most empowering messages about eluding Tricky People was presented by Detective J.J. Bittenbinder. He explains, "Anytime you have a lure, and [the abductor] starts the lure, it's a dialogue with the child. As soon as the dialogue starts, and the kid says 'no' and walks away, I don't care what lure it is, it's over...You don't allow a dialogue." The more the dialogue continues, the more engaged the child becomes and the more easily he or she will be seduced by the scripts of the molester or abductor. But the child has one powerful response, which will allow him to stop the lure in its tracks. If your child understands this one simple rule "cut the dialogue! cut the conversation!" his chances of being lured by strangers is reduced dramatically.

If a stranger comes to you
And starts to lay a rap
Don't hang around
Don't fall for his trap

~ Lyrics from *"G.O.M.F."*
Can't Fool Me!
Yello Dyno Records

The message of "cutting the dialogue or conversation" brings with it a source of power for the child. Children are at an extreme disadvantage when faced with an adult's size and mental capability. A child may think, "How can I stay safe? What power do I have over a big adult?" Parents and teachers can answer:

You've got your eyes that can see
You've got your ears that can hear
You've got your heart that can feel
You've got your feet that can get up
And run like the wind

~ Lyrics from *"G.O.M.F."*
Can't Fool Me!
Yello Dyno Records

When children understand that they have the choice to "cut the conversation," and use their powers to stay away from Tricky People, they will understand that they can keep themselves safe.

ACTION STEPS

1. **Instruct your child how and when to "cut the conversation."**

The rules regarding talking to strangers apply here: if an unfamiliar person tries to start a conversation, your child should "not make the connection." Instead, he should do whatever he has to do to "cut the conversation." He should look away, walk away, and, if necessary, yell for help and run away. The same rule applies even when it is someone he knows well. If he feels uncomfortable or unsafe tell him he has the right to "cut the conversation."

2. **Test your child's ability to "cut the conversation."**

Practice a variety of engaging "lines" that might attract your child to respond, such as, "That's a cool skateboard you're using – where did you get it?" or "You're so pretty. Have you ever modeled?" Then, have your child show you how she would "cut the conversation" and get out of there.

9
TAKE THREE STEPS BACK

"The first thing we have to do to maximize the safety of our children when they are not in the presence of a caretaking adult is to teach them to stay an *arm's reach plus* away from people they don't know even if they have to back up to do it."

— Sherryll Kerns Kraiser, "Preventing Abuse and Abduction by Strangers," *The Safe Child Book*

Take three steps back
Take three steps back
That's how you can begin
Take three steps back
Take three steps back
Then run like the wind

~ Lyrics from *"Tricky People"*
Can't Fool Me!
Yello Dyno Records

Many predators have caught their victims simply by reaching out and grabbing them. Teach your children to stay at least three arm lengths away from any adult or child who makes them feel uncomfortable or unsafe. This appearently very simple safety rule is, in fact based on a very thorough understanding of bio-mechanics and is one of the most effective tools that a child has to keep himself safe. (As further reference see Part 2 *The Yello Dyno Method*, David Ham's explanation of bio-mechanics.)

Also, research shows that cars are involved in 80 percent of abductions. Many have occurred when an adult calls a child over to his car and asks for directions. When the child gets close enough, the adult grabs her and pulls her into the vehicle. Crime experts say that the average adult simply does not ask a child for directions. Therefore, if a child is approached for directions, this is a red flag. Your child should keep her distance!

ACTION STEPS

1. **Teach your child to stay at least three steps away from anyone who makes him feel uncomfortable or unsafe.**

   Have your child back three steps away from you and then reach towards him. He will see first hand that you can't easily grab him. It is a very empowering moment for a child. Practice with role-playing games. You can be a stranger, angry adult or even a bully. Have your child demonstrate moving three steps back until he gets it right.

2. **Instruct your child to keep a safe distance if an adult asks her for help or directions.**

   Your child can either ignore the adult, say she doesn't know, tell the adult to go ask another adult for help, or just run away.

10

RUN LIKE THE WIND

"The point is that nowadays, to run like hell from a suspicious stranger is the right thing for a kid to do."

— "Never Talk to Strangers & Watch Out for Nice Guys, Too," *Newsweek*

Take three steps back
Take three steps back
That's how you can begin
Take three steps back
Take three steps back
Then run like the wind

~ Lyrics from *"Tricky People"*
Can't Fool Me!
Yello Dyno Records

Stranger abudctions are in the news all too frequently; the stories of the attempted abductions, of the children who got away are often overlooked. When these stories are reported by the media, we usually find that the reason the children got away was because they used learned safety skills. Running is one such skill. The success stories often include children who trusted their instincts when they felt scared, and who ran to a safe place.

While it seems easy from an adult's perspective that if you are in danger to get out of there, the biological programing of a child is different.

> "In general, young children (unable to successfully fight or flee) utilize a predominant dissociative response (freeze or surrender pattern)."
>
> ~ Bruce D. Perry, M.D.,Ph.D.,
> "Childhood Trauma, the Neurobiology of Adaptation,"
> Child Trauma Programs, *CIVITAS*

If a child is not given an alternative pattern of response through education and role playing that "kicks in" to replace the freeze and surrender patterning, then they are being left open to unnecessary harm. In most instances, a child being threatened by a predator, stranger or acquaintance, or even a bully at school, is safer if she gets away: *run like the wind.*

In one example, from a Newsweek article, two girls were playing by a pond near their homes in Illinois. When a stranger slowed down in his car and began watching them, the girls ran. One of the girls said, "I was upset we had to leave but I knew it was the right thing to do."

In addition to running, children should also understand that if they feel scared and decide to run to safety they can do anything necessary to get away, even dropping their school books or backpack, so that they will not be slowed down. Detective J.J. Bittenbinder tells the story of one little girl whose father had warned her never to lose her school books or she would be punished. So one day, while a man cornered and molested her, she hung onto her new school books. Children should know that their safety is more important than any book, clothing, or other personal item. Material things can be replaced – your child cannot.

ACTION STEPS

1. **Tell your children to run to a safe place if they or are scared.**

   Advise your children to run to the nearest public place such as a fast food restaurant or to a place where there are other people. Children should also know the "safe houses" along any route that they travel regularly. If someone is following them in a vehicle, generally they should turn and run in the opposite direction from where the vehicle is going or to the nearest safe place, depending on the circumstances. To help scare the person away and get other people's attention, they should also remember to yell while running.

2. **Make sure that your children are not embarrassed to run.**

   You can test your children's willingness to actually run (while yelling) at a park or in your neighborhood.

3. **Check their safety knowledge with "what–if" games.**

   Periodically, as your children grows up, quiz them on how to handle specific situations. Make sure that your children at some point would run if they were scared.

4.   Don't reinforce the wrong messages.

Don't, for example, tell your children "never to lose or damage belongings such as school books". Safety should always come first. Help your children be tough targets by telling them not to hesitate if they feel scared. They should drop their school books, backpack, or whatever they are carrying – and run. They should also know that if they drop their personal items, such as school books or even a shoe, these items will provide a trail of evidence that you can use to find them.

11

YELL! YELL! YELL!

"The only thing that might have saved Polly that night, says her aunt Juliete, is if she and her friends had screamed for help...Children need to learn to resist and scream no matter what."
> – "America's Child," *People*

"Do your children a favor. Encourage them to scream. It is an important defense tool. Don't raise a silent victim. You owe this to your children."
> – Letter writer to *Dear Abby*

Children have a natural talent for yelling—and they can use it to protect themselves. Too often, from the time children are little, adults tell them not to yell. But when in trouble, a child who yells may be the safest child. Screams are meant to alert others to danger, whether real or imagined.

Parents should encourage their children to scream if they are ever in danger, and parents should prepare children to use this self–defense technique whenever they need it. Child abductors in prisons today say that if their potential victims made any noise, they left them alone. Surely we do not know if screaming would have saved some abducted children such as Polly Klaas, but perhaps it would have provided an opportunity for someone to have attempted to save them. Experts advise parents to tell their children: yell as loud as you can; yell as hard as you can; yell to attract someone to help you; yell to scare the perpetrator away.

Another barrier to the effectiveness of this powerful safety tool is a child's embarrassment. Teens, for sure, and even some children as young as ten would rather not draw attention to themselves. They would choose to be quiet, and take a chance that they are wrong. But if they are being abducted, attention from a helpful adult is exactly what they need. They must understand that it is better to be safe at all costs than to avoid embarrassment.

As well as screaming, children must learn to yell out key phrases, such as, "This is not my father!" This is critical because if a child is being taken from a public area, passersby may just think the child is throwing a temper tantrum. The dramatic case in England where two adolescent boys abducted a two-year-old from a mall is a heart-wrenching example. People in the mall that day said that they did, in fact, remember the two boys leading a crying child outside, but they assumed the boy was the brother of one of the older boys. Shortly after that, the child was murdered. If the child had yelled, "This is not my brother!" he might have been saved.

ACTION STEPS

1. **Train your child to make a verbal commotion if anyone ever tries to grab her.**

Let your child know she can use her "outside voice," inside, if she ever feels unsafe. Help your child practice yelling deeply from the gut so that she can break into an attention-getting yell at a moment's notice. A weak yell from the throat will not be effective. Your child should also practice yelling specific descriptive statements such as "I need help!" or "This is not my father!" and "I'm being kidnapped." Without practice, a child may be too scared at the moment to yell correctly. It seems simple, but almost no one does it right at the moment they really need it.

2. **Explain that safety is more important than possible embarrassment.**

If your child resists yelling because it feels silly or embarrassing, explain that it is much more important to save himself from danger than to worry about being embarrassed for a few minutes. Tell your child that his voice is an important power over bigger people. Explain that many children have foiled Tricky People by scaring them away with a long, loud scream from the gut. Remind them that Tricky People don't want other people to know they are tricky.

12

BREAK AWAY!

"I don't care if they have a weapon, *don't* go with them. Kick, scream, break things, scratch, go for the crotch, the eyeballs...anything."

> – Scared mother's advice to her ten-year-old daughter, "Fears of the Unspeakable Invade a Tidy Pink Bedroom," *Newsweek*

"I wasn't scared of the gun, I was just scared to get into that pickup truck."

"Had you thought what might happen if you did get into that pickup truck?"

"I wouldn't be here talking to you."

> – Exchange with a twelve-year-old who broke away from an abductor, Today Show, *NBC*

M any parents are signing up their children for martial arts courses because they believe that with those skills their children will be able to defend themselves better against would-be abductors. In fact, experts including law enforcement officers and martial arts masters say that almost without exception, children will not be able to physically defend themselves against an attack by an adult. Actually, the primary benefit of learning martial arts is the confidence and self-esteem chiildren gain from the mental and physical discipline.

While children cannot "beat up" an adult, that is not to say that they should not put up a struggle if they are ever grabbed. In fact, many children have gotten away from attackers by biting, kicking, and spitting, while yelling at the top of their lungs. Most convicted child abductors have said that they leave children alone the minute they make any noise or fight back. Therefore, your children should know that in some situations they should put up a fight and try to break away. Sometimes a child's odds for survival are much better if he resists than if he does not. However, some perpetrators do get more violent if they are angered. So the best safety education provides your children with the reassurance that they can make the right decision in a specific situation. They should be able to judge when to fight, when to make a scene, and when to be quiet and wait for an opportunity to run. If children know the basic safety rules they will be better prepared to do this.

In most cases, rather than worrying about physically defending themselves, children should use their heads and *stay away* from any threatening situation. Sensei David Ham says that an objective in Aikido, a non-violent martial art, is to understand "ma-ai" or distance. Children should keep their distance no matter what. If they are ever approached, they should first take three steps back, then, if the situation feels wrong, they should yell for help and "run like the wind" to safety. In one case, a twelve-year-old escaped from a potential abductor because she followed the advice her mother gave her: "God forbid someone grabs you, but if they do – kick, punch, bite, spit. Do what you have to to get away." In this case, the potential abductor grabbed the girl's backpack. She faked a seizure, and while pretending she had to sit down, she wiggled out of her backpack and ran.

ACTION STEPS

1. Tell your child to break away if anyone grabs him.

Your child should not wait to struggle and put up a fight; he should resist right away to scare off the attacker. The first stage of an attempted abduction is the point where the attacker is the most vulnerable, unsure of himself, and subject to surprise. Adult self-defense classes instruct women to repel an attacker by engaging in activities that will throw the person off-guard such as pretending to vomit or faking a seizure.

2. Practice letting your child "break away" from you.

Grab your child and have him struggle and fight to get free. This will show him that strength alone is not enough.

3. Remind your children to practice safety skills so they will never be grabbed in the first place.

All of the safety rules presented in this book will help children use their heads and steer clear of dangerous situations.

4.   Instruct your child to not allow herself to be put into a vehicle or to be taken anywhere.

Your child should do whatever she must do to avoid this. If a person tells the child to be quiet, to come along and she won't be hurt, that person is lying. Remind your child of PC, Privacy and Control, that abductors need to take a child away from public places to a place that is private and where the abductor will be in control.

5.   Instruct your child never to go with a person holding a weapon.

While this is a really tough point to address, keep in mind that if a child is threatened by an attacker with a weapon and the child goes with the abductor, his chances of survival are much lower than if he had put up resistance from the very start and got away. In the case of a robbery this may not be the right thing to do because the motive is different.

13

Don't Keep Secrets That Make You Feel Uncomfortable

"Since 85 to 90 percent of perpetrators are known to the children, sexual abuse cannot take place without secrecy. Therefore, one of the first things a potential perpetrator will do is find out if the child can keep a secret. If a child steadfastly refuses, most abusers will not risk moving ahead."

> — Sherryll Kerns Kraiser,
> "Preventing Sexual Abuse,"
> *The Safe Child Book*

This is one of the simplest and more powerful lessons you can teach your baby or teen. A child as young as three years old can be taught to say, "We don't keep secrets in our family." They don't even have to know about the dangers they might face. In fact, your child should be taught that there should be no secrets in your family. Secrecy is the main reason why abuse occurs over a long period of time, and with so many children. Secrecy strengthens the adult's power and control over the child, isolates the child from others, and helps maintain the physical abuse. Potential abusers may use lines such as, "We won't tell anyone about our private game, okay?" If an adult requests that the child keep a secret, that is the alert for trouble. A child should know that anyone who tries to get him to keep quiet about something they are doing is not a friend, even if Mom or Dad refers to them as a friend. A child should also be warned that abusers will use threats such as saying, "Go ahead and tell, no one will believe you." Abusers have been known to threaten to hurt a child, his pet, or his loved ones unless he keeps a secret. But a child should know that those threats are usually hollow.

Abusers also may twist the concept of secrecy to make the child feel that he or she is a "partner" in the sexual activity. According to author Jan Hindman, in *Abuses in Sexual Abuse Prevention Programs*, molesters might use lines such as:

"Do you have any idea what your mother would do if she knew the kinds of touching *we've* been doing?"

"If your breasts hadn't grown, I would never have allowed you to touch me like this."

"I could tell that you like this or I never would have done it."

"Because I love you so much, I won't tell your mother what you've been doing with me."

These approaches, which are almost too difficult for a normal, loving parent to hear, make it painfully clear why you must be sure your child will not keep bad secrets.

Sometimes a child may not confide in an adult about a troubling situation because she does not want to tattle or because she is afraid her parents will be angry with her or will not believe her. A child should feel confident that you will believe her and will not be angry with her for telling.

Parents should also understand that a child will not always tell about abusive situations in a direct manner. For example, if Uncle Bill is touching your child's private area, she may say to you, "Uncle Bill smells bad." Parents need to really listen to their child and understand what she may actually mean when she makes negative comments about, acts uncomfortable around or hides from a particular adult.

An added benefit we have seen over the last sixteen years is that children who have grown up with the belief that they have the right to be safe are more likely to speak up if they feel they or others are in danger even when peer pressure is to be silent.

ACTION STEPS

1. Teach your child to say, "We don't keep secrets in my family."

Your child should not keep secrets from you, especially secrets about an adult or older child who is bothering or trying to get him to keep a secret. Encourage your child to share any secret that makes him feel unsafe or uncomfortable. Instruct your child that if an adult tries to get him to keep a secret or says something like, "You don't need to tell your mom and dad, I'll tell them later," your child's response should be, "No, I don't keep secrets from mom and dad and I'm going to tell."

2. Explain that whispering and secrets with friends are okay, as long as they are not dangerous.

A child may confuse secrets with whispering, with surprises (like birthday gifts), or with secrets between friends such as friendship clubs. A child should be taught the difference between okay secrets, which are fun and harmless, and bad secrets, which could hurt him or someone else if he doesn't tell. Surprises are things that make people happy and that get told eventually, whereas secrets are never told.

3. Teach your child that there is a difference between privacy and secrecy.

Privacy means keeping something to yourself, and a child's privacy deserves respect. Private secrets might include her feelings about a friend or a poem she wrote, but doesn't want anyone to read. Secrecy means that you are bound not to tell. If there is pain, shame, or embarrassment surrounding the secret, then something is wrong.

4. Help your child understand that a touch that makes him feel uncomfortable or unsafe is not his fault.

If someone touches your child in a way that is not okay and makes him feel uncomfortable, tell your child that you will do your best to help him. Tell him you may be upset by what happened but not angry with him and no matter what happens, you will always love him. Also, reassure him that you will deal with the adult who harmed him.

14

TELL UNTIL SOMEONE LISTENS

"Part of the process was I would pick children that were non–assertive, that I knew wouldn't tell."

> – Convicted child molester,
> "The Crusaders," *NBC*

"Now, consider: If children valued their sexuality as much as (or more than) their bicycles, and if they realized that sexual abuse is like having their bicycle stolen, then abuse would be reported (and resisted whenever possible) without hesitation."

> – Jan Hindman, "Abuses to Sexual Abuse
> Prevention Programs,"
> *The Hindman Foundation*

In one sexual abuse case reported on 20/20, a young girl was molested by a trusted family member for two years. She finally overcame her fears and told someone, and the person was tried and jailed. By telling, she got the abuse to stop. Now her advice to other kids is: "If no one listens to them, they should keep on telling until someone will listen to them." This should be every parent's advice to their own children. Surprising as it may seem, children experiencing abuse may have to tell as many as nine people to get someone's attention, and 95% of the time the children are telling the truth.

Children may be reluctant to tell their parents about unusual situations with adults or older children; for example, when they have been shown pornography or touched inappropriately. Part of the problem is that the abuser often leads the child to believe that it is his fault because he has "attracted" the abuser. The child is often told how he will cause pain to many people he loves, and in some cases be the cause of the family being broken up. To get a child not to tell, abusers use a variety of threats such as, "Your parents won't believe you," "I'll kill your puppy," or "Your mother won't hug and kiss you anymore." A child needs to know that most of these threats are hollow, that you will always love him, and that he needs to tell you about disturbing situations no matter what. Even if your child gets the person to stop bothering him, the abuser will usually go looking for another child. If your child tells, then there is a chance that the abuser will be caught and stopped. Also, it is important to report incidents to the authorities so that the potential abuser can be found.

Statistics say that girls traditionally report molestation four to one over boys, but this gap is beginning to narrow. Why do boys hesitate to tell? Two reasons. One, boys are more susceptible to humiliation. Boys do not like to admit to themselves, their friends, or their families that anything like molestation could have happened to them. The stigma of the action is too great for them to bear. And two, boys fear that if their parents become worried about them they will respond by placing more restrictions on them. Boys resist close supervision, so they don't tell their parents about things that bother them. But this kind of thinking could mean trouble. One young boy had been bothered repeatedly by a man during his morning paper route. He told his younger brother that a guy was "bugging" him, but made his brother promise not to tell his parents. Two weeks later he was abducted and murdered.

In regards to stranger abductions, parents should respond carefully to their children's fears. For example, if your child tells you that someone was following him home from school, you should not focus on correcting him for not following the correct path home. Instead, provide a nurturing context for him to discuss high-risk situations. Each time we listen to our children and believe them, we teach them that honoring their feelings and telling the truth are more important than making mistakes. Although they may need correction as well, the fact that they had the courage to tell the truth is really more important. At the very least, let your children know that you will reduce your disciplinary actions for any mistakes they made such as taking the wrong path home. This can help give them the confidence to discuss very serious situations, should they arise in the future.

We must teach our children, age-appropriately, what is normal, and that involving children in sexual activities is not right. Be sure you give your children the right to say "no," and then tell. They will have a very good chance of being passed by because the abuser does not want to be known. Unfortunately, all children may not be able to resist the sexual advances of a determined adult or older child. If a child who has been abused tells right away, he is more likely to have a quick and successful recovery.

ACTION STEPS

1.   Give your child the power to tell.

As soon as your child is vocal, make him understand that it is necessary to tell a trusted adult if anyone is touching or scaring him . A child should tell if someone asks him to keep a secret, gives him money or a gift, makes him feel uncomfortable, or threatens him. Instruct your child to tell, especially if an adult says not to tell, and if the adult threatens your child in any way. If your child is not sure if an adult's behavior is "bad," let your child know that he can ask you and you will help him decide. Also, make sure he understands that it is better to tell you or someone else later, than not to tell at all.

2.   Encourage your child to be firm with a potential abuser.

Teach your child to say "no" to a person who is bothering him. Then if the adult doesn't stop, your child should say, "Stop or I'll tell on you."

3.   Instruct your child to look for help until she gets it.

To be sure your child knows whom to go to for help, describe a variety of scenarios and ask whom your child would talk to in each case. For example, what would your child do if a man followed her to school and tried to start a conversation? Would she tell her mother, father, aunt, minister, teacher, or some other adult? Ask her whom she would talk to if the first person wasn't available. Let your child know that it is never too late to tell and ask for help, even months or years later.

4. Teach your children to tell if they see anything suspicious.

Children should be watchful and aware of potentially dangerous situations, for example, someone hanging around the school playground. They should try to describe threatening strangers as best as they can, including height, size, color of hair, the type of car they were driving, and the license plate number. They can even write the license plate number in the dirt. Children have often been the ones to successfully describe suspicious people. You can practice testing your children's memory by periodically asking them to glance at some adult, then turn around and describe the adult. You can even make a game of memorizing license plates, car colors, and descriptions.

15

ALWAYS ASK FIRST

"Don't go anywhere with anyone unless your mother
or father or another adult they have told you to trust,
says it's OK every time."

> — Irene van der Zande,
> "Strangers," *The KIDPOWER Guide*

How can parents make sure children are safe when
they can't be with them all of the time? One way is
to communicate with them. Children should
understand that their parents or guardians need to know
where they are at all times. This includes teens. With the
advent of the inexpensive cell phone, I would recommend
that as soon as you find yourself unable to keep clear tabs on
your children, give them a cell phone. This is particularly
helpful with teens. A cell phone becomes an "electronic leash"
that can keep the door of communication open when they are
away from you. I've been pleasantly surprised to see how
many times my own teens have contacted me when they were
in need of my support.

Children should always ask their parents or guardians first
before going anywhere or if they change their plans. Children
should also know that they can call their parents if they ever
need a ride home from anywhere. To reinforce this rule and
honor their children, parents should also call their children
and communicate with them when they are away from home.

1. **Teach your children always to ask your permission before going anywhere.**

   Whether going to a friend's house, to help a neighbor, or to the store, children should ask an adult's permission first. They should also tell you or their caregiver if their plans change for any reason. To make sure they understand this safety rule, ask them to identify all of the various situations where it is important for them to check first with you before they go anywhere or do anything.

2. **Give your children a checklist of adults they can trust.**

   Children need clear guidelines about adults with whom they are allowed to travel without checking first, such as their school teachers or grandparents. Have your children practice saying, "I'll check with my mom first," whenever anyone who is not on your "approved" list, asks them to go somewhere. Always be on time to pick up your children anywhere, such as school, sports practice, or dance classes. Children who linger alone are more vulnerable to abductors.

3. **Be sure that you keep in touch with your children when you are apart.**

   To make this safety rule a family rule, you should let your

children know where you can be reached by phone. When you are traveling, you should leave an itinerary with your children.

4. Teach your child to call if he or she ever needs a ride home.

For example, if a friend's parent was supposed to take your child home and suddenly could not make the trip, your child should call you before going with someone else.

16

ALWAYS HAVE A BUDDY

"Children who are alone make easy targets for strangers."

   – "Careful, Not Fearful,"
     Sesame Street Parents' Guide

We've all heard that children should use the buddy system; but it is such a simple idea that we tend to overlook how valuable it can be in so many situations. Once again this rule works for all ages. The buddy system can be a valuable tool for a child for several reasons:

(1) a predator is ususally looking for a child who is alone;

(2) if there's a problem the second child can go for help;

(3) when two or more children are together they are more likely to make a good decision; and

(4) two children are more difficult for an abductor to handle than one.

Using the buddy system means *staying together.* Police and martial arts instructors teach that when a person is just twenty-one feet away from another person it may be too much distance to be of any help in an emergency.

Make the buddy system a family rule. Children should always be with another person when they are away from home.

ACTION STEPS

1. **Make it a family safety rule for your child to always have a buddy.**

   Whenever he goes anywhere, such as to a playground, to the mall, or to a public restroom, your child should have a companion. Make sure your child understands that it is safer to be with others than it is to be alone. If anything happens, a friend will be there to help. One special note: children should *always* have a buddy (preferably an adult) when they go to public restrooms. Restrooms in malls, fast food restaurants, and highway rest areas have become places where people (including gang members) looking for trouble, tend to hang out.

2. **Make the buddy system a habit.**

   It is commonly known that if you practice something for thirty days it will become a habit. For one month, structure or reinforce the use of the buddy system with your children. It will become a family habit before you know it.

17

WALK TALL!

"Teach your kid to be alert."
— "Better Safe Than Sorry," *Starweek*

> *So if your parents get lost*
> *It's your turn to be the boss*
> *I'll be walkin' real tall*
> *And in no time at all*
> *They'll be laughin' and cryin'*
> *They showed up in no time*

> ~ Lyrics from *"If Your Parents Get Lost"*
> *Can't Fool Me!*
> Yello Dyno Records

Children who are alone and are not paying attention to their surroundings are more likely to be manipulated and overpowered by aductors and other predators. Children should stay alert to avert danger. Parents need to teach their children to walk tall and appear to have confidence – even if they are scared and don't feel confident. Acting confident can be very useful when it comes to staying safe. Street safety includes walking purposefully, putting a bounce in your step, looking around you, and being alert like a deer to the people coming and going around you. If someone makes you feel uncomfortable, turn and look that person straight in the eyes and then go to a safe place or to a woman and ask for help. Always look as though you have to be at a certain place at a specific time.

ACTION STEP

Practice walking purposefully with your child.

You can help your child understand this concept by showing how to "walk tall" – looking confident, alert, and unafraid. Your child should also stay alert to the world around her, for example, the people nearby and the part of town she is in. It is important not to overcompensate, however. Your child should not try to look like she is *looking* for trouble or she may attract a bully. Also, if a child feels frightened for any reason, she should try to calm down and focus on using her personal safety skills to get home safely.

136

18

USE THE TELEPHONE

"Children who don't know their address and telephone number are missing a major defense if they should get lost...They have no way of getting home or calling for help."

— 'Careful, Not Fearful,"
Sesame Street Parents' Guide

It really is so simple
It's actually fun
"O" for Operator
Or dial "9-1-1"
Say your name and problem
Say your address too
Sing your phone number
I'm so proud of you

~ Lyrics from *"Help Me Operator"*
Can't Fool Me!
Yello Dyno Records

Once a six-year-old girl was abducted by a man who asked her for directions and then pulled her into his car. After forty-eight hours of frantic searching by the community, posting posters, and newscasts of the incident, the man got scared and dropped the child off in town – right next to a telephone. The girl knew to call "911" for emergencies and the police picked her up right away.

All children need to know how to use the telephone and to memorize important telephone numbers. They also need to know their full name, their parents' names, and their address. They need to know how to call "911" or "0" for operator. They should be instructed how to use all types of telephones including pay phones, office phones, and hotel phones. They should know to never call "911" to make a prank call.

Remember, music is one of the easiest ways to teach children to memorize information such as their telephone numbers. Many parents have said that they just couldn't get their children to remember their area code and home phone number until the numbers were set to music.

When teaching their children their home telephone numbers, remember that they also need the area code. If a child is abducted, he or she can easily be transported into another area code or out-of-state. While searching for their missing children, parents have been known to call their telephone number in every area code to see if their missing child has called.

ACTION STEPS

1. **Teach your children your telephone number including the area code as soon as they become verbal.**

Music makes memorization easy. You can make up your own little song or purchase sing-along music such as Yello Dyno's *Can't Fool Me!* album. The song "Help Me Operator" is especially designed to make it easy for children to remember their telephone numbers (as well as learn to dial "911"or "0"). Older children should also memorize their parents' work numbers and cell phone numbers and the number of a trusted neighbor or family member. Keep these numbers written down near your home phone for easy access, and have your children carry this information on them or in their backpacks. Additionally, children should know their address and their parents' or guardians' full names.

2. **Teach your children that they can dial "9-1-1" or "0" for emergencies (or other emergency numbers in some areas).**

Some experts believe it is always best for children to call "911" or "0" in an emergency, even before calling home. Calling home might actually slow things down. Dialing an emergency number is almost sure to get fast help. If "911" in your area has advanced services, the address and phone number of the caller will appear on the operators' screens. Be sure that young children do not confuse "911" with "nine–eleven." Since there is no number "11" on the telephone dial, they may get confused. Additionally, children should know that in most places they can dial the operator without money and reverse the charges for a call home. In an emergency, instruct your children to give their name, problem, and address to the operator who answers. The information and how it is delivered by the child helps the operator evaluate whether the call is genuine or a prank. Children should be warned never to call an emergency number to play pranks. When they really need help, they might not be believed, like the boy who cried, "Wolf!"

3. Teach your child how to dial from several kinds of phones.

Home phones, cell phones, pay phones, hotel phones, and business phones all work differently. You don't want your child's efforts to reach you thwarted because she didn't know how to use the only telephone that was available. For example, hotel phones often require the caller to dial "9" or "8" first, and business phones require that you first select an outgoing line. In hotels, you can dial "0" to get the hotel operator who will then dial "911." It is extremely important to actually practice with your child on real phones, not just verbally explain how to use them.

4. Plan ahead for emergencies.

If your child feels threatened in his home, one trick is to dial "911" and leave the phone off the hook. The operator will be able to hear everything, learn the source of the call, and dispatch help.

19

TAKE THE SAFE ROUTE HOME

"Children love to find the shortest way home: it makes them feel smart and powerful. Criminals often look for their victims in these out-of-the-way places."

– "How to Raise a Street Smart Kid," *HBO*

The safest way to get home from school, friends' homes, or anywhere children go regularly is to take the same route each time. This way children become familiar with the route and with the location of places where they can go for help along the way, such as businesses or "safe houses." Also, if children take the same route home every day, parents can accurately gauge the time it takes them. If a child is ever missing, parents can backtrack on the route to search for the child.

1. If your child walks home from school, instruct him to take the same route home every day.

Encourage your child to never take shortcuts. Walk his regular route with him and plot out where he should run if he is ever scared. Look for public places such as convenience stores, "safe houses," and for payphones along the route.

2. Instruct your child to go directly to her destination after school.

Whether going home, to a babysitter's house, to a neighbor's home, or to the library, your child should go directly to that location. Make it a rule that she must get your permission to take a different route home, for any reason.

3. Teach your child to avoid unknown routes.

If, for any reason, your child ends up on an unknown route home, she definitely should not go down alleys, side streets, or walk through empty lots. It is always better to stick to heavily trafficked streets and walk purposefully down the middle of the sidewalk.

4.   Instruct your child to go to a place of business or a "safe house" if he is ever scared.

If your child is approached by a stranger on the way home or feels that someone may be following behind, he needs to know where to go to find safety. Play "what-if" games to illustrate this rule. For example, where would he go if a man in a car slowed down nearby while he was walking home?

5.   Instruct your child to sit near the bus driver or near a mother with children when she has to ride public transportation.

Your child should also remain aware of the people who are sitting around her.

So if your parents get lost
It's your turn to be the boss
I'll be walkin' real tall
And in no time at all
They'll be laughin' and cryin'
They showed up in no time

~ Lyrics from *"If Your Parents Get Lost"*
Can't Fool Me!
Yello Dyno Records

Lost and Found: A Mother's True Story

"One day last year, my three children and I had been walking through the park. There was a big festival going on and there were probably thousands of people. I turned around and my daughter had walked one way and we had walked the other. I panicked because I didn't see her anywhere. Fortunately she knew what to do. She found a police officer and told him, 'Her mommy was lost, but it was okay because she'd be back real soon!'

It was almost verbatim quoting the words from the song and it just warmed my heart that she knew what to do at the age of four. She wasn't scared. I was the one who was in hysterics and crying and it's so funny because she looked at me and said, 'It's okay, Mom.' And she started laughing and she said, 'That's just like the song. You'll be laughing and crying. I never understood that, but now I know what it means!'"

20

FOLLOW YOUR LOST AND FOUND PLAN

I'm awalkin' through the mall
I'm awalkin' real tall
I'm findin' help right here
I'll betcha mom's real scared
Mom's probably just runnin' behind
She'll do better next time

~ Lyrics from *"If Your Parents Get Lost"*
Can't Fool Me!
Yello Dyno Records

Before your child ever gets lost and has to face this frightening situation alone, teach her what to do and how to get help. If a child is separated from you or lost, she will often freeze because she is not sure where to go or what to do. A child who is not prepared to handle the situation may have visions of "strangers" lurking behind every corner. This is self-defeating. She needs to be calm so that she can focus on staying safe and getting found. A child with a "lost and found" plan will be less scared and, therefore, less likely to find herself in greater trouble.

ACTION STEPS

1. Prepare your child with a plan before he is ever lost.

Tell your child that if he is lost in a public place, he should stay calm and alert. A child's natural response when lost is to wander around, which must be avoided. Generally, he should stay within the area where he last saw you. He should keep his eyes open for someone who can help him, such as a police officer, store clerk, bus driver, or a mother or grandmother with children. Your child should approach that person and say that he is lost. Then he should give the person his name and his parents' names, and ask the person to page his parents over the loudspeaker, if available. If appropriate, the child can give his address and telephone number to the person helping him.

2. Instruct your child never to leave a public area to look for you.

If lost, your child should never go into an area where he could get into greater trouble such as an office, dark hallway, bathroom, storeroom, parking lot or alley. He should stay within the public area and not leave the store or go to the back office of the store with anyone.

3.   Plan ahead when on an outing.

When you are out in a public place with your children, such as in a mall or theme park, agree beforehand on a meeting spot in case you get separated. For example, agree to meet at a bench near a fountain or in front of a particular store. You should instruct very young children to stay near the spot where they last saw you; tell them you will retrace your steps to find them, so they should not wander.

4.   Regularly review with your child what she should do if she is ever lost.

Your child will need reminders as she grows up. Test her comprehension of your "lost and found" plan by having her describe it to you periodically.

5.   Tell your child that if she is ever lost or taken you will look for her until she is found.

Your child will feel more confident and less scared knowing that you will never stop looking for her if she is ever lost.

21

FOLLOW HOME ALONE
SAFETY RULES

"While it's sometimes necessary for eight or nine-
year-olds to be home alone, the data show that it's a
frightening experience for them. Be sure the child
knows how to lock and unlock the doors and what to
do if a stranger calls or knocks on the door. Give
them phone numbers of people to call if there's any
problem, and give them coping strategies, rather
than just saying, 'This is good practice for you.'"

— "How Parents Can Talk to Their Kids,"
Newsweek

A guideline for deciding when you could feel
comfortable leaving your children home alone is when
you think they could handle a crisis. Even if you never
leave your house when your children are there, there are times
when you are unavailable. For example, when you are in the
shower, in the garden, or taking a nap, they are on their own.
When your child is alone at home, he will be the only one
available to answer the door or telephone, so he should know
exactly how to handle these situations. It is critical that he
does not give any specific information over the phone, such as
his name, your name, your address, or that he is home alone.
Establish concrete guidelines for your children when they are
by themselves at home. Prepare them so that they feel
confident in as many situations as possible.

ACTION STEPS

1. **Teach your child never to tell anyone that she is home alone.**

In fact, your child should not give any information to a phone caller or a person at the door. You may want to instruct your child to let your answering machine screen all phone calls. If someone does reach her on the telephone or knocks on the door, she needs to tell the person that her parent or guardian is busy and will call them back later. You can also prepare a statement that is more specific to your family. For example, if you garden regularly, your child could tell callers you are busy in the garden. If you nap in the afternoon, your child could inform callers that you are napping and will call them back later. Your child should not be persuaded to open the door for anyone who has not been approved, such as a person delivering flowers, a repair man, a neighbor, anyone in a uniform (even a police officer), or someone who says there is an emergency and that he needs to come in and use the phone.

2. **Practice "home alone" skills.**

When your child is home alone, check on her skills by calling her and also knocking on the door. Have her practice saying things like, "My mother is taking a nap. She'll call you back." To further clarify this in your child's mind, practice several "what-if" situations. Ask your child, for example, "What if a policeman comes to the door and says there is an accident or other emergency in the neighborhood and says you have to open the door?" Let your child answer; if necessary, help her to find the right response. In this situation she could tell the officer that she will call the police department for confirmation before opening the door, or that he should go to another house.

3. Make sure your child knows whom to call in an emergency.

Keep all important phone numbers such as for trustworthy neighbors and your workplace in a convenient place. Also review when to call "911" or "0" for operator in an emergency.

4. Make sure children five years of age and older know how to lock and unlock all of your doors and windows.

They should also know how to work the alarm system if you have one.

5. Review other "home alone" emergency plans, such as what to do in case of a fire.

Conduct home fire drills regularly. Many safety-related organizations such as local fire departments provide this type of information. Be sure to keep all emergency telephone numbers near your telephone, including the phone number for the local hospital and the poison control center.

22

NEVER LEAVE YOUR YOUNG CHILD UNATTENDED

"If one mother will listen and realize that all it takes is a second. Go in and answer the phone, go in and grab a Pepsi out of the refrigerator...You come back out and your kid ain't going to be there."

— Mother of three-year-old who was abducted and murdered. "Kids and Strangers," Cincinnati, *WKRC−TV 12*

Most parents feel they keep a close eye on their children, and they don't often worry about someone walking off with them. Yet there is case after case where a parent has turned her back for ten minutes, five minutes, and even one minute and her child was gone. Statisically it is a very rare occurence but when it happens statistics don't matter. In some instances, the abduction was described as occurring right under the parent's nose. There is the case of six-year-old Melissa Lee Brannen, who was taken from a neighborhood Christmas party while her mother turned to get her coat and hug a friend good-bye. Five-year-old Michael Dunahee was playing on a playground; when his parents returned five minutes later he was gone. Seven-year-old Ashley Estell went to the playground while her brother played soccer for just a few minutes; she was abducted and killed.

What are parents to do? How can we keep our eyes on our children every second of every day? Clearly, we cannot. The community, parents and children all need to become partners in helping to keep kids safe. From the parents' perspective, they have to be cautious so that the odds that their children will ever be harmed are reduced. To start with, until children are about five to six years old, parents should be vigilant about not letting their children out of their sight. Parents and guardians need to remember that they are the primary source of defense for young children. As your children grow older, enforce the buddy system and have them ask first before they go anywhere.

Parents should realize that if they are with their children at a playground or public pool, for example, they must *be with them*. If they are talking to another adult, their children are technically on their own. Remember, police and martial arts experts say that if your children are just twenty-one feet away from you they could get into danger and you would not necessarily be able to help them.

ACTION STEPS

1. Do not let children under five or six years old out of your sight.

Also teach young children not to wander off in crowds and public places.

2. Teach your children that they must not run away from you.

Some small children are amazingly fast, and since they are so small, they can easily get lost in a crowd. Teach them that they must never run away from you or a caregiver. In fact, they should always stay close by your side.

3. Never threaten to abandon your child.

It's easy to become tired or frustrated with a slow-moving or temperamental child when in a public place such as a mall. However, threatening to leave the child and walking away is clearly not a safe way to handle the situation. Instead, carry the child, or place him in a stroller.

23
USE THE CORRECT
VOCABULARY

"Show me a kid that knows nothing about sex and
I'll show you my next victim."
    –"The Crusaders," *NBC*

"If [children] don't have the vocabulary to talk about
their body parts, then if something happens they
can't tell anybody. They know that it's off-limits to
talk about. They can't get help."
    – Dr. Ian Russ, Ph.D., The Home Show, *ABC*

C aring parents are the best source of any information
that leads to children's sexual education. One of the
first steps is to give them the names of their private
parts. Private parts include the genital area, the buttocks, and
the breasts – essentially the area covered by their underwear
and bathing suits. If parents aren't comfortable with the
clinical names they could use the phrase "private parts" in
general conversation. Most children can't identify their body
parts or they find it too embarrassing to talk about because
that is the behavior handed down from their parents. If abuse
occurs they do not have the vocabulary to clearly describe the
abuse. This has often weakened the defense of a child in an
abuse trial. But young children can be taught to speak openly
and naturally about their bodies. By learning the names of
their body parts instead of the slang terms, children receive a
subtle message that their genitalia and those of others are
important and worthy of discussion in respectful language.

ACTION STEP

Give your children names for their private parts.

At the age of two or three, while children are learning names for their body parts such as toes and fingers, they are receptive, curious, and open. This is the time to introduce words such as "penis" and "vagina." If this subject is too uncomfortable for you to deal with, consider obtaining one of the many children's educational books to assist you.

24

FOLLOW HOUSE AND CAR SAFETY RULES

"It's believed that Polly Klaas's killer came in through an unlocked back door."

— Child Abductions: "What a Mom Must Know," *McCall's*

Sometimes obvious breaches of basic safety rules are overlooked for the sake of convenience, such as leaving a sleeping child in the car for a few minutes while you run into a store. Often child abductors are looking for just such an opportunity. In an example that terrified parents across the country, Polly Klaas's abductor and murderer is believed to have gone right through an open window or door in the house. For this reason, parents in small towns can no longer assume that they do not have to follow the same safety rules as parents who live in the city. As we've seen on television, our mobile society makes every house in every city and town a potential target. Appropriate safety guidelines must be considered in every home.

For added safety, the local police in many communities will meet with groups of families to describe how they can keep their homes safer; often they will even help set up block watch programs. It never hurts to have your neighbors watching out for your safety and you watching out for theirs; in fact, police say these are some of the safest neighborhoods.

ACTION STEPS

1. **Lock the doors and windows of your home with good locks, such as deadbolts.**

2. **Be sure your house has good lighting.**

   All entries should have lights that can be turned on from inside the house. Flood lights allow you to look into your yard at night if you hear any noises.

3. **If necessary, install an alarm system in your home and use it.**

   Some neighborhoods are more susceptible to trouble than others, so many families have home alarm systems.

4. **Provide easy access to telephones from every room.**

   You may want to install child monitors in the bedrooms of younger children.

5. **Never leave children in the car while you run an errand — even for a minute.**

6. **Help set up an organized "block watch" program in your neighborhood.**

   Contact your local police department for more information.

25

ESTABLISH SCHOOL SAFETY RULES

"Check and see if your school has a call-back program...Make sure the schools in your area at least inform the parents if the students do not attend school. That's one little step you can do today."
— Oprah Winfrey,
The Oprah Winfrey Show, *ABC*

School safety has taken a whole new dimension in the 21st century. For a more in-depth understanding please read Part Four on Protecting Your Children From Violent Kids. Not coincidentally, schools environments are reflecting the increase in violence from bullies to classroom avengers to non-custodial kidnappings to child molesters. In some instances abductors target a child in the morning as he is walking to school, then take the child in the afternoon while he is walking home. Parents need to be vigilant to ensure that their children's schools are ensuring children's safety. Two basics are call-back programs if your child doesn't come to school, and requiring adults to sign-in when they visit the school and sign-out children at the school office.

ACTION STEPS

1. Establish firm school pick-up permission rules.

Make sure that your school and daycare center will not give your child to anyone without your specific written instructions and proper identification. Child I.D. cards, which identify the correct parent or guardian, can be especially good for this purpose.

2. Require immediate notification if a child is absent from school.

If one of your children is absent, a school official should call you at home or at work, to notify you. That way, if your child is lost on the way to school, a search can begin immediately and precious hours won't be lost. Insist that your children's schools and daycare centers offer a program that notifies parents immediately if a child is absent. If necessary, help set up a notification program in your children's schools.

26

DON'T ADVERTISE YOUR CHILD'S NAME

"Don't put your child's name, first or last, visibly on hats, caps, jackets, bikes, wagons, etc. Remember, a child responds to a first name. A person using that name will automatically not be thought of as a stranger."

— "Prevention Tips for All Ages,"
Missing Children Report

Putting your children's names on the outside of their clothing or other personal possessions gives abductors an inside track, because children can let their guard down if a person calls them by name. A child may believe that this person knows him or knows his parents, and may believe that it is okay to go somewhere with that person. Proper identification on your child is important. It just needs to be concealed. For example, children can have their name on I.D. jewelry (on the inside where it's not visible) or on an I.D. card that they carry in their pocket or purse.

ACTION STEP

Make sure your child's name does not appear prominently on any of her possessions, such as clothes, bicycles, or school books.

If you want your child to wear an I.D. bracelet or other identifying item, be sure her name is not easily visible. On most I.D. jewelry the engraving is small and hard to read unless held under proper light, so these are generally fine.

27
CARRY PROPER I.D.

"You'd be surprised how many times we go to a parent and ask them, 'Give us a good picture of your child so we can get it on the news or we can get it distributed out,' and they don't have a clear picture, the child is not by himself, and it's not recent. Sometimes it's as much as five years old; on an eight-year-old that's a lot of difference. They (parents) need to have current pictures of these kids."

> – Sergeant Judy, Dallas Police Dept.,
> Spectrum, *Channel 5 News*

"There are so many families that don't even have pictures of their kids, much less recent ones. They don't have their exact height or weight measurements. You've got to think about keeping things like that," said Detective Larry Hanna, another investigator in the missing persons unit.

> – Parents Warned to be Prepared,
> *Las Vegas Review – Journal/Sun*

Proper child I.D. works. Parents and guardians should carry an I.D. card for each one of their children in their wallets. Then if you think that your child is missing or lost, you can respond immediately by handing the I.D. card over to the authorities on the spot. This speeds up the search for the lost child immeasurably. Authorities agree that the faster parents act, the faster they can find their child.

It is well documented by police that when a child is lost it is very difficult for emotionally distraught parents to think clearly and remember the correct actions to take. At a time like this, it is sometimes impossible even for loving parents to correctly describe their child, let alone think of the steps to take to find him. "He's about three feet tall. He has blond hair ...no, well...it used to be blond...it's more toward light brown now..." Imagine how many little boys or girls might fit a verbal description of your child in a mall on a Saturday afternoon! The following story illustrates this point.

> "I was feeling very stressed and had a real fear of not knowing what happened to my daughter, and these feelings made it hard to remember and to relay to the police many of her important characteristics. Angela's Yello Dyno I.D. card helped speak for me because it contained all her vital information and special identifying features. With the help of the I.D. card, which I kept in my wallet, the police were able to help find my daughter quickly."
> — New Castle, DE., *Parent*

When we are frightened or panicky our body jumps into the "fight or flight" response. Large amounts of adrenaline are dumped into our bloodstream. Many of our functions slow down or even shut down so that we can focus on exactly what we need to do to respond to the emergency. In these situations, we tend to develop tunnel vision, where we can lose sight of everything but the emergency at hand. In the case of a lost child, all of our signals are shouting, "Find my child!" What parent wants to try and remember the proper emergency procedures, or to stand at a counter and struggle to identify his child to security officers at a time like this?

Proper child identification is critical at this moment. But what is proper child I.D.? Few parents know the answer and many security professionals have never really thought it through. Since showing concern for missing children gains media attention and reflects community concern, I.D.s are often used as promotional items. Offering the I.D. makes the sponsor look good, but too often little attention is given to the function, content, and quality of the I.D., even though parents may at some time really need to use these I.D.s! That is why it's important to make sure that the I.D. card contains all of the necessary information in a format that is useful at the time of the crisis.

Yello Dyno has conducted extensive research over the years, including talking to law enforcement officials and investigators who work to find missing children, to establish what makes a child I.D. valuable. Four crucial points arose from our research:

1. The I.D. information must be in the parents' possession at the moment their child is lost, which is why laminated, wallet-sized I.D. cards are the best;

2. The I.D. card must contain the specific information that security or law enforcement officers need, presented in a specific format;

3. The child I.D. card must be up to date; and

4. The card should contain emergency instructions for the parent which will help them do the right thing in a high-stress situation, when it is most difficult to think clearly.

Many child I.D. products are not complete and may give parents a false sense of security. Furthermore, most child I.D. products are not true *immediate response* child I.D.s. Most, such as "passport" type I.D. kits or police home record files, are stored at home and, therefore, are generally useful only when a child is missing for a long time.

To respond quickly to a missing child report, law enforcement officers need certain information. Most important is a color photograph of your child and your child's physical description. They also need your child's birth date, key physical identifiers, medical emergency information, and parent or guardian information. Surprisingly, a child's nickname can also be essential, because a child under seven often will not answer to his or her formal name when lost or under stress. A good fingerprint on the I.D. card can also be helpful if you do not have a full set of fingerprints filed at home.

For further information about I.D. cards and other child security products and services, see Appendix E.

ACTION STEPS

1. **Carry a child I.D. card with correct information in your wallet at all times.**

   The Yello Dyno I.D. card is a good example of the information you need to provide authorities if one of your children is ever lost or missing. (See pictures in Appendix E.)

2. **Provide all of your child's caregivers with your child's I.D. cards.**

   You are not the only person who will spend time with your child in public places. You should ensure your child's safety when she is with babysitters, grandparents, friends of the family, etc.

3. **Update your childrens' I.D. cards every year.**

   Your children grow and change rapidly from year to year, so the I.D. cards you carry will be much more valuable if they are current.

4. **Make a mental note of what your child is wearing each day.**

   You should be able to accurately describe your child if he is ever lost or missing. His clothes could help distinguish your child from the crowd.

5. Provide your child with an I.D. card or other I.D. products.

Personal I.D. might be in the form of bracelets, shoe tags, or necklaces. Teens should also carry an I.D. card with them at all times. They not only provide identifying information, but may also include special emergency hotline telephone numbers if your child ever finds himself in trouble.

28

KNOW THE PEOPLE IN YOUR CHILD'S LIFE

"'All the kids on the block knew him,' she said. 'In fact, he bought bikes for them to ride. But they could never take them home'...The first mother said she had doubts about Allen, but because he was so helpful, she gave him the benefit of the doubt."

– "Child Pornography Arrest Shocks Neighbors,"
Austin American-Statesman

It is amazing how many incidents of child abuse occur in situations where children spend lots of time with adults whom their parents don't even know. Molesters gravitate toward children. They often look for jobs or volunteer opportunities where they will be in close proximity to large numbers of children. Parents cannot automatically assume that every coach, every scout leader, and every neighbor is a person with whom they should let their children be alone.

It deserves repeating: child molesters nearly always look like "nice guys." On the surface they can be very kind, charming people. But there are uncountable stories about how large numbers of children are molested by people their parents thought were safe. One convicted molester says that within a week of meeting him, one set of parents let him baby-sit their children, one of whom he molested. He says that because he was a youth group supervisor and looked clean-cut, they blindly trusted him with their child. Remember, child molesters often cloak themselves behind a mask of being a "good Samaritan" type person when in fact they are a "wolf in sheep's clothing".

The only way to keep children safe is to check out the people they spend time with. In particular, parents should be alert if another adult gives their child a great deal of attention. There must be some reason why. As Major Calvin Jackson, a leading forensics expert and child abuse investigator, has said, "If an adult likes spending more time with your child than you do, the chances are you have a problem. Parents should become suspicious of these individuals and become vigilant."

However, parents do not have to go overboard to protect their children. The majority of the people working with children are devoted professionals who simply love working with children. Parents just have to be smart. If something seems fishy, it just might be. Just as children need to trust their instincts, parents also need to trust theirs.

This safety rule boils down to one simple guideline: don't blindly accept new people into your childrens' lives. This means that parents need to get to know their children's friends and their friends' parents. They should communicate with their children and find out with whom they are spending their time. Parents should also be aware that many molesters, after being discovered in one community, will move to another community and start over.

ACTION STEPS

1. **Be involved in your child's activities and know her friends.**

Check out your child's friends' homes and meet her parents before letting your child sleep over, or go on any outings. Keep track of her friends' names, addresses, and telephone numbers. If your child likes spending a lot of time at any particular friend's or neighbor's home, drop in from time to time unexpectedly to check on her and see what the kids are up to. Also be wary of adults who display an inappropriate level of interest in your child — such as by taking her shopping or showering her with gifts.

2. **Communicate with your child.**

Ask your child whom he spends time with, what those people are like, and what he does when they are together. Listen and watch carefully for anything that sounds out of the ordinary. Watch your child's behavior after he has spent time with a new friend, whether it's a peer or an adult. If his personality starts changing with that person's influence, you should find out why.

3. Do not base your trust of people on superficial appearances.

Remain aware of the potential for abuse. Besides his friends, thoroughly check out the adults with whom your child spends time. Ask for references from babysitters, daycare operators, and other adults with whom you entrust your child's care. Also ask for references from any adult who will be supervising your child away from school grounds, such as a coach, scout leader, or youth group leader. Check out the references or network with parents who have. Be particularly alert to an adult who is new in town. Find out if the person knows anyone locally who can vouch for him.

29

PROMOTE YOUR CHILD'S SELF-ESTEEM

"Once children experience the power to keep themselves safe, it affects other areas of their life. Self-esteem and confidence soar. We want to teach children that they have the right to be safe and to prevent them from becoming victims...Children who have had a sense of their power, and who have been taught to think for themselves, are the safest children of all."

— "You've Got the POWER!"
Warrior Spirit, Video

"I believe it's time that everybody in America started treating their children differently...We have to make sure our children understand that they have self-esteem..."

— Mark Klaas (Polly's father), *Donahue*

Strong self-esteem can be children's best defense in staying safe. For one thing, children with positive self-esteem will have the confidence to perform all of the important safety rules that will help keep them safe. Parents will be making a huge investment in their children's welfare by taking the time to promote self-esteem. Moreover, self-esteem will enhance other important areas of your children's welfare, by giving them the confidence to avoid youth violence and peer pressure to experiment with drugs.

Often parents say that they hesitate to approach the topic of personal safety with their children for fear it will scare them and break down their self-confidence. But it's the way parents handle this topic that determines how it is internalized by a child. Safety education is an important part of helping children develop realistic and balanced perspectives about people and the world they live in, as they grow up.

A child's self-esteem comes from developing confidence in his or her abilities and skills. Many police and investigators feel the real value of martial arts classes is to help children's self-confidence grow. After all, it is unrealistic to expect a sixty-pound child to fight it out with a two-hundred-pound man. Instead, knowing he or she should cause a commotion, yell, resist, and then run to a safe place are some of a child's best defenses. Confident children perform these actions the best.

Building self-esteem in kids doesn't require that much time or effort. Simple things over time can work wonders. For example, including a child in the family's decision-making process, whether it is planning and cooking a meal or helping to plant a garden, shows that parents respect their children's thoughts and opinions. Building self-confidence can begin with little steps such as this example, related by my husband, Dennis:

> "The other day I was at Taco Bell and my young son wanted another tostada. I realized this would be a great opportunity to help build his confidence and comfort in speaking to an adult. I told him that he could go buy his tostada and that I would be watching. I gave him a dollar and off he went. After navigating through some cool teens, a frazzled mom, and a bored cashier, he pulled it off. He returned with the change, his tostada, and a big grin. It seems small, but it was very important to him. Little things like this accumulate to build self-esteem in a child."

ACTION STEPS

1. **Look for your children's unique qualities and encourage them.**

   While recognizing your children's unique qualities, pay attention to their strengths and weaknesses as they relate to personal safety. For example, you may have an extremely friendly child who loves to talk to people. That child will require extra instruction about why she should not make friends with people she doesn't know until you also get to know those people.

2. **Reinforce your love often.**

   Children need to know they are loved, so it is important to reinforce your love frequently. Tell your children that you will never stop loving them, no matter what; and that if they are ever lost, you will never stop looking for them either.

3. **Be aware and present safety education carefully to your children.**

   Don't project your fears and don't be unnecessarily dramatic. Fear can damage self-esteem, and the confidence that springs from self-esteem underlies many of these safety rules. It can also be weakening, not empowering, to be too graphic about the consequences. After all, when you teach your child to look both ways before crossing the street you don't describe in vivid detail what might happen if he gets hit by a car.

4. Involve your child in adult activities.

For example, while shopping you can let your child pay the cashier. This will develop her confidence in interacting with adults she does not know and help her learn to assert herself in the world of adults.

5. Learn more about developing your child's self-esteem.

There are hundreds of books on this topic. Visit your local library or bookstore to find a book that suits your needs.

30
LISTEN TO YOUR CHILD

"If you talk to your children and they talk to you, you establish an open relationship with your children before you need it, not afterwards."

> – J.J. Bittenbinder,
> "Street Smarts: Straight Talk for Kids,"
> Teens and Parents, *PBS*

Experts have described child abductors and molesters as the best child psychologists. It is the parents' job to put the odds in their children's favor. One of the reasons that communication between parents and children is important is that children are easily swayed by the "scripts" or "lures" of molesters.

Major Calvin Jackson tells this true story, which he experienced during his many years as a child abuse investigator:

> "In one dramatic case, the person molesting children was a prominent member of the medical community. Parents often used the fatherly physician to provide treatment for their children. During interviews of families who used the doctor, it was disclosed that most of the children did not like the physician, and in fact cried and resisted vehemently when told they would have to see him. Parents attributed the fear to a general dislike for doctors, although some children informed the parents they did not like what the

doctor did to them. The parents never asked what it was he did. In several instances the children described how he 'examined' them, requiring them to remove their garments, when in fact he was supposed to only check for minor ailments. Further, the parents did not make a distinction between their children's behavior when they visited other physicians and when they visited the molesting physician. The children did not resist being treated by other physicians. The unfortunate bottom line to this situation is that there were 123 verifiable instances of sexual child molestation raised against the doctor at the time of his conviction."

This story offers a classic example of parents' not listening to their children and, when they do listen, of not really *understanding* what their children are saying. Unfortunately, this is among the most common mistakes parents make. We all want to be the best parents we can possibly be, but as we rush from one responsibility to the next, our time with our children often diminishes to just moments each day. In that short time, we mostly just cover the day-to-day basics. For example, an after-school greeting might go a lot like this: "Did your day go well at school? Did you have a snack yet? You look tired. You'd better try and go to bed earlier tonight. Did that cough bother you at school today? Do you have homework? You left your bed unmade this morning and you need to tidy up your room before you go out to play. Could you also help me bring in the groceries? Your father is working late tonight. I have to go pick up your brother at his friend's house." This is not a likely time for deep communication, is it?

We listen to our children "on the fly," so to speak. This limits our capability to hear subtle fluctuations in their voices and to let things settle and see what is behind seemingly simple statements. Parents need to find the time of day that works best for them to check in with their children, whether it's right after school, during dinner, or just before bed.

Listening to our children often means stepping outside of our own inner world and our own problems, and really focusing on our children. We have all experienced that satisfied expression on our childrens' faces when we give them our full attention. There is no doubt that they feel special. We naturally give the courtesy of our attention to adults when they speak, but it is often a courtesy we do not extend to our own children. Clinical psychologist Lawrence Kutner, Ph.D., believes that talking "with" our children is different from talking "to" them. In his book, *Parent and Child*, he acknowledges, "Communicating effectively with a child often requires that a parent combine the deductive skills of Sherlock Holmes with the boundless tact and patience of an ambassador." So, if at first you don't succeed, give your children repeated chances to express their opinions, fears, or hopes.

Listening to your children may one day mean having to hear something that you find difficult to accept. Be aware that a child being molested or bothered may not speak about it directly. For example, your child may say to you, "Uncle John smells bad." If you were to respond, "That's not a nice thing to say about your father's brother," your child may take it to mean that you don't care and won't really listen if she were to tell you that Uncle John is coming into her room at night and fondling her. A simple response like, "What do you mean he smells bad?" might lead you in unexpected directions.

This open, loving relationship between parents and their children has to begin early in life. Children need to be raised with a strong sense that you will always love them and listen openly to them, even when they do something bad. Be sure to let them know that while you may not like their actions or behavior, you still love them.

Love. Nurturance. Belief. Empowerment. These are the four pillars that will provide your child with the inner strength he or she needs to stay safe. We need confident children, children who can be alone and take care of themselves – especially in today's uncertain world. By talking with and listening to your children, you will establish open communication and a sense of trust. This will encourage them to discuss their inner feelings and confide in you, and will set a pattern that will carry you and your children successfully into the future.

ACTION STEPS

1. Do your best to listen to your children.

Try to figure out what they might really be saying. Remember that they may not always speak directly about things that are bothering them.

2. Even if your child is misbehaving, your love should still be communicated.

Let your child know that while you do not like his behavior and wish he would stop, it doesn't mean you don't love him.

3. Establish a line of communication with your child.

Talk frankly with your child about the people in the world who might bother him. Child education experts say that you have to tell your ten-year-old what you want your teen to know.

4. Never belittle your childrens' fears.

Our children are individuals. They are part of us, yet uniquely their own. They may have fears that we see as unrealistic. That doesn't mean that we should say things such as, "Oh, you shouldn't be afraid of that." Instead, we should talk with them about their fears, giving them room to express the fears and then offering a wider perspective for them to understand why their fears don't have to be so scary.

5. Discuss family issues at regular times.

Set up specific periods of time, such as after dinner, when every member of the family tells about their day or discusses things that are bothering them.

6. Give your children support when they make mistakes.

All children will make mistakes, such as forgetting to get your permission when they go to a friend's house one afternoon. You should assure your children that even if you are annoyed with them for the mistake, you still love them. When your children are honest about their mistakes, it can be encouraging to show them that you appreciate their honesty, for example, by reducing the disciplinary measures.

7. Encourage your children to seek assistance from others.

As much as you might want to be, you may not be available for your children at the exact moment they need you. This is why you should ensure that your children know trustworthy people in addition to you with whom they can talk. Choose those people carefully, whether it's a family member, friend, teacher, or child-care provider. This idea of building a family network to raise children is not new. In fact, an old African proverb says, "It takes a village to raise a child."

CHECKLIST

30 PROVEN WAYS TO PROTECT YOUR CHILD FROM BECOMING LOST, ABDUCTED, ABUSED OR VICTIMIZED

✓ 21 CHILD GUIDELINES

☐ **1. Trust Your Instincts.** One of the most important ways to keep your child strong and free is for him to understand that he can get help if someone makes him feel uncomfortable or unsafe.

☐ **2. Beware of Tricky People.** It's not what someone looks like or how well you know him, it's what he asks you to do that matters.

☐ **3. My Body's Mine!** Your child needs to understand that her body is hers, and that means that she has the right to choose the level of physical affection that feels comfortable.

☐ **4. Identify Strangers.** Because a child cannot tell from the outside if a person is bad or not, you need to teach him what is OK to do at different ages.

☐ **5. Go to the Right Strangers for Help.** Your child needs to know what kind of strangers to go to for help if she is ever lost or in trouble.

☐ **6. Avoid Privacy and Control (PC).** Tell your child to avoid being in a location that gives PC to someone who makes him feel uncomfortable or unsafe.

☐ **7. You Can Say "No!"** A child who can say "no" to an adult when he is uncomfortable or scared will be the child who has a chance to keep himself safe.

☐ **8. Cut the Conversation!** A child has one powerful response that will allow him to stop powerful lures in their tracks... cut the dialogue!

☐ **9. Take Three Steps Back.** Teach your child to stay at least three arm-lengths away from anyone who makes him feel unsafe or uncomfortable.

☐ **10. Run Like the Wind.** Your child needs to know that it is OK to run away if she feels she is in danger.

☐ **11. Yell! Yell! Yell!** Your child can use his natural talent for yelling to protect himself.

☐ **12. Break Away!** While your child cannot "beat up" an adult, she must put up a struggle if she is ever grabbed.

☐ **13. Don't Keep Secrets** that make you feel uncomfortable. Your child should not keep secrets from parents or guardians.

☐ **14. Tell Until Someone Listens.** Empower your child to tell a parent or someone he trusts whenever he has a problem, and keep telling until someone listens.

☐ **15. Always Ask First.** Teach your child to always ask a parent or caregiver before going anywhere.

☐ **16. Always Have a Buddy.** Ensure that your child always has a buddy when walking to school or in public places.

☐ **17. Walk Tall!** Teach your child to always walk purposefully and stay alert.

☐ **18. Use the Telephone.** Instruct your child to learn her telephone numbers, including area code, how to use various telephones, and when and how to dial "911" and "0."

☐ **19. Take the Safe Route Home.** Make sure your child always takes the same route home everyday from school and from friends' homes.

☐ **20. Follow Your Lost and Found Plan.** Your child needs to know what to do and how to get help if he is ever lost.

☐ **21. Follow Home Alone Safety Rules.** Teach your child how to behave when home alone.

✓ 9 PARENT GUIDELINES

☐ **22. Never Leave Your Young Child Unattended.** Children under five years old are too young to be on their own.

☐ **23. Use the Correct Vocabulary.** Teach children the correct names of their private parts.

☐ **24. Follow House and Car Safety Rules.** Parents should not overlook the obvious safety rules, even when they are busy.

☐ **25. Establish School Safety Rules.** Ensure that your child's school follows proper safety guidelines.

☐ **26. Don't Advertise Your Child's Name.** Do not put your child's name visibly on any personal items.

☐ **27. Carry Proper I.D.** Carry an up-to-date child I.D. card for each of your children at all times, and give one to other caregivers.

☐ **28. Know the People in Your Child's Life.** Be involved in your child's activities and know his friends.

☐ **29. Promote Your Child's Self–Esteem.** Strong self-esteem can be a child's best tool for staying safe.

☐ **30. Listen to Your Child.** If you talk and listen to your child and she talks and listens to you, this establishes an open relationship *before* you need it, not afterwards.

PART FOUR

PROTECTING YOUR CHILD FROM VIOLENT KIDS

PROTECTING YOUR CHILD FROM VIOLENT KIDS

"One million U.S. students took guns to school in 1998."
— *Parents Resource Institute for Drug Addiction*

"They do so primarily because they feel threatened and can't count on adults to protect them."
— "Lost Boys: Why Our Sons Turn Violent and How We Can Save Them,"1997 CDC Survey

"Luke Woodham of Pearl, Miss., was a short, fat boy who was beaten and ridiculed by his peers. Mitchell Johnson of Jonesboro, Ark., was a pudgy outcast. And Eric Harris and Dylan Klebold of Littleton were disturbed loners whom classmates taunted as often as Harris and Klebold taunted them. All four teens took revenge by killing their schoolmates. Bullied, they became bullies themselves."
— Anna Mulrine, *U.S. News,* Cover Story 5/3/99

The day after the Littleton, Colorado School Massacre I was driving my 13-year-old son and 15-year-old daughter to school. My daughter was overly quiet and I noticed a worried look on her face. "What's up?" I asked. Coming out of a deep train of thought she said, "How do I know I'm safe at my school?" I didn't have the right answer for her. I was able to tell her, as a mom, that I thought she was safe but I knew my words did not ring true. Because of the need to protect my own children and because of my background in child safety, I hope the answers I have found will help you protect yours. If you ask your children who the bullies are at school, they can rattle off their names with no problem. The National School Safety Center now calls bullying "the most enduring and underrated problem in American schools." Bullying leaves its mark on 1 in 4 children. It's no laughing matter. Twenty years ago it might have meant ending up with a bloody nose. Today it may be a trip to the emergency room or worse. The role bullies have played in triggering a new type of violent child, "Classroom Avengers," will have to be addressed. Identifying violent kids may save your child's life, but how do you recognize one? Not all of the kids who fit this profile will go into a school and shoot multiple victims, but statistically they will commit acts of violence in their life. In helping parents and children recognize adults who are predators, the first lesson I teach is that it's not what someone looks like that matters — it's their behavior that matters. It's the same thing with kids who hurt kids — it's not what they look like, it's their behavior that matters. With the knowledge in this part of the book, you will learn how to recognize these potentially violent boys. This knowledge will not only help you to help them but, most importantly, it will enable you to protect your own child.

Bullies are obvious, but the Classroom Avengers are more difficult to recognize because they generally don't exhibit overt "bullying" behavior. However, if you know what to look for, they give countless signs to alert those around them to the impending tragedy.

What is the behavior of a Classroom Avenger? He may spend countless hours on the Internet, or be an expert at video games. He's usually a good student, his behavior is normal, adults like him, and his dress is usually in keeping with teens of his own age. He has little or no previous history of delinquent behavior and he is not known to have a psychiatric problem. Over-all he's an okay kid but most kids think he's a bit of a nerd. He may be the quiet kid seated next to your daughter in class. If your daughter is the gentle, nurturing type, she has probably told him that the other kids pick on him too much. Her consoling him may actually cause him to fantasize that she is his girlfriend and a small slight on her part may risk her life. Your son may sit in the desk on the other side of him. Being outgoing and one of the most popular kids at school, he may find no harm in teasing this nerdish kid. It's not meant to hurt, but those small jabs all during the year may build to trigger a Classroom Avenger to "defend his honor." As with any toxicity, some children are more vulnerable to violence than others.

Who are the most vulnerable? The boys who have shocked us to our core by entering our schools and killing our children and teachers. Their faces have paraded across our magazines and in our media. They are described as "super predators," "monsters" and "crazies." We try to distance ourselves from them, but as a mother, when I look into their eyes I can't help but wonder what went wrong. They are children who have committed the most atrocious acts, but they are still "children." They don't look like monsters; in fact, they look like normal kids. If I dare to look closer, they look like the boy next door and even worse, maybe my own son. Are these unpredictable, random acts? No, they are not, if you know what to look for. At first it seems easier to alienate these boys and their families but that only leaves us vulnerable. These boys are symptoms of an epidemic that started years ago in the inner cities, because that was the most vulnerable segment of the population. Just as teen pregnancy and latchkey kids were once common in the inner cities and in the poorest communities, now urban violence by teens, that once seemed so far removed from middle America, has entered our suburban and rural schools. The epidemic has invaded our country and much more deeply than many of us would like to believe. When we send our teenagers off to school imagining that they could never encounter lethal youth violence, it leaves them dangerously vulnerable. The fact is that almost every child now goes to school along with some troubled child who could commit acts of lethal violence. While this epidemic permeated urban America years ago, its rural and suburban mutated-form is the "Classroom Avenger."

One of the most dramatic points in the profile of the Classroom Avengers is that they come from families who give the appearance of being "superficially normal," but underneath they are often quite dysfunctional.

Some other factors that contribute to the development of violent kids are:

Divorce

"Divorce, separation and/or frequent episodes of intense friction between parents, and parents and child, is the norm...Explicit or covert anger and hostility are the prevailing emotions in the family, accompanied by parent-child power struggles and battles over control...Discipline, however, is overly harsh and applied inconsistently. One or more of the Classroom Avengers' first-degree relatives may be mentally ill, personality disordered or a substance abuser."

– James P. McGee, Ph.D. & Caren R. DeBernardo, Psy.D., *The Classroom Avenger*

Abuse

"Key to preventing violent behavior is preventing child abuse."

– American Academy of
Child & Adolescent Psychiatry

Neglect

"Since the late 1960's the amount of time parents spend with their children has dropped from an average of thirty hours per week to seventeen."

> – Lipsky and Abrams, 1994; Galston, Dec. 2, 1991
> Shirley R. Steinberg and Joe L. Kincheloe
> *Kinder-Culture*

Violence

"The average child will witness at least 8,000 murders on TV by the time he or she leaves elementary school, along with more than 100,000 assorted acts of violence."

> – Sisela Bok, "Mayhem"
> *American Psychological Association*

"With the solid emotional, behavioral, cognitive and social anchors provided by a healthy home and community, this pervasive media violence does not "cause" violence, but it does contribute to a pervasive view that the world is a much more dangerous place than it really is. In children exposed to violence in the home, these media images of power and violence are major sources of "cultural" values, reinforcing what they have seen modeled at home. And the beliefs and actions of all children reflect the world they are raised in. The violence in our streets started in our homes."

> – Bruce D. Perry, M.D., Ph.D.,
> "Neurodevelopmental Adaptation to
> Violence:How Children Survive the
> Intragenerational Vortex of Violence,"
> *CIVITAS Child Trauma Programs*

With such a toxic social environment, the demand for parental involvement increases. But parents are less available than ever because today's economic climate demands that both parents work to make ends meet, either by choice or necessity. Some studies show that mothers still do 80% of the household work and the rearing of children.

> "Whatever its origins, a parent's psychological unavailability is a form of child maltreatment, and maltreatment plays a central role in the development of bad behavior and aggression in children."
>
> — James Garbarino, Ph.D.,
> *Lost Boys: Why Our Sons Turn Violent and How We Can Save Them*

Classroom Avengers, while superficially passive, are deeply disturbed and can be easily misunderstood. They may have the appearance of normality, but their behavior is a response to a hostile environment that has rejected them. Their behavior has become a form of protection. The depression, shame, rage, alienation and bloated self-centeredness is masked by a countenance of apparent normality. Neglect can continue without disturbing the status quo. A parent can appear to be parenting and the child can appear to be "normal." How can a parent actually be parenting and miss so many signs of distress?

> "Is it possible for parents to miss homicidal rage? Where were the Harrises and the Klebolds when their sons were watching Natural Born Killers over and over? Have they ever played Doom and the other blood-soaked computer games that occupied their children? Did these 'educated professionals' take a look at the hate-filled web site their kids created? Were the Harrises aware of the pipe-bomb factory that was in their two-car garage? The kid down the street was aware of it, and he's 10 years old."
>
> — Amy Dickinson,
> "Where Were the Parents?" *Time*

When you understand what to look for, there was no mistaking that these boys were in serious trouble. Dylan Klebold's and Eric Harris's families as well as the Littleton Community, the police, their teachers, the parents of their friends, and the other children were given countless opportunities to recognize the difficulty these boys were in and act to prevent this tragedy. Only one family tried but no one took them seriously.

Some have asked, could Dylan and Eric really have known what they were doing? Were they partially the product of violent video games? Marines are trained on Quake and Doom. As such, did these boys understand the difference between fantasy and reality?

Fantasy or Reality?

"Video games are highly structured and programmed universes. Either you play the game according to a fairly rigorous set of rules or you lose. Thus, if the game is about kicking, punching and killing your opponent, then in order to win you must do exactly that."

> – Shirley R. Steinberg and Joe. L. Kincheloe,
> *"Kinder-Culture"*

We've been assuming as adults that all this information is being logged by the brain as "imaginary," but is it? Recently I was out with my son and a 12-year-old friend of his. We were approached by a friendly dog and my son's friend shrunk back. His reaction was fearful. "I hate dogs!" he stated. I asked him why he hated dogs, and he said he had seen five people bitten by a Doberman pincher. I asked him when and where. "I saw it on TV," he said. "But it wasn't real," I replied. He then said heatedly, "It doesn't matter. I saw it. I hate dogs."

Children as old as six years old still think that if you die you will miraculously come back to life. But even more important, 13-and 14-year-olds who are old enough to kill still do not have a clear concept of death. Video games, movies and the media bombard our children with images of death divorced from the real consequences of violent actions.

> "When he opened fire, Michael said, he was trying to get people to notice him...He didn't think the light-calibered Ruger could kill..."
> — Paducah, KY, "Michael Carneal,"
> Jonah Blank, *U.S. News*

Obviously, Michael did not understand the difference between fantasy and reality. To the extent our cultural "entertainments" blur the line between fantasy and reality, we will all pay the price.

The purpose of this section of the book is to help you prevent the reoccurrence of these tragedies in your own lives. The knowledge and "personal safety tools" will give you both the awareness and the assurance you need *to act* to protect your children. Recognizing those who are in trouble does not take a Ph.D. All it takes is knowing the signs of trouble and taking time to listen to your children.

Your Child Knows Best

Ask your children who the troublemakers are in their class or school: the "strange" ones or the ones everyone picks on. You will be surprised how much information they can give you. Children are much more in touch with their survival instincts, and they do not rationalize or deny behavior. They are great allies in helping you identify whom to check into. From fifth grade on, begin sharing the following points with your children so they know what to watch out for. Knowledge empowers children. It does not create fear. In fact, it removes fear. You should have little doubt by now that our children today live with a level of fear most of us never experienced growing up.

There is a fundamental lesson I have been teaching for more than ten years: "We don't keep secrets. If someone asks us to do something that makes us feel uncomfortable or unsafe, then we tell an adult we trust." This key *Safety Rule*, along with the balance of the program, encourages children to speak up when in danger. Because of this patterning, which reinforces the belief they have the right to be safe, a strong base of self-confidence is built in the child, beyond just peer acceptance. This gives you a dramatic advantage in protecting your child or teen.

Another critical component for your child's safety is that there is communication and mutual support between the parent, the administration and the teachers at your child's school.

> "I never thought it could happen at my school. I just recently got out of the hospital. I was a victim of a shooting at my school. I've been teaching for 20 years and I never thought it could happen at my school. Some of the kids knew about it before it happened, but they didn't want to say anything — they have a code of honor and they did not want to tattle-tale. But someone has to stand up, someone has to take a stand because, if you don't, then somebody else is going to get hurt."
>
> – Gregory Carter, Teacher, Richmond, Virginia

When evaluating a school's "safety net" you should be met with positive support for your concerns. The answers for these questions should already be written policy. If not, your inquiry in writing should compel the administration to consider the issues. The following questions are from *Protecting the Gift: Keeping Children and Teenagers Safe* by Gavin de Becker, America's leading expert on predicting violent behavior.

8 Questions to Evaluate a Safe School

1. Are there school policies addressing violence, weapons, drug use, sexual abuse, child-on-child sexual abuse, unauthorized visitors?

2. Are background investigations performed on all staff?

3. Does the screening process apply to all employees (teachers, janitors, lunchroom staff, security personnel, part-time employees, volunteers, bus drivers, etc.)?

4. Can my child call me at any time?

5. How does the school address special situations (custody disputes, child kidnapping concerns, etc.)?

6. Are acts of violence or criminality at the school documented? Are statistics maintained?

7. Are teachers formally notified when a child with a history of serious misconduct is enrolled at the school?

8. Will I be informed of teacher misconduct that might have an impact on the safety or well-being of my child?

In Part One, Chapter Four, Who Are "The Bad Guys"?, you will find *"Eight Red Flags for Identifying Child Molesters."* That information has helped many parents and teachers prevent and remove their children from dangerous situations.

The following list of *Imminent Warning Signs of "Kids Who May Kill or Commit Suicide"* is to help you identify a dangerous child. My intent is to protect normal children and if possible to help troubled children. The warning signs are not a call to arms. Being able to identify a child who will become a Classroom Avenger is difficult, at best, but identifying a child who has the potential to do serious harm is not. As with the Eight Red Flags, I recommend that you look for several of these warning signs to be present at once. One or two are not generally enough to take action. A child who exhibits multiple signs repeatedly, (and with increasing intensity) is a likely candidate for violence. Some behavior requires immediate attention, such as obsession with fire setting, cruelty to animals, or adult sexual behavior even in children as young as six years old. For the child's sake (and to prevent triggering an incident) avoid labeling, isolating or punishing any child who fits this profile. Be sure you are aware of what is "normal" behavior for different age groups so that you do not misinterpret typical behavior. Remember, most of us were not perfect as teens and some of us made some pretty stupid mistakes.

> "Surveys show that most boys and many girls exhibit some delinquent behavior during their teenage years, with more than 60% engaging in some combination of aggressive acts, drug abuse, arson and vandalism."
>
> — James Garbarino, Ph.D.,
> *Lost Boys: Why Our Sons Turn Violent and How We Can Save Them*

Confer with other adults to see if they have the same view and concerns before acting. If you agree, then approach the school counselors, police and/or the parents of the child appropriately. If you are close to the family, decide if it is beneficial for you to approach them first. Be sure to show your concern for their child and be supportive. Don't attack their parenting. In most cases the parents will not be open to your suggestions because the problem stems from within the family dynamics. Remember, do not try to handle this on your own. Include professionals who are trained to handle potentially difficult and dangerous situations.

Imminent Warning Signs of
'Kids Who May Kill or Commit Suicide'

1. Recent Stressful Event: "Breakup" with presumed or real girlfriend, victimization (persecution) by peer group, conflict with parent, school personnel or authority figure.

2. Excessive feelings of isolation and being alone; if associated with behavior that is aggressive or violent, take note.

3. Dramatic drops in grades or attendance at school.

4. Considered "weird" or dangerous by peers. Detailed threats of lethal violence – verbally, in writings and/or drawings.

5. Preoccupied with weapons, explosives or other incendiary devices.

6. Severe rage – "out of control," for seemingly minor reasons.

7. Overt self-injurious behaviors or threats of suicide. Cruelty to animals and smaller children. Fascination with fire and fire-setting.

This is admittedly tough stuff. While we are learning to protect children from violent kids, we should review briefly the characteristics of normal children.

Five Characteristics Common to Emotionally Healthy Children

1. Personality: They are generally friendly and can be outgoing or shy, but not "withdrawn."

2. Relationships: They have good relationships with siblings, parents, other adults and authority figures.

3. Peer Acceptance: They are accepted among their peers. This does not necessarily mean "popular."

4. Outlook: They have enthusiasm about the present and the future and often have specific career aspirations.

5. Activities: They participate in constructive group activities such as student government, theater and the arts, choir, band, sports, scouting, 4-H, and traditional religious groups.

Many exceptional people do not fit the traditional mold and struggle with "the system." There is a pervasive subculture in many schools that says "being different is bad." This is wrong and should not be tolerated. Many unique individuals (for example, Albert Einstein and Buckminster Fuller) fall through the cracks of mainstream educational and social systems, but still become productive and valuable citizens (if not outright great citizens). What you are looking for is a troubled individual, generally with an *escalating* history of generally negative behavior.

Great people can come out of adversity and difficult childhoods. The care and guidance of just one adult can change the entire course of a child's life, even if they have all the negative traits previously discussed. Consider taking the hand of such a child.

Characteristics Common to Violent Kids

1. Loners and/or social outcasts.

2. Physically healthy: not likely to be physically handicapped or disabled.

3. Attend public school, no participation in pro-social groups or "normal" pastimes; socially immature.

4. Members of alienated groups or gangs.

5. Relationship conflicts with peers and adults.

6. Poor parent and sibling relationships; child abuse.

7. Family history of mental illness, personality disorders or substance abuse (but only about 10% of violent kids have severe mental illness). Depression, suicidal tendencies.

8. As infants — colicky, temperamental, delayed milestones, history of bed-wetting. Problems with attachment and bonding.

9. Display chronic anger; anger and power struggles within the family.

10. Distrustful and secretive with adults in authority.

11. Negative self-image and/or unstable self-esteem.

12. Inappropriate access to, possession of, and use of firearms.

13. Violent fantasies, strong attraction to real and fictional violence in media, movies, video games and music.

14. Premeditation/planning/surveillance of targets.

15. Victims of bullying since preschool.

16. Multiple psychological stresses imagined or real, including rejection, discipline, humiliation.

17. Inability to accept responsibility and blame.

18. Cruelty to animals; fascination with fire/fire-setting.

Classroom Avengers[1] vs Urban Violent Kids Characteristics
CLASSROOM AVENGERS

1. Caucasian race.

2. Middle income, reside in rural or small community residence in south or northwest.

3. Fair to excellent academic performance; average to above average IQ.

4. Appearance of normality to adults: no history of serious school misbehavior or conduct disorder.

5. Superficially "normal" dysfunctional family (hidden anger and hostility).

6. Illegal drug and alcohol use uncommon, or some experimentation. Prescribed psychiatric medication by pediatricians or general practitioners who are not skilled in psychiatric care is more likely.

7. Strong school interest. The school is the center of their social arena.

8. Superficially respectful toward teachers and authority figures.

9. "Geeks or nerds" who are rejected by mainstream students. Rarely instigate physical confrontation.

10. "Covert" vandalism and dishonesty.

11. Target: females, highly functioning students and authority figures.

12. Motive: vengeance and achievement of power and/or status.

(1) The Classroom Avenger is a new phenomenon. This information is not intended to be a definitive portrait and as new information becomes available some characteristics are sure to change.

Classroom Avengers¹ vs Urban Violent Kids Characteristics

URBAN VIOLENT KIDS

1. Minority races.

2. Lower income, reside in large city.

3. Consistently poor academic performance; below or average IQ.

4. Severe and evident conduct disorder.

5. Obvious family history of problems: divorce, multiple moves, financial stress, abuse, alienation, etc.

6. Illegal drug and alcohol use.

7. Low school interest. The center of the social arena is outside of the school.

8. Extremely belligerent and disrespectful toward teachers and authority figures.

9. "Cool Kids" who have patterns of impulsive and chronic hitting, intimidating and bullying behaviors.

10. Well documented history of extensive criminal and/or delinquent behavior.

11. Target: could be just about anyone.

12. Motive: to harm but usually have secondary motive; disputes, robbery or rape.

"One million U.S. students took guns to school in 1998."
  – *Parents Resource Institute*
  for Drug Addiction

12 ACTION STEPS

1. **Don't give up or let go of your child too early.**

   Most parents take a "mental break" from raising their child between the ages of ten and twelve. It appears as a "breather." The child knows the safety basics and is not yet stepping into the dangers of the teen years. But because of the media influence and the size of schools today, the turmoil of the teen years is starting younger and younger. Be alert to shifts in your child's behavior, sleep pattern, friends or performance in school.

2. **The teen years are a time of identity formation.**

   Be sure you know your child's role models — who she wants to be like and why.

3. **Teens need more privacy, however spending the vast majority of their time behind closed doors is not healthy.**

4. **Know where your children are physically and mentally.**

5.   Teach your child from a young age not to bully others.

Cartoons teach the opposite. When your child has the painful experience of being bullied, remind him that another child feels the same way when he bullies him. Listen to your child when he tells you about someone who is repeatedly bullying him or if he is bragging about bullying another child. Step in and help him learn appropriate behavior. Seek professional help if the pattern keeps getting stronger.

6.   For a child who has an "explosive temper".

Teach your child not to respond with aggressive behavior or derogatory comments to others, as this may be taken as threats causing the threatened child to lose his temper. Teach your child that a kind, gentle but firm response helps to keep him emotionally connected and reinforces non-aggressive behavior. If your teen is encountering an aggressive person at school, tell him to be kind but to keep his distance and advise the school counselor of the situation. Parents, school counselors and teachers must respect a student's need to be anonymous if they expect a student to speak up.

7.   Help your child realize that actions have consequences.

Violence has a price. On an ongoing basis, share your views and understanding with your child of the effects of the violence and aggression that he sees, either in video games and movies or that he possibly encounters in school or in the neighborhood.

8.   Apply discipline consistently, without anger.

This will help your child learn that there are consequences for misbehavior. If anger is a key element in your family dynamics, seek professional help.

9.   Encourage your child to share her thoughts and feelings.

Your child's sense of worth is established by how you, as the parent, respond. This is a life pattern. If you have a problem with your child commonly responding with anger or withdrawing from you, it is a cover for a deeper emotional problem. Seek professional help.

10.   It is a misconception that your teen has to cut all connection to you.

In fact, the opposite is true. Teens and parents are made to believe by the media that teens need to be "on their own," and abandon their families. The opposite is actually the truth. Teens want and need more than ever to know there is strong family support behind them.

11.   Always check with friends to see if they have guns and if they are securely locked up before your child plays there.

12.   Remember that a child is the reflection of the family, so get to know the families of your child's friends.

Take time to discuss your views and concerns with them. No two families parent exactly the same. Be sure to agree on the big issues, while perhaps yielding on the small ones.

Food for Thought

"The correlation between media violence and aggression is stronger than the correlation between second hand smoke and lung cancer and condom use and HIV prevention."

> – Brad J. Bushman, Ph.D., "New ISU Study looks
> At Weak Coverage of Media Violence Research,"
> Department of Psychology Publication,
> Iowa State University

"The overall youth homicide rate dropped in 1997, but the rate among small town and rural youth increased by 38 percent. That statistic highlights my conviction that no longer can any of us believe that we and our children are immune to lethal youth violence, because today almost every teenager in America goes to school with a kid who is troubled enough to become the next killer – the chances are that kid has access to the weapons necessary to do so."

> – James Garbarino, Ph.D., *Lost Boys: Why Our
> Sons Turn Violent and How We Can Save Them*

"More police and more courts and more prisons and better investigative techniques are fine, but the only way crime is going to go down is if all of us simply stop accepting and tolerating it in our families, our friends, and our associates. This is the lesson from other countries with far lower numbers than ours. Only this type of grassroots solution, in my opinion, will be effective. Crime is a moral problem. It can only be resolved on a moral level."

> – John Douglas and Mark Olshaker, *Mind Hunter*

Food for Thought

"So while you may be able to keep your son from owning one (a gun), if you try to talk him out of wanting one, you are up against a pretty strong argument. 'You mean I shouldn't want a device that grants me power and identity, makes me feel dangerous and safe at the same time, instantly makes me the dominant male, and connects me to my evolutionary essence? Come on, Mom, get real!'"

> – Gavin De Becker, *Protecting The Gift: Keeping Children and Teenagers Safe (and Parents Sane)*

"By the time a child reaches the age of eighteen, approximately one in four will have been impacted directly by some form of traumatic event (e.g., natural disaster, MVA, domestic violence, physical or sexual abuse)."

> – Bruce D. Perry, M.D., Ph.D., G. Michael Gomez, M.D., "Role of the EMS Provider in Crisis Intervention," *CIVITAS Child Trauma Programs*

"If a child feels he has to be fearful all the time, it breeds cynicism and distrust. He'll tend to see others as essentially bad. He may also become an adult who takes no chances, which is very limiting – because without risk, he's not likely to be successful in life. Fear in itself is a form of victimization."

> – Jack Levin, Ph.D., Director of the Program for the Study of Violence at Northwestern University in Boston in *Redbook*, February 1998

PART FIVE

PLAYING IT SAFE ON THE INTERNET

PLAYING IT SAFE ON THE INTERNET

"A new Web site appears every 22 seconds, more than 3,900 new sites every day. Today at least 85 of those new sites will be selling commercial pornography."
— WebChaperone Fact Sheet,
Webco International

C hild predators have found an unguarded playground on the Internet. With the rapid growth of the Internet, it is impossible for law enforcement to effectively patrol the millions of Internet highways; therefore the primary protection of children has to be in the hands of parents and schools. Literally overnight, cyberspace has become a street in our town that children can walk down without our knowledge. With a click of a key, they could walk into a striptease joint, an X-rated movie or be charmed by a child predator in a chat room. In the past, our children did not usually encounter such options until they had the mental and emotional maturity to cope. State laws required that they be at least 18 years old to enter these adult establishments. In cyberspace our children are being lured as early as they can use a mouse.

Once again, our first line of defense as parents and educators is to educate ourselves. Our second line of defense is to educate our children. Knowledge is like a lamppost that is put up in a dark alley. The criminals scurry away in fear of detection. There are easy steps that we as parents can take to learn more about the Web and prevent online dangers. If you are not computer literate, begin by increasing your own computer literacy. You might even have your computer-savvy child escort you through cyberspace.

You will be stunned to find that links to XXX rated sites often appear along with appropriate results when your child does innocent searches. Predators use these innocent words to catch unsuspecting children. The same phrase will also bring up different results on different search engines, and different results on different days depending on the popularity of sites. No word blocks are going to stop these requests, and the law doesn't allow anyone to put in print what will appear in front of their eyes. The sites that would be banned by parents are the sites being discussed and visited by children.

Sixth, seventh and eighth-graders are naturally curious about their bodies and sex as they go through all the changes of puberty. Remember that teens want to belong. Group peer pressure and the sexual bombardment from the media could lead your child to a site he or she will regret.

Some curious boy is going to go look at pictures at some point. Don't think your child is the exception. Explain that curiosity is natural. Tell your child about pornography. If you don't, some schoolmate will. Who would you rather have educate your child? Let your child know that the pornographic sites on the net are not examples of a loving relationship, but rather expressions of people filled with pain. Also let them know that these images hurt the mind and once they are in the mind they will always be there.

This story from an old Readers Digest is a wonderful way to explain to children why they might want to wait. A young girl asked her father a question and she was too young to understand the answer. He pointed to his packed suitcase for his business trip and asked her to put it in the car for him. She laughed and said it was way too heavy for her to lift. He said, "It is the same with your question. The answer is too heavy for you to carry right now, but I will be glad to answer it when you are older."

The need to teach your child the street smarts of cyberspace is obvious. As is age appropriate, discuss what your child might encounter. Many Internet carriers offer blocks to help keep kids out of adult Web sites, but this is not a complete solution. A computer-literate child can break through any block if they really want to. If you don't believe me, ask a few of your child's friends who are really into computers. Even if you have blocks on your computer, do your child's friends have blocks on their computers?

It is vital to remember that child predators traditionally prey on the most vulnerable children. Their approach on the Web is the same as in real life. They look for children who are in need of attention, who have low self-esteem, are loners or are uneasy with social skills. Children whose parents both work full time or are going through a divorce are often good candidates.

Child molesters are superb listeners. Why? Because they are so obsessed with luring children. The hunt, known as "grooming," is almost as thrilling to some predators as the conquest.

The Internet has become an incredible resource for predators because they can literally have unlimited and unsupervised "grooming" time with your child. It is missed as abuse because there is no initial physical contact. *Your child may be at home, but that doesn't mean that your child's mind and heart are not being affected.* It has been common in cases that involve the Internet that a child can become so obsessed with her online friend, particularly if she is unhappy in her day-to-day life, that common sense goes out the window. Children naturally want to believe that someone is good and they apply their values to those they are talking to online. They all to easily come to trust this stranger, just as they do a "charming" stranger that they might meet in the mall. If they are not trained on how to recognize behavior that means danger, over time this relationship can replace a child's interest in real relationships and day-to-day activities. A child can move into an online fantasy world created by a predator who could endanger their life. It becomes brainwashing by a "spider" who is literally spinning a web to lure your child into meeting them. With continued contact, the predator leads the child into playing as active a role in the relationship as he does. This "spinning" includes the repeated use of inappropriate material, so your child will eventually accept part of the responsibilty. This creates a bond of silence. This attachment, often incredibly intense, can be closely guarded and protected by the child. Because the victim may believe she is "in love" with the offender, she may warn him if you are outwardly too upset. Keep your composure, learn what is going on and then approach professionals for help if appropriate.

Remember, you have your child's best interest at heart, so you may have to put on your detective's hat and learn before your child does what is the safest and best way to surf the web.

Investigating Web-Sites Yourself

Let's face the hard facts. We hear stories of child molesters in chat rooms posing as teens to lure our children. Is this true? Yes. Of course this is not always the case, but it does happen.

Understanding the enemy gives us the power to protect our children from them. There is an organization that supports molesting children. They are highly organized and vocal about their beliefs. NAMBLA, North American Man Boy Love Association, believes that it is natural to have sex with children. It is active in changing legislation to lower the age of consent and is trying to change the view of this behavior to a freedom of choice issue rather than a crime. Parents John Walsh and Maureen Kanka (mother of Megan) never knew about this group until it was too late for their children. They both tell of their shock to learn that such a group exists.

Not only does it exist, it has a Web site you can visit. The organization does not break the "law." It provides support through the Internet to child molesters who would normally find no avenue of support for their behavior. They believe they are fighting a historic battle to free children to be able to choose to participate in these relationships. They seem to overlook that these are not two consenting adults but a child and an adult. Their philosophy can be viewed at NAMBLA's site at http://www.nambla.org/. There are no inappropriate pictures on this site. The need to teach your child the "street smarts" of cyberspace is obvious.

To see the options that may entice your child, try typing key words on two or three of the Internet search engines. Innocuous words can have shocking results. For instance, try doing a search for "japanimation" at www.excite.com. If you don't know about "japanimation" and "anime," your older children almost certainly will. These innocent cartoon characters that have become household names and faces to our children, are also pornographic characters on the Internet. When you do this search, you will be given options for sites to visit. You do not have to enter these sites. The descriptions of the sites are enough to let you know that you do not want your child going there. You'll be stunned at what is available under this seemingly innocent search in animation. That is certainly enough to let you know that the Internet needs parental involvement, and that the need to teach your child the "street smarts" of cyberspace is obvious.

Now, as parents, let's step back to our adolescence and remember those challenging years. Peer acceptance was so important and those "popular kids" just had it so good. So when the Internet comes up in discussions and the sites that would be banned by parents are discussed, what's the cool thing to do? Go look. So instead of waiting for a crisis, join your child on the web and lead him or her on a safe journey.

A Mom's True Story

When my daughter was 14 years old and wanted to start going into chat rooms, I joined her for her first voyage. She was quite excited. I asked her what screen name she would use. Having just seen the latest Batman movie, she picked the name "Poison Ivy 14" after one of the characters. I wasn't happy with her choice and certainly didn't like her including her age, but I knew it was an innocent choice and several others had their age after their names in the chat room. This was my opportunity to be there with her and help her learn.

What I didn't tell her about was that there was another character by that name. In fact there are three R-rated movies named Poison Ivy. They commonly rent at video stores. Each movie is about a teen-age girl, Poison Ivy, who uses sex to wreak havoc, including seducing older men. What a choice of names she had picked!

No sooner was she on and chatting away with several "unknowns," than she began to receive particular attention from one man. When I had her ask questions about him, he said he was an auto mechanic from Canada. I asked my daughter if she thought it was a little odd that this man was on the Internet on a Friday night and not out with friends. She didn't think much of it and they kept chatting back and forth.

After about half an hour I asked her to ask him how old he was. He replied that he was 42 years old. Since she had already put her age up there for everyone to see, I knew he knew that he was talking to a young girl. The conversation between them was certainly not one that should hold the interest of an adult.

As a twist to their conversation, I suggested she tell him that she wasn't really 14 years old but to give him my age since I was older than he was. She confessed to him that she really wasn't 14 years old. He sent back a reassuring reply that it really didn't matter. Then he asked her how old she really was.

She said, "Oh, you really don't want to know." "Why not?" he replied, "I'm enjoying our conversation." "OK," my daughter said, "I'm 48." At that, he left the chat room and was never to be heard from again, at least not as "that person."

This was a simple and sheltered experience for a mother and daughter, but the following true case from the National Center for Missing and Exploited Children will show you how dangerous it really can be when the web is used to trap our children.

> "On September 26, 2000, NCMEC's CyberTipline received a lead from a lawyer representing the owner/operator of an adult-oriented fantasy telephone service. One of the workers was continually receiving calls from a New York City resident, who told her he had been previously convicted for child rape in California and was now routinely stalking and abducting young women in New York. After confirming the information they had received, staffers from NCMEC's Exploited Child Unit performed multiple database searches in an attempt to locate the man within the city. Analysts contacted the California Department of Justice and found that the suspect was a registered sex offender with a 22-page "rap sheet," whose crimes ranged from sexual offenses to bomb threats. He had also served a prison term for sexually abusing a minor, indecent exposure, and aggravated harassment. This information was immediately forwarded to the New York Police Department's Computer Investigations and Technology Unit, and Detective Kathleen Heavey took on the case. Heavey

posed online as a 13-year-old girl to get additional information from the suspect, and she learned that he was teaching elementary and middle schoolers at a Brooklyn school, as well as posing as the head of an online modeling agency. When police arrested the perpetrator, they searched his residence and recovered child pornography in the form of movies, photographs, and digital images – many in which he was shown molesting young girls. It was also discovered that he made frequent trips to Buffalo, New York, where he stayed in a hotel room and lured young females. The suspect was arrested on charges of disseminating indecent materials to minors and failure to register with the state as a sex offender. Additional victims – at the school, the modeling agency, and in other states – are being continually uncovered, and the case is still under investigation."

This story is shocking but it is important for us to know what we are up against. On the other side of the coin, there are organizations and police officers who are working side by side with us to protect our children. One such person is Officer Harold Jones, MCSE, a police officer for over 24 years, who served on the Riverside Ohio Police Department near Dayton, Ohio for 14 years. He twice received the medal of valor – the highest award given to a living police officer. Currently a reserve officer for the Riverside Police Department, he works in the detective section handling High Technology Crimes. He has spoken at national conferences for the High Tech Crime Investigator Association. Officer Jones also instructs various organizations and law enforcement officers around the world on computer related crime issues; specifically "Identity Theft" and online child predators. Being happily married to Sarah, a lovely English lady, and the father of two beautiful children, he has written most of the following section from his family to yours in the hope of helping you protect your children online.

Note: Some technical information is in PC language. Mac users will have to make appropriate adjustments.

Law Enforcement has Lost 10 Years in their Fight Against Child Predators Because of the Internet.

Having survived 24 years as a police officer, I have seen first hand all the crimes that plague our country. Domestic violence seems to always travel at the same pace. Alcohol abuse continues to destroy families, and drunken drivers still are the number one cause of car accidents. Drugs that gained popularity in the 60's have swept our nation and are probably at the root of more domestic deaths and violent crimes than anything else. My work now focuses on tracking criminals on the Internet.

What will be the verdict on the Internet's role in crime? The jury is still out. What we do know is that the Internet has put law enforcement back at least 10 years in their fight against child predators. With 56% of Americans online (NBC stat 9/17/02) comes the issue of cyber crime, and in particular, the risk to our children. Prior to the Internet, the preferential sexual offender had to physically arrive at the environments needed to prey upon our children. For example, they had to physically drive by the playground and/or be a coach on a little league baseball team and chance some wise adult becoming aware of their nefarious activity. To gain active support for their views and obsessions they had to meet in person and this too was a risky business.

Now he (or she) can sit at home and connect to one Internet relay chat server that contains as many as 24,000 chat rooms. In total anonymity, he can chat with our children, or exchange ideas with other offenders thus honing his skills even finer. He can present any description he chooses and pretend to be any kind of upright person he wishes to be. Our children and anyone else for that matter cannot tell if the person on the other computer is truthful or dishonest.

Here are some things that we as parents can do to stop this forward motion of crime and those preying upon our innocent children. A valuable tool is learning the language of the web.

Listen and Learn the Lingo

Kids are still kids. Think back. Didn't you have words for things that only you and your friends used?

CODE:	MEANING:
POS	Parents Over Shoulder
P911	My parents are coming, watch your language
TA/SA	Teacher / Sibling Alert
:OX	Shhh! It's a secret.
CTN	Can't Talk Now

> — Secret codes used by kids in chat rooms,
> *Oprah website: Kids' Secret Chat Codes*

You don't have to become a computer technician to keep your child safe, but you do need to know the basics about computers. If you hear terms you're not familiar with, write them down and buy a computer dictionary to look them up. Even easier, just ask your child what the words mean: listen and learn the lingo. If you sense something is amiss, ask your child. You might be surprised at how easily the answer comes. Often a child is most willing to share their newfound knowledge and might even enjoy teaching you about the computer and the Internet. If you need more help you can log on to sites that will help you learn or you could take a course at the local community college.

Computers have many of their own terms coming fresh out of the box. IBM, Hard Disk, Mac, Dos, Hard Drive, RAM, Buffers, Web Page, Cache, USB1, USB2, Wireless 802.11B, web pages, to name a few. Some of the more interesting words to listen for are terms like IRC, ICQ, AIM, or just the phrase Instant Messenger. All of these refer to messaging online and these messages can occur live, instantly, and for the cost of a local phone call by either party.

IRC stands for 'Internet Relay Chat'.

ICQ refers to the term 'I Seek You'.

AIM references to 'AOL Instant Messenger'.

Most of the time the term is tied to the first letter of the word or phrase. Instant messenger programs allow you to detect a friend online, type a short message like "Hello, you there?" The receiving party can see the message, simply type a reply and hit the enter key. The reply can be seen in about 2 seconds, much like a momentarily delayed phone call, but it is on the computer screen. Either party can also send a file, picture, song, or video via instant messenger programs.

Listening for the keywords of the trade may help thwart dangerous connections. Predators often befriend a child by sending pictures of the child's favorite music group, baseball team, movie star, etc. This lends itself to the child becoming relaxed with the predator and the relationship grows from there. The two begin to exchange data, pictures or whatever until the predator gradually introduces the victim to sexual content. This may begin with what the child believes is an accidental file transfer. It often serves to spike the child's curiosity resulting in sexual discussions that open the door for more frank discussion. Now the predator has the child where he wants him. What started out as an online musical song transfer has now grown to discussion about sexual conduct and it keeps going from there.

Another safety measure for parents and teachers is to listen for the words "Web Page" or "URL." Both reference a page or file that has been created with graphics and pictures on a computer and then sent to a larger computer to be "hosted" or broadcast to the Internet by a company that is in the business of hosting web pages. This is how most of the world is doing business these days and how many predators are reaching out to children on a regular basis.

One common scam is to throw up a false modeling page for young girls. The predator asks for pictures of young girls, (or boys) and then contacts the child promising fame and fortune with an "in person photo shoot." A good way to evaluate an offer is that if it seems to good to be true, it probably is.

Another typical scam is to create a web page loaded with free information about popular rock stars. This is designed to attract a child of the age and gender preferred by the predator, to visit the site and email the Webmaster who is the offender himself. This begins the slow and careful process of contact between the predator and the prey.

Search Engines are one of the best resources parents have to protect their children online. Some of the most popular are www.yahoo.com, www.google.com, www.alltheweb.com and www.aol.com. Learn to use them to look up most anything, particularly to learn about the computer and the web.

One often-overlooked resource available to parents is the very vehicle that many parents fear, the computer itself. Computers have become much more user friendly and most programs have a HELP mode. The book, *How Computers Work* by Ron White and Timothy Downs is an excellent source of learning how a computer works and it has excellent pictures to ease the learning process.

If your family creates a web page for friends and relatives to view pictures, as well as updates on family happenings, be careful not to place any geographical identifying information on that page, or school and sport team names. Strongly discourage your child from posting any picture of himself or herself on any web page that has public access. Pictures can be copied off the web and traded between other predators as teaser type files online.

Many business websites post employee's biographical information. Limit it to business information and be very careful what you post. You can easily be traced from information being broadcast on the net. At the same time, being able to trace whom your child is contacting or websites they are visiting can also work in your favor.

File Searches That Can Clue You in to Your Child's Interests

First of all, to determine if your child is visiting any dangerous websites, use "Control-H" while browsing the web to see the history of websites that have been accessed recently.

Then, it is a good idea to search for common file-forms of pictures on a regular basis to assure you that all is going smoothly. To do a search for pictures click on START. A menu will pop up. Go up to the word FIND or SEARCH. Depending on which version of Microsoft Windows you might be using, left click on that and when you see the new box pop up, it will have a space near the top where you can type characters. In Windows 98 it will say FIND: ALL FILES and you need to click on that in the little white block titled NAMED. In Windows 2000 you will see a box come up called SEARCH RESULTS. These boxes are only for you to type the name of the files you want to see. In that box asking for the file name, type the following characters:

*.jpg – After typing this hit the enter key to send the computer on its search

*.bmp – After typing this hit the enter key to send the computer on its search

*.gif – After typing this hit the enter key to send the computer on its search

Each of the three searches above starts a search for the three main types of photos available today. Each search will usually yield many results. The asterisk followed by a period before each file format tells the computer, "I want to see any picture that ends in the extension of jpg, gif, or bmp. I don't care what the first part of the title is." You can then look over the list of files on the computer. If you see a name that looks out of place, double click on it to view that picture. A typical out of place name might be something like littleboy12.jpg or meage42.bmp. Each name indicates something that may reveal the contents of that picture. Littleboy12.jpg is probably of a 12-year-old boy. Meage42.jpg is probably of an adult aged 42. Each name is a good clue that the picture may not be what you want your child to have. If you find inappropriate pictures, action must be taken.

An easier approach is to purchase any of the various graphic viewing software programs on the market. One of the many excellent pieces of software is "Thumbs Plus." This program will do an automatic scan of your hard drive and show you all the folders on your computer that contain photos of any kind. It will also color code folders so they are easy to spot. Double click on that folder and Thumbs Plus will automatically show all pictures in a thumb nail view. You can learn more about this software at www.cerious.com. Obviously, this will also reveal if your computer is mysteriously holding pictures, particularly pornographic photos. There are many good software programs on the market for this purpose.

Parents – be aware of what pictures are available on the web: countless sites now offer home pages with explicit images that are designed to draw in paying customers and many sites are completely free. Not all nude pictures are illegal by the mere fact they exist. The question is – who drew your child to those photos and how old is the person possessing them? Often a predator will not send nude photos in the early stages of developing a relationship with the child. The picture may look like a perfectly normal, fully dressed person. However if you see a photo of an adult or teen you don't know on the computer, ask your child who it is and where it came from. Pictures and personal communications are most commonly tramsmitted as email.

Email Issues

Most cases will involve email because the new form of Internet offender is often more comfortable communicating by email than verbally.

One important issue is to make sure your email program is configured to show "Full Headers." Headers contain much valuable information that law enforcement or corporate investigators can use to determine who wrote the message and where he or she is. If you find an email that is unacceptable print it out.

Ask your child to show you the email that the picture was attached to. Print out a copy of that email with full headers attached. Do not forward it electronically to the police department, or to a family member for a second opinion. Every time it goes through an email server computer, it has lines added to the very headers that may help you find your suspect. Don't clutter up your potential evidence with email forwarding. Print it out and hand carry it.

Also, if you are suspicious of your child's contacts, don't accept the statement that the child deleted that email. Sometimes the child for any variety of reasons may choose to try and cover up the relationship. Email is not always gone just because someone hit the delete key. In the program, Outlook Express, it can take up to three steps to truly remove an email from a server, not just the "one step" method of clicking on the email and hitting delete.

Recovering email can require swift movement. Some providers of Internet service hold that mail 2 days and some hold it 30 days. It depends entirely on the company and the policy of that email provider. Always remember to try and print the full email in question and try to include the headers.

Email is huge on the Internet and the companies that provide Internet access are fully burdened keeping storage space for all emails that travel over the Internet. Because of this, all Internet Service Providers (ISP) delete emails at the earliest possible time.

If you don't know what else to do and you are not comfortable configuring the program, disconnect the machine from the wall and secure it until more technical help can take over. Remember that time is of the essence in dealing with Internet Service Providers.

If you think there is evidence of, or even a chance of a predator contacting your child by email, you must act quickly to get help from the police or from other investigators. You don't need to secure the monitor and keyboard, just the machine (CPU), if at all possible (except self-contained computers). Officials will be able to take that machine and if necessary get inside it, and even potentially log into your child's account with the proper permissions and legal footing. From there they can access those emails, and view buddy lists and the like.

Buddy Lists

Buddy Lists are just what the name implies: a list of online buddies and the screen names they have made up for themselves. There are many programs that use these items such as America On Line, MSN Networks, Yahoo, and the list goes on. These are people your child has listed to keep track of in their Internet software programs, and that he wants to be aware of when he signs on to the Internet: this is similar to an address book that stays open all the time while a person is on the Internet. It is simple to get an online account, acquire an instant messenger program and create a screen name. Your screen name is how your are known in the cyber community. The information about whose accounts these buddy lists are actually linked to is held on the service providers' server computers.

For example, if your America Online buddy name is "Happytom794b33," that name and other identifier information will be found at America Online Headquarters in Dulles, Virginia. If a law officer has probable cause to inquire with official court documents to discover your identity (assuming you use AOL as your Internet service provider), the law officer working an official investigation can acquire this information.

Instant Messaging (IM)

Another method of commuication that is extremely popular with children is "Instant Messaging." Often children will do their home work and leave the computer on and chat back and forth with classmates throughout the evening. Instant messaging is rapidly growing. It originally started in the early home computing days with programs like ICQ (Short term for "I Seek You"). ICQ has around 80 million users. AOL has 1.32 BILLION instant messages a day as of mid 2002. Many corporate employees stay in contact across the country using IM software and instant messages, but children make up a large portion of the IM audience. Unless the user of the software has configured the software to make use of "Logging", these messages will not be saved. They appear, and when they are gone they are gone. No records of the messages are kept at the Internet Service Providers' location. If you have cause to see your child online receiving instant messages, it would be a good idea to actually sit and read them with your child to monitor the contents. If you see inappropriate content, write down the screen name and the service provider your child is using, and if possible, what type of instant message it is such as Yahoo, AOL, MSN, etc.

This information may prove invaluable if an incident ever develops. Instant messages are available on small hand held devices now. They are about the size of a regular pager. Cell phones can also receive instant messages.

IM is big business and is here to stay. Any concerned parents must be aware of what is being sent to their children. This may require monitoring software to help you maintain your parental control, and there are many available in the market place today.

Parental Controls

Check the software used by your children to see if it can be configured to function under the umbrella of parental controls. Probably the most notable of these is America Online. For example, if you have an account with AOL and create a new screen name under the "master account" for your child to use, AOL asks if the screen name is for a child. If you answer in the affirmative, AOL will ask you the approximate age and will allow you to limit your child's access. You can set it up so your child is not able to receive Instant Messages, access certain chat rooms where inappropriate material may be discussed, or visit certain web pages containing adult content. Certain file downloads may be blocked; certain times of the day limitations may be set, and the list goes on and on.

Other software programs on the market offer varying forms of parental control. This is a highly valuable feature so check to see what controls may be included with the software you are using. There are also more drastic measures that you may choose to use as your children get older called 'montoring software.'

Monitoring Software

'Monitoring software' is by definition a software that can be installed on a computer to record everything that goes on within that machine involving a user of said machine. To make use of this kind of software one must decide to install it either: (i) in what is referred to as stealth or undercover mode, or (ii) out in the open where the users are fully aware they are being watched. In this non-stealth mode, some software even displays a warning banner to the user when booting up (starting) the computer. If nothing suspicious is going on, this might be a good deterrent to underage computer users if they are reminded every time they boot up that they are being watched.

Many forms of monitoring software are available on the market. These software programs do 'screen captures' and often monitor 'keystrokes actually typed' and then record those items for later playback. They can often capture and record 'instant messenger messages' and most anything that the user may see on the screen. They also capture 'passwords' that when typed, appear as an asterisk on the screen, and then disclose to the installer what the password is. They can track 'dialog box changes' and use of all applications on the computer. Some have the ability to email the installer copies of the information requested, and even send silent copies of emails received and sent to the email address of the installer's choice. This is done without making use of the standard email program already installed on the machine, so that no sent items are displayed in the regular email program. Many employers are now turning to these pieces of software to monitor the activity of employees. According to the July 2002 issue of PC Magazine (www.pcmag.com) approximately 63% of employers monitor their employees. These software programs can often be purchased and downloaded directly over the Internet. The cost ranges from $30 to approximately $100 with a wide variety on the market. PC Magazine, July 2002, did a useful comparison of the software available.

There are also 'keystroke logging hardware devices' available, which attach directly to the PC itself. Often they are attached between the computer and the keyboard or can be built directly into the keyboard and become a part of the keyboard itself. All keystrokes reveal themselves in the logs kept by these machines. These devices do not capture screen shots of items appearing on the screen, but restrict themselves to keystrokes. They start at approximately $70 dollars and go upwards to several hundred dollars.

Other useful software programs for filtering your child's use of the Internet are Cybersitter, Cyber Patrol or Net Nanny. The software costs about $40–50 and acts as a digital chaperone, blocking any inappropriate content. These programs work by checking which sites your child visits against a list of disapproved sites, compiled by the makers of the software.

Any concerned parent or guardian could find these types of software helpful in monitoring what children see on the computer. If while monitoring your child you encounter a problem, you should contact the police and consult an attorney if they advise, to learn about any legal issues.

Most important in this age of online child dangers is that parents continue to communicate – talk and talk some more with your child and your child's peers. Let them know that they can bring any online mistake to your attention, and let them know that no matter how bad it is, you can work it out together. Education of the "real dangers," including the following Action Steps are the best weapons in the fight against online predators.

Just as you know your child's day-to-day world, you must know your child's cyber world. With the knowledge Officer Harold Jones and I have shared with you, the Internet should be an amazing tool for safely traveling the Super Highway with your child.

ALARMS THAT MEAN
PARENTS SHOULD TAKE ACTION

1. If your child spends excessive amounts of time online, particularly with one person, one chat room or one group.

2. If your child is becoming removed from the family.

3. If your child mentions how her Internet friend is more undestanding than you are.

4. If your child doesn't want to share information about people and messages he has received online.

5. If the computer screen suddenly goes dark when you enter the room to see your child.

6. If your child uses an unusual number of discs to retrieve information and/or is hiding discs, it may mean that adult images are being downloaded or secret correspondence is being saved.

7. If your child is online late at night.

ACTION STEPS
FOR PARENTS

1. **Knowledge replaces fear with strength and conficence.**

   Cutting kids off from the Web will not work. It is too powerful. It is an exciting and incredible educational resource that you will want for your children. Spend time with your children online. Just as you chose when your children first rode a bike and will decide when they will drive, you'll want to be there to guide them through the virtual world. So arm yourself and your children with knowledge.

2. **Keep communication open.**

   Parents who have used The Yello Dyno Program since their children were young, have found that one Yello Dyno Rule has kept the door of communication open even when their children become teen-agers: "In our family we don't keep secrets that make us feel unsafe or uncomfortable." You will be amazed over time at how many situations fit into that category! If you add this to your family "do's" now, be ready to listen! You're more likely to hear when your children encounter disturbing situations in all areas of life. They will most likely come to you for support and for answers when they encounter embarrassing or disturbing information on the net. Upsetting things happen. Help your children learn how

229

to deal with the problem. Help them learn the proper solution rather than taking their privilege of going online away from them.

3. Work together.

Teens are learning how to be independent, so don't be surprised if they process the information first and come to you a few days or even a week later for your input. Remind them that if they encounter someone in a chat room who makes them feel uncomfortable or unsafe, they should tell you. Together you can notify the service provider.

4. Watch the clock.

Limit the time your kids spend on the Internet just as you do TV and time spent on the phone. What you want is a well-rounded individual, and moderation is the key. Also remember that time at home is a good stabilizing time for kids, and if they are in other worlds through electronic media, i.e. Internet, TV, video games and phones, they are not "at home" or there with you.

5. Monitor activity.

Because our children are sitting right in our homes, it doesn't seem like they could be in danger. Since there is no legal structure that ensures honesty, truth and information that will not corrupt the minds of naive children, do not underestimate what they can encounter. With children under 16, keep the computer in areas where it is easy for you to supervise, or make a point of casually visiting your teen unexpectedly when he is on the net.

ACTION STEPS
FOR CHILDREN

1. **Make sure she picks a screen name that will attract the kind of friends she would like.**

    She should never use a name that is negative, belittling or provocative.

2. **Tell your child to only send photos with your permission.**

3. **Tell your child that if he encounters inappropriate or offensive messages, never respond to them.**

4. **Make sure he knows to never give anyone his password on line.**

5. **Your child should never fill out surveys or register at sites without your permission.**

6. **Tell your child that if he or she wants to meet an on-line friend in person for the first time, you must be present.**

7. A person may not be who he says he is.

Make sure your child understands that someone she might meet in a chat room, may not really be a child.

8. Your child should never give out personal information to anyone online that you and he or she does not know in person, and if someone is asking too many questions, your child should alert you.

Your child must be smart and not give his age, name, address, phone number, parent's work address or phone number.

He should not give out the make, color or model of the family cars.

He should not give out information about his school including name, location, and school colors. Landmarks around the school or home, such as names of a mall or resturant or state park, should not be given out. All of these types of information makes it easy to locate a school or home online and on a map.

He should not discuss his extra-curricular activities such as sports, dance lessons, church groups, or hobbies. These types of activities can reveal how to find your child.

He should not discuss personal fears, worries or problems he has with his friends or family, or how often and when he is home alone.

APPENDICES

The following two Appendices (A & B) are written by Seth Goldstein, Esq., who is a leading authority on child abuse. Appendix A is exerpted from *The Sexual Exploitation of Children*. Used by child abuse investigators across the country, it is considered the foremost textbook on the topic. Appendix B is entirely new material, and will be extremely useful for those that need to protect their child in the legal system.

Goldstein gained much of his knowledge while working as a city police officer and investigator for the Santa Clara and Napa County, California, District Attorney's Office, where he specialized in child abuse cases for thirteen years. During his years in the field, he worked one-on-one with many children and their families to bring child predators to trial. Goldstein was one of the founding members on the Board of Directors of the National Center for Missing and Exploited Children, as well as participating in the group that developed the investigative techniques that have become the standard in the professional field. The training curriculum they developed is used by the U.S. Department of Justice.

Reprinted with permission of the author and publishers.

APPENDIX A

THE TRICKS USED BY TRICKY PEOPLE

One of the hardest topics for parents to understand and comprehend is the variety of "methods" that child molesters and abductors use to get physically close to children. One of the primary reasons that this topic is difficult to confront is because the approaches used by adults who seduce children appear, to the untrained eye, to be normal behavior. In order to help parents keep their children safe from these approaches, we have compiled the following list of eleven methods and styles of seduction commonly used by child abductors and molesters. (This list is an expansion of the list of lures cited in "Beware of Tricky People," Chapter 3.) According to Goldstein, the following common characteristics of sexual exploitation have been compiled from the vast number of child sexual abuse cases that have occurred in this country.

As you'll see from the following material, child molesters are very clever. They have tried-and-true ways to get access to children, and to disguise their inappropriate(and unlawful) activities from the eyes of caring adults. Basically, their approaches with children are similar to the persuasive sexual approaches adults use with other adults; however, children don't have the sophistication to understand what is happening. The fact is, the child molester pursues his prey with a purpose, and will use any method that works. Goldstein makes a direct comparison between stalking prey and the seduction of children. "The offender, once he has targeted a child, will track down and methodically approach the child and begin to work on seducing him. All the while, the molester performs actions that appear, on the surface, to be normal when in actuality he is introducing the child to sexuality."

All parents and guardians of children should understand these methods and styles of seduction used by child molesters so that they can keep their eyes and ears open for inappropriate actions, and help children live their young lives free from molesters desires.

Methods and Styles Of Seduction
from *The Sexual Exploitation of Children*
by Seth Goldstein, Esq.

Affection and Attention
For the most part, a child is seduced in the same way that one adult seduces another. The offender takes him places, buys him things, impresses the child, makes the child feel loved and indebted to the offender, then he becomes physical with the child. It starts subtly, by holding hands, an arm over the shoulder, a hand in the lap, eventually graduating to more explicit conduct.

Mislabeling the Activity
Another common method of seducing a child is to misrepresent what the offender is actually doing. This could mean tricking the child into performing a sex act by using a legitimate activity to achieve physical contact with the child. In one case, a man who engaged in sexual activities with eight-

to-nine-year-old boys liked to play a game called "monster," in which he would wrestle with the boys and touch their genitals and other areas. All of this was accomplished without the child's knowing what was actually going on. From this kind of activity, the offender will graduate to more blatant touching. After the child feels more comfortable with the idea of the offender breaking the barrier of "personal space," the offender will advance to sexual play.

A common ploy to trick the child into an act is to tell the child that what is being done is for a purpose other than the real one. For example, a young child was seduced into posing for photographers after being told that the offender was making pictures for a publisher of medical books to assist doctors in teaching others about sex.

Misrepresentation of Moral Values

Since a child possesses little experience or knowledge, the offender is often easily able to convince the child that sex with an adult is a legitimate activity. It is easy to understand why children acquiesce to the demands of the child molester, considering the vast literature on sex with children and sex manuals that are on the market. These are often left out and available for children to "discover" by accident or are specifically shown to the child by the offender. In many cases, children have been shown films that are either sexually graphic or suggestive.

Slow/Subtle Exposure to the Concept of Sexual Activity

By constantly talking to the child about sexual activities, the offender slowly indoctrinates the child into the world of sex.

Curiosity

Another style of seduction is to arouse the child's curiosity. This is often done by leaving sexually oriented materials out and available to the children. The seduction includes leaving sexual aids in areas where children can find them, which leads to conversations about sexual matters.

Narcotics and Alcohol

The use of narcotics and alcohol by the child molester is commonplace. What better way to get a child to a place he wouldn't ordinarily go than to provide him with something he can't ordinarily get? The use of alcohol is mostly limited to the older child; however, it is also a common denominator in some cases involving young children.

Misuse of Authority

This may take two forms. In the first, the offender takes advantage of his power, as in the following example. On several outings, a Boy Scout leader told the children in his troop to disrobe. Over a period of time he graduated from fondling them to orally copulating with them. Each time he told them not to tell anyone.

In the second type of misuse of authority, the offender takes advantage of a position of special trust and represents the activity as legitimate, using his authority, stature, and position to convince the child that what he wants is okay.

Rewards and Bribes

A very common style of seduction is the use of rewards. Sometimes the child is told in advance what he will receive if he cooperates with the offender. Other times the offender doesn't tell the child until after the act. Soon the child learns that by doing what the offender wants, he can have his own way. The reward may be as elaborate as a car or as simple as an ice cream cone, depending on the circumstances.

Children are easily lured by promises to make them Hollywood stars. The hopes of grandeur, and comparisons made by the offender between the child and the child's idols, often make them easy prey. Modern advertising is often shown to the child, especially advertising that accents the sexuality of young children, to convince the child of the propriety of the acts.

Blackmail

Once the child has been placed in a compromising situation – sexually or otherwise – the offender can obtain some control over the child by threatening exposure. The offender knows that the child feels guilty and is wrought by shame. The offender also knows that most children have very little self-esteem or confidence, and feel helpless in the situation they are in.

A deep concern of many children who have a close relationship with an offender is the fear of being taken away, out of the family situation. This threat may be expressed or implied by the offender, or may be developed by the child with no direct threats being made.

Use of Pornography

Both child and adult pornography is often used by the child molester to seduce the child. In addition to misrepresenting moral standards, the pornography can be used to demonstrate the acts in which the offender wishes to engage. It may also be used to stimulate the child's interest in the depicted activities and to lower the child's inhibitions.

Threats

Rarely is a threat of harm used to get the child to comply with the act. The only time a threat becomes necessary is to keep the child quiet and to continue participating in the activities that the offender desires. For the most part, threats are made that imply negative consequences for both the victim and the offender if there is disclosure.

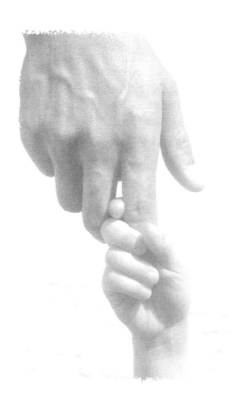

APPENDIX B

PROTECTING YOUR CHILD IN THE LEGAL SYSTEM

S adly, the majority of molestation cases involve people known to the child. This means that it is more likely that your child may be victimized by a family member. If that person is a parent or someone you or the child knows, there are many things that will happen that will involve the system and the courts.

Reporting

Once a suspected child abuse report is made to the authorities, they have a mandate to investigate. In a ground-breaking case in California[1], one parent successfully sued a police department for refusing to investigate on behalf of his child after that child was returned to the other parent, and that parent further abused the child. How much time an agency will take to investigate will vary depending upon the circumstances of each case. If a law enforcement (police) agency is called, they will interview witnesses and collect evidence. Then, if they determine a crime can be proved, an arrest is likely to follow and/or a referral to a prosecutor may be made. In most law enforcement agencies, the original

---

1. Alejo v. City of Alhambra, (1999) 75 Cal.App.4th 1180

investigating officer will be in uniform. If you think that this will be a problem, when the original call is made, you will need to first contact the investigating detective unit directly, or ask for a supervisor and tell them of your concerns.

Should the case be prosecuted, it is important to understand that the prosecutor is the attorney for the state, not the victim. He does not and may not represent the victim's interests in court. In most prosecutor's offices, there is an office of a victim advocate. However, this is not an attorney, and is primarily a person who will help the victim and his or her family through the court process. These people will often be the gatekeeper for Victims of Crime compensation funds. A prosecution of an offender may take up to a year or more to actually get to a trial.

There are often hearings held before the trial and you and/or your child may be called to testify. In the investigative phase of a case, you and/or your child may refuse[2] to talk with police or defense investigators. However, if served with a subpoena, you and/or your child must appear. Refusal could result in serious consequences and/or dismissal of your child's case. In one case a parent refused to cooperate by not allowing the child to testify or talk to the authorities. The child was removed from both parents and taken into protective custody. In another, the parent was arrested for failure to appear and later, jailed for contempt. If you do not feel it is in your child's best interests to cooperate, you should contact a private attorney.

Generally, when a parent, any relative or anyone in the child's household is responsible for a molestation, a social services agency may become involved to assure the child's safety. While the police are responsible for determining if a crime is involved, the social services agency, on the other

---

2. However, see discussion on Failure to Protect herein.

hand, is responsible for ensuring that the family protects the child.

Any parent who is felt to be a risk to the child may be removed from the child's proximity. The social worker may see that a restraining or protective order is placed on the offending parent, and threaten the non-offending parent with arrest if they allow a violation of that order. This may also translate into taking a child into protective custody, if the parents are unable to assure the child's protection.

Failure to cooperate with the social worker has serious consequences. Parents have been known to be charged, criminally, with failure to protect their children when the social worker believes that the child was subjected to unnecessary risk by the non-offending parent. This has resulted in the child being taken away from both parents and placed with other relatives, or with total strangers, in a foster home, as illustrated above.

Four Separate Court Systems Involved

Besides the criminal courts, a juvenile or dependency court may become involved. In the juvenile court, the judge must determine if the child was a victim of abuse. If so, the judge must decide if the state should become responsible for the child, where the child should reside and with whom. In most states, even though a person has molested a child, the courts are required to return the child into the family and bring the offending parent back into the child's life. This is a process called reunification. There are some circumstances where reunification may not be required, however, they are not necessarily favored by the courts. For example, a father was accused of molesting his daughter. The social worker removed the child from the home until there was an assurance of the child's safety in that environment, after which, she was returned to the home.

The father, however, was ordered to live away from the family. He was allowed visits and engaged in therapy to try to deal with his problem. As he continued in therapy, he was given more and more time with the child and was, eventually, allowed back into the home.

In most states, both parents are entitled to an attorney if a petition of protection is filed in the juvenile court. Some states appoint those attorneys. The child is also entitled to a separate attorney in many states. If an attorney appears for the social service agency, they sometimes are also representing the child. This is a precarious position and parents should be leery of having a government lawyer representing their child when the government is trying to take the child away. Most children are protected in this fashion. However, the government lawyer has a divided loyalty if he is representing the social services agency and the child. The interests and objectives of the agency and the child could be diametrically opposed to one-another. In one case, the social worker wanted the child removed from the family home. The attorney for that agency advocated for removal. However, the child wanted to go back to the home since the offending parent was living somewhere else. These two interests conflict. An attorney should not be in such a position that he represents two persons with such divergent interests as these.

This is also where it gets sticky. A parent's failure to cooperate or participate in this court process could result in termination of parental rights. If the judge finds that neither parent is able or willing to protect the child, it could terminate those parents' parental rights. This means your child will no longer be your child. For example, if a mother doesn't believe that her child was abused by her husband and refuses to keep that parent away or cooperate with the authorities, the court could take the child away from both parents and put the child up for adoption.

The third court system involved is the family or conciliation court. Where the juvenile court was responsible to assure that the child is protected from the world, the family court must decide, between the parents, what is the best living situation for that child. When ordering visitation and custody, the family court will often defer to the rulings in the criminal and juvenile courts. At times, the police and social workers find insufficient evidence to proceed in their respective courts, leaving the family court to rely upon its own resources to rule on the protection of the child.

In this situation, too often, parents who are trying to protect their children are considered to be a thorn in the side of the system. They are disbelieved and distrusted. This is a critical decision point for a parent trying to protect his or her child from an abusive co-parent. When the suspicion first surfaces, a non-offending parent must decide whether or not to retain an attorney to assure the child is protected, and players in the system conduct a proper investigation. In one case, a mother reported that her young child was observed continually engaged in sexualized behavior. She said that her daughter told her that 'daddy' hurt her 'pee pee'. After initial interviews, the social worker and police officer felt they were unable to establish that anything happened and refused to file a criminal complaint or petition of protection. The mother's only option was to go to family court and seek a change in custody and protective order.

The civil court is the fourth court that may be involved, where a personal injury action might be filed or where a civil restraining order is obtained. When a family member, a member of a church, school or other family friend molests your child, you may sue them on behalf of the child and, often, yourself. If the offender lives, works or has a likelihood of coming in contact with your child, you may need a restraining or protective order. If the offender has rights to see the child ie: a parent or, in some states, grandparent, you should seriously consider a restraining order.

Expectations of the System

In the criminal courts, the victim and his or her family is expected to cooperate with the authorities in the prosecution of the case. The prosecutor will expect to have access to whatever information (s)he will need to assure the jury will believe the child. The defense attorney will also be seeking evidence to support his client's position. Either may try to obtain medical or psychiatric records of the child or other members of the family. The courts expect that witnesses and the child's family will cooperate with all efforts to legally obtain this information. If the defense attorney tries to obtain such records, the prosecutor may not be able to prevent it from happening. If the prosecution itself seeks these records or is unable to stop the defense request, it may be necessary to hire a lawyer to do so. You must not rely on the prosecutor to warn you or inform you that you will need an attorney. You must be vigilant and assert that right on your own. In a case where a neighbor had molested a child and some other boys, the neighbor sought the boy's school records to try to discredit the boy. The parents had to hire a private attorney who was able to successfully protect the records.

Expectations of Family

In most situations, parents expect that they will be treated fairly and properly informed. In most situations this happens. However, in too many cases where personalities and policy clash with the family's expectations, legal rights get trampled and the unexpected happens. Parents have had children, literally, ripped from their embrace when a social worker or police officer got the wrong idea.

Need for Advocacy

Often a law enforcement agency has different priorities than the parent reporting the crime. Considering the large number of cases law enforcement must investigate, they often will not be able to get to a case as fast as a parent would want.

The investigator may not agree with the complaining parent about the need to prosecute. Constant calls from an anxious parent often backfire and the investigator will lose interest. Threats of complaints to be made to supervisors or superiors often result in negative outcomes for the advocating parent. This is where tactful and subtle advocacy is necessary.

As has been said, because the parent and child often are not represented, there is a need for advocacy. An attorney who is experienced in all four court arenas should be sought at the earliest possible time. Securing evidence and proper posturing of the case from the outset will help to assure that the authorities do their jobs properly. When this happens, the child's ability to be protected is greatly enhanced. Advocacy that assures the authorities have properly and completely done their jobs will provide more credible evidence if the civil courts become the only recourse to protect the child.

Need for Active Involvement

The biggest mistake a parent can make is to totally rely upon the government to do the right thing. Most of the time a child's case will be handled correctly. However, a parent must be vigilant throughout the process to ensure the case doesn't languish and isn't prematurely dropped. Prosecutors and law enforcement are often overloaded with cases. Too often, the expedient path is taken, rather than that which secures justice. Prosecutors are elected officials. They and their staff need to know you support their efforts to protect your community. They also need to be informed of your expectations concerning your individual case and in return, they should inform you of their intentions. You may not always agree and it will be necessary to monitor their efforts. There is no requirement that a prosecutor must inform the victim and/or his/her family of the disposition of a case. By making your presence and your interest known, you are more likely to be satisfied with the end result.

Resources

Local victim advocate groups may be found on the Internet and in the phone book. Referral services of local bar associations may be of assistance in finding a competent and experienced attorney. However, the most reliable way to find an attorney is a referral from someone who has had a good experience with an attorney. You will want an attorney who knows and practices in all of the areas of law mentioned in this section. In particular, you want someone who knows about child abuse and who has experience dealing with this very difficult area of litigation. In these matters, the right attorney can mean the difference between the child being protected and that child being abused again by the system or the offender.

For additional resources, see page 300.

References for Appendix B

California Office of Criminal Justice Planning. (1996) *The California Children's Justice Act Task Force: Report for 1996.* Sacramento, OCJP

Conte, J. R. and Shore, D. (1982) *Social Work and Child Sexual Abuse,* New York, Haworth

Conte, J. R. ed, (2002) *Critical Issues in Child Sexual Abuse:* Historical Legal, and Psychological Perspectives, Thousand Oaks, Sage

DePanfilis, D. and Salus, M. K. (1992) *A Coordinated Response to Child Abuse and Neglect: A Basic Manual,* Wash., D.C., U.S. Dept. of Health and Human Services

Dubowitz, H. and DePanflis, D., edis (2000) *Handbook for Child Protection Practice,* Thousand Oaks, Sage.

Edwards, L. (1987) *The Relationship of Family and Juvenile Courts in Child Abuse Cases,* Santa Clara Law Review, Vol. 27, No.2

Edwards, L. and Sagatun, I. J. (1995) *Child Abuse and the Legal System.* Chicago, Nelson-Hall

Feller, J. N., et al. (1992) *Working With the Courts in Child Protection.* Wash. D.C., U.S. Dept. of Health and Human Services

Finklehor, D. (1979) *Sexually Victimized Children.* New York, Free Press

Finklehor, D. and Associates (1986) *A Sourcebook on Child Sexual Abuse,* Thousand Oaks, Sage

Goldstein, S. (2000), *Sorting Out Allegations of Child Abuse in Custody and Visitation Cases:* The Problem of System Failure, in Crook L. and St. Charles, E. Expose: The Failure of Family Courts to Protect Children from Abuse in Custody Disputes: A Resource Book for Lawmakers, Judges, Attorneys, and Mental Health Professionals. Los Gatos, Ca. Our Children Our Future Charitable Foundation

Haralambie, A. M. (1999) *Child Sexual Abuse in Civil Cases: A guide to Custody and Tort Actions,* Chicago, American Bar Association

Melton, G. B. and Barry, F. D. (1994) *Protecting Children from Abuse and Neglect,* New York, Guilford

Myers, J. E. B.(1997) *A Mother's Nightmare - Incest: A Practical Legal Guide for Parents and Professionals,* Thousand Oaks, Sage

National Research Council (1993) *Understanding Child Abuse and Neglect,* Wash., D.C., National Academy Press

Packard Foundation (1998) *The Future of Children: Protecting Children From Abuse and Neglect,* Los Angeles, Vol. 8, No. 1

Rosen, L. N. and Etlin, M. (1996) *The Hostage Child: Sexual Abuse Allegations in Custody Disputes,* Indianapolis, Indiana University Press

Schecter, S. and Edleson, J. *Effective Intervention In Domestic Violence Cases: Guidelines for Policy and Practice.* Reno, Council of Juvenile and Family Court Judges

Villmoare, E. and Benvenuti, J. California *Victims of Crime Handbook: A Guide to Legal Rights and Benefits for California Crime Victims,* Sacramento, Victims of Crime Resource Center, McGeorge School of Law

Winner, K. (1996) *Divorced From Justice: The Abuse of Women and Children by Divorce Lawyers and Judges,* New York, Regan

Whitfield, C. L., et al (2001) *Misinformation Concerning Child Sexual Abuse and Adult Survivors,* New York, Haworth

Zorza, J. (1999) *Why Courts Are Reluctant to Believe and Respond to Allegations of Incest.* in Schwartz, B. ed. *The Sex Offender: Theoretical Advances, Treating Special Populations and Legal Developments.* Kingston, N.J. Civic Research Institute, Vol. III

APPENDIX C

CHILD SECURITY PRODUCTS & SERVICES

To help keep your children safe, you may want to consider purchasing some of the many child security products and services in the marketplace. This section will give you an overview of most of the child security products that are available, and provide you with the relative advantages and limitations of each one. (We have omitted the products and services that are new and require further development and testing.)

It is important to evaluate the child safety products and services before you purchase them so that you can avoid two key problems: 1. developing a feeling of security just because you have purchased a safety product or service, when, in fact, the product or service may not be truly as effective as is claimed (parents must always keep in mind that no product or service replaces solid personal safety education); and 2. purchasing a child safety product or service from a non-reputable company. There are several companies offering parents child security products; most are reputable, but unfortunately there are a handful of companies who are little more than opportunists seeking to capitalize on parents' fears. Many of these companies have either failed, have poor or misrepresented products, or limited, incomplete, or wrong information. For the most effective products and for the greatest security of your privacy, you should only deal with reputable child security companies or organizations. Before purchasing child security products or services, you should ask yourself: Are these tools really helpful? The following information will give you a frame of reference for evaluation; and because rarely is one product or service enough to ensure your child's security, the information in this section will also help you plan a complete child security system for your children.

Child Identification Products and Services

Child identification. What exactly does that mean? In today's world it means more than just giving authorities a sketchy description of your child. "He's three-and-a-half feet tall, blond hair, and blue jeans . . ." That type of information means nothing in today's crowded amusement parks, malls, and ball parks. As mentioned earlier, 10,000 people may pass through the average mall on a typical Saturday afternoon. Compounding the confusing issue of child identification is the wide variety of child I.D. products on the market (the selection is growing as several companies move to enter the marketplace). How is a parent supposed to know whether the I.D. products being advertised in Sunday's paper are products that they really need or just another product that will give them a sense of security, but, in reality, do nothing to help protect their child?

While identification products and services are an important part of a complete family safety program, remember this one important fact: child I.D. products are for *after a problem occurs.* Just like insurance, you hope you never actually have to use it, but you should be prepared. Here are the child I.D. products you need to know about:

Child Identification (I.D.) Cards

A child I.D. card is the most convenient and effective form of child identification because parents and guardians carry the I.D. cards in their purses and wallets just like a driver's license. There is no better way for parents to instantly provide identification of their lost or missing child to authorities. For maximum benefit, these child I.D. cards must be properly prepared and contain the exact information that is required by authorities to find a lost or missing child. (See the chapter called "Carry Proper I.D. – It's Critical" for a listing of the key information necessary on a child I.D. card.) Some I.D. cards also carry medical emergency information, which can be valuable if your child has special medical requirements. Also, I.D. cards should be laminated whenever possible, so that they do not become smudged, bent, or tattered. Unfortunately, many I.D. cards are incomplete or poorly made. To be truly effective, every parent and guardian should carry I.D. cards for each of their children. You should also keep an extra card handy for babysitters, relatives, or friends to carry when they are watching your child.

It's also valuable for children to carry I.D. cards on themselves. If they are injured or lost, the identifying information can help medical and law enforcement personnel assist them and contact you. Keep in mind that the cards should be concealed so that no one can gain access to the information. Your children can keep the cards in their backpacks, wallets, fanny packs or purses.

Child I.D. cards have been used successfully many times in real-life situations. These cards can be obtained from child identification and security companies, non-profits and agencies, do-it-yourself kits, through malls or business promotions and occasionally from police.

Note: For families' privacy and security, we do not recommend that any personal information, such as photographs, fingerprints, and videos, be kept by anyone but the child's parents or guardians.

DNA I.D

DNA is, without question, the future of identification. DNA analysis is considered the most important advance in forensics since fingerprinting. DNA use in U.S. courts has skyrocketed, freeing people who were unfairly prosecuted and sentenced, and putting criminals away who had previously beaten the system. The FBI has implemented a national DNA database, called CODIS, to track people by their DNA. The U.S. Army started a genetic depository in 1992 that will eventually include the DNA of every American in uniform. The U.S. Army's goal is to have no more "unknown soldiers."

DNA I.D. (also known as "genetic fingerprinting") is the only virtually 100 percent positive and permanent identification method. For example, photographs fade and must be updated, and fingerprints can smear or be difficult to acquire (getting a proper child's fingerprint can be very difficult), but each person's DNA remains the same for his entire life. DNA (deoxyribonucleic acid) molecules are that part of the human physiology which carry the genetic "blueprint" that makes each person unique. Each person's genetic makeup is exclusive and permanent. As such, DNA fingerprinting can provide reliable identification even when it may be impossible to recover an actual fingerprint. Further, DNA I.D. is generally admissible in court, and can be invaluable in reuniting parents with their children in the case of parental abductions, kidnappings, accidents, and natural disasters.

DNA identification is now available to families in an easy-to-use, at-home kit. With the "do-it-yourself" DNA Pak, it takes parents only minutes to capture, preserve, and store their children's genetic fingerprints. The DNA Pak provides a way of properly taking, recording, and storing genetic samples in a patented, tamper-proof system. It is a way of properly storing genetic samples, not the actual DNA test; if the DNA sample is ever needed to make a genetic match, the process is usually initiated by law enforcement or some other agency. Beware of suggestions to make your own DNA I.D. While storing DNA samples at home can be simple with a specially made medical package, it can be completely ineffective without the right procedures. The DNA Pak can also be a part of your at-home fact file. By combining an up-to-date child I.D. card and DNA I.D., parents can have a valuable child identification system.

Fingerprints

Fingerprinting children is one of the most popular child identification methods used by organizations, especially at community events and malls. Many parents are led to believe that a set of fingerprints will keep their child safe. However, fingerprints of children do nothing to prevent abduction, and they are not a replacement for Immediate Response I.D. cards. They are generally only valuable if a child is missing long-term. What's more, fingerprints of children are extremely difficult to get, even by professionals such as police. In fact, authorities find that up to 75 percent of the fingerprints taken of children may be of little value. The reason is that the lines on a child's fingers are very fine. That's why foot and palm prints are often taken of very young children. It therefore takes a special touch to ensure that the ink is not too heavy or too light, that the correct angle on the finger is used, and that at least 10 of the ridges and valleys of the pattern are clear. For this reason, parents should be sure that fingerprints are taken by people trained to take fingerprints of children and who do so regularly. Whenever possible, they should avoid trying to do it themselves at home; however, this is better than nothing until you can get them done by professionals. Fingerprints of your child, either one good one or a whole set, should be kept in an at-home fact file. If you only have one clear print, it should be the index finger of the right or left hand (depending on whether the child is right or left handed), because that is the finger your child is most likely to touch with and leave a readable print behind.

Home I.D. Record File

Another important child identification method is a child I.D. home record file stored in a safe place. An at-home I.D. record of your child provides thorough identification of a lost child. Again, however, it does not replace proper I.D. that you carry on your person. The advantage of a home record file is that it can contain more information than a wallet I.D. card, and is useful primarily for more long-term missing children.

Parents should assemble an at-home identification packet for each of their children. Include in this packet:

- Recent photographs of your child (the photographs need to be straight on to be useful for identification, reproduction, and photo-aging techniques), including a clear, color head and shoulders view that accurately depicts what your child looks like;
- An accurate physical description of your child including height and weight, hair and eye color, scars and birthmarks, glasses, braces, earrings;
- Up-to-date medical and dental records;
- Fingerprints (see above);
- A videotape of your child; and
- Any information that could help identify or locate your child, for example the names, addresses and numbers of friends, common play areas, mannerisms, and habits.

Parents should store this information in a safe place in their home. Also, they should consider carrying a copy of this information with them if they are on an extended vacation. Since children grow and change quickly, parents should update this information at least once every year. While some sources recommend four times a year for preschoolers, that is not practical for most busy families. Do it as often as you can manage, but for sure once a year. If you have a properly organized home record file, it will be much easier to update.

Photographs

There are very specific requirements needed for a photograph to be useful in finding a child. As mentioned above, a good photo means a clear, color head and shoulders view that accurately depicts what your child looks like. It must be a front view and be very sharp. Because children grow and change quickly, photos must be updated regularly.

Video Tapes

Video footage of your child provides authorities an opportunity to see the child from a variety of angles. Be sure to keep the videos safely at home in a fact file. You do not have to pay a lot of money for any "special" kinds of video footage, just use your video camera or borrow a friend's. From time to time, some video operations and businesses offer special child video promotions in some communities.

Child I.D. Jewelry

The value of I.D. jewelry-bracelets, necklaces and shoe tags is fundamentally the same as the child carrying their own I.D. card. If your child is injured or can't communicate for whatever reason, the I.D. can help law enforcement and medical personnel contact you. However, so you don't advertise your child's name, the information on the bracelet and shoe tags should be on the inside only. Also, the engraving on necklaces should be fine enough so that no one can read it unless they are very close and hold the tag correctly in the light. Shoe tags are better than iron-on labels because children usually have fewer shoes than they do pants and shirts. Also, the tags can be transferred to new shoes as your child grows. The drawback, of course, is that if you are going to use them, they should be on all the child's shoes. The value of a bracelet or necklace is that you only need one and it is always on your child. I.D. jewelry can often be purchased at mall "kiosks," jewelry stores and flea markets.

Iron-On I.D. Labels

Iron-on I.D. labels are generally sold in two forms. One type has your child's name, address, and telephone number. The other type is generally issued as part of a "child registration" service. The only information that appears on the label is your child's name and a central contact number, which is often an 800 number. If you register with such a service, make sure you are careful about who is keeping personal information on your child.

There are two fundamental problems with iron-on labels. The first problem is just one of practicality. It is difficult for parents to keep current labels in all the articles of clothing of a growing child. Not only do children grow rapidly, they lose things and they destroy things. As a result, for many busy parents it is almost impossible to stay current with labels. The second problem is that law enforcement, medics, or other people who may be assisting your child in an emergency may not even notice the labels on your child's clothing. whereas I.D. jewelry is generally easy to spot.

Photo-aging Techniques

Increasingly, photo-aging techniques have had a great measure of success. In this process, a photo of a child is "age progressed" to try and determine what a child, who was last seen years ago, may look like today. However, parents must keep in mind that this technique is only educated guesswork. It cannot identify a lost child with 100% accuracy. Up until recently, the process of age progressed photos was tedious and time consuming, often taking up to 36 hours by a professional police artist or medical illustrator. Recently, computerized age progression technology has been developed. To age progress a child's photo, the artists enhance the facial features based on the child's parents' and siblings' features. To be effective, parents must be involved in the process because they can provide key descriptions of family members. While computerized age progression is faster, it is still a painstaking process, where specially trained artists must work on one section of the child's face at a time. While not necessarily an accurate depiction of the child at his or her current age, this process can give the families some measure of hope in rekindling public interest and generating new leads.

Personal Alarms, Monitoring and Tracking Devices

The jury is still out on these devices. The problem with all of them is that, by themselves, they can give parents a false sense of security. Personal alarms emit a piercing shriek or siren when the child pulls a pin or activates it by some other method. While they may be great attention-getters, the other side of the coin is that people don't necessarily respond to alarms because they have become desensitized to this type of noise. Do you respond to car alarms in a parking lot? Unless you can see a child being harmed as a result of an alarm, they provide little value. Better than an alarm is a child who knows how to properly scream, "This is not my mom!" or other appropriate phrases.

As for monitors, the purpose of monitoring devices is to listen to what is going on in the child's world. Some monitors are two-way with the adult and child each wearing units. These are best suited for listening in on babies and young children in another area of the home but once outside the home, they have very limited use. This is not the same as a two-way radio for older children, which has a wide variety of uses.

The purpose of tracking devices is to allow adults to pinpoint a child's location within a certain range. With satellite technology and GPS (Global Positioning), these are becoming increasingly sophisticated. They are kind of like a kid version of a "LoJack" (the hidden transponder you put in a secret place on a vehicle so it can be tracked if stolen). This concept has the "cool factor," but a piece of technology should not be purchased as a replacement for proper child security education.

"No neighborhood watch or electronic device can replace solid safety rules and emergency strategies for children," stated an article in the Austin American-Statesman on January 29, 1994.

That's even truer today than it was then. If parents feel strongly about using alarms, monitors and/or tracking devices, they must remember one important thing: they are not fail-safe so you cannot depend solely on them. Among the problems: your child may forget it when he leaves the house, the batteries may fail, it may get damaged in play, and it may not perform as promised. Their voice and street smarts will never be left at home and will not run out of battery power. If you purchase an alarm, monitor or tracking device, do so as a complement to a family safety program, which includes well-rounded education. Make sure to purchase the devices from reputable companies.

Martial Arts

Gaining skill in a martial art can be a valuable personal safety tool, but not for the reasons most people think. Most experts agree that martial arts classes will not help a child physically defend himself against an adult attacker. According to Officer Dan "The Hulk" Razzano: "I don't care what kind of belt they have. Black belt. Green belt. A six-year-old is not going to beat an older person out there in a street brawl when the person wants to get the child." (HBO's "How to Raise a Street Smart Kid," video). Often children see images on TV or at the movies of children "beating up" adults, and they think they can do it, too. Remember a few years back the movie, "Three Ninjas"? It's a great example. It's a fun family movie – but no reality whatsoever. In fact, if a child tries to fight back with an adult, he may only further enrage the person. This area of personal safety must be approached with caution. Although there are times to fight, no doubt, the child may be better off waiting for an opportunity to escape.

However, according to those involved in martial arts, the skills learned do have important benefits. At the very least, your child can gain much needed confidence, self-esteem, and important life skills. The right kind of martial arts training helps educate the mind and the body. That can be truly powerful safety training. According to Sensei David Ham, member of the Aikikai Foundation (Japan), "When a child stops fighting and starts taking positive action to remain safe is when self-defense really works. And taking positive action is only possible with proper safety training." Furthermore, when children gain confidence through self-defense they realize that they don't generally need to fight to stay safe. Instead, they learn to steer clear of problems in the first place. The bottom line: the best way for a child to defend himself against an attacker is to use his common sense and personal safety skills.

Educational Products

As you know, we think these are the most important products of all. However, just because an educational product is on the market does not mean that it is a good product; or even if it is valuable, that does not mean it is a complete child security system. You must use discrimination, and apply sensible personal safety principles like the ones you will learn in *Raising Safe Kids in an Unsafe World*. If you do purchase a safety educational product or enroll your child in a safety education program, be sure to review, test and challenge what your child has learned so you can help customize it to the unique circumstances of your child and your family situation.

There is a variety of safety education products, including music, books, computer games and videos, that are generally available from your local library, bookstores, music stores, video stores, or direct from private organizations. Programs offered in communities or through schools should also be considered.

The Yello Dyno Program, which includes seminars, books, music, literature, and identification products and services, is also available to schools, daycare centers, churches, civic organizations and business sponsors.

APPENDIX D
YELLO DYNO
SAFETY MUSIC

Music: The Charming Way to Safer Children

A song is more than just words and a melody. It is a singer, a mood, a setting, a story and characters. With educational songs – particularly safety education – the creators of music have a further responsibility because they have to impart valuable educational concepts into enjoyable songs that children will want to hear again and again. It's much harder than it sounds!

What's more, we wanted to create safety education songs which the difficult-to-reach ten-to-twelve-year-olds would enjoy as much as the four-to-nine-year-olds. Today's pre-teens are just too sophisticated for what they perceive as "kiddy" music, and too often educational music talks down to children. We know that to make music truly effective, kids have to like it. So our goal was to create great songs that just happened to have a message. In fact, we wanted to weave safety education into music that is so enjoyable children don't even realize how strong an effect the songs have on them. The best educational songs should be so memorable that children can remember the words at the (often stressful) moment that they need the information contained in the song.

To accomplish this task, we called on the talents of some of the music industry's best and brightest. Many of the music and educational professionals involved in this first album, *Can't Fool Me!*, were as inspired as we were to be a part of the important project of getting valuable safety information to children. To ensure that this music is as valuable as it can be, every word, every lyric, every singer, and the musical style of every song was chosen specifically to accomplish a particular safety objective.

The main character of our safety education program for children is Yello Dyno. He is the ultimate big brother to every child. He is big, strong, and, unless you mess with his kids, he is friendly to everyone. Kids say he's "cool" – the utmost praise from four-to-twelve-year-olds. Most importantly, he knows all of the important safety rules and cares most about sharing them with children.

It is only through music that the safety rules can evoke the deep, strong, emotional, and psychological lessons for children. On the following pages are the wonderful lyrics to the eight songs on the children's personal safety album, *Can't Fool Me!*, with a little bit of background on how and why we created each song.

"My daughter, Sofia, who I adore, loves Yello Dyno. Every little girl and boy, especially those who have less, have the right to learn how to protect themselves without fear. Your program represents that opportunity. As a father, I have no words to thank you for having the courage to fulfill your mission in life...in benefit of millions of kids...including mine."

– Luis Banck, husband of Susy, and father of Sofi Banck, Puebla, México.

David Ham

Songwriter and Producer of Can't Fool Me!™

During his remarkable career, David has traveled the world creating radio, television, and billboard communication, and is one of the leading jingle writers of our time. Adept at creating "mnemonic hooks," his unforgettable music and lyrics have won over 1,000 broadcast awards, including nine Clio nominations, six Best of Canada Awards, and three International Broadcast Awards. A loving father, David is also an accomplished Aikido instructor (non-violent martial art).

This combination of musical talent, love for children, and personal safety expertise makes David the perfect choice for writing and producing this special children's music. He writes dynamic songs that have the ability to educate, excite and empower children to stay free from danger. Through Aikido, David has learned that safety concepts come from the heart and that love is the foundation of strength. He has also, miraculously, helped take this difficult subject and make it non-fearful and accessible. Yello Dyno's *Can't Fool Me!* is sure to be added to his long list of awards.

"There are ways to teach children about keeping themselves safe that will not scare them, and the new *Can't Fool Me!* album is one of them. This music is upbeat, sophisticated and very well produced. I loved it!"

— P.J. Swift, parent, children's radio producer, Santa Cruz, California

THE YELLO DYNO YELL

Like an energetic pep rally, Yello Dyno himself leads off the *Can't Fool Me!* safety music concert to a "foot-stomping" start by teaching boys and girls how to yell for help properly. With his cool, soulful Blues Brothers personality, he cuts right through children's lack of understanding about what makes a from-the-gut yell that will truly attract attention. Yello Dyno's playful dialogue breaks down children's natural embarrassment about yelling to attract attention to themselves in public places. And Yello Dyno also teaches children important phrases to yell if they are ever in trouble, such as "This is not my dad!" What kid won't love being let in on the ancient "Paleozoic secret" of yelling?

Intro Announcer: *Ladies and Gentlemen ...What all y'all have been waitin' for ... would you welcome ... quiet down now ... quiet down ... would you please welcome ... that Purveyor of Protection, that paleontolic personality, that barry totin', foot-stompin', tail-thumpin', safety maven o' soul ... brothers and sisters... give it up for Yello Dyno!*

YD: *(laugh) YEAH!*

[Audience claps enthusiastically]

YD: *Let me hear you say YEAH!*

Crowd: *Yeah*

YD: *Let me hear you say YEAH!*

Crowd: *Yeah*

YD: *Let me hear you say YEAH!*

Crowd: *Yeah*

YD: *YEAH!*

Crowd: *Yeah*

YD: *YEAH!*

Crowd: *Yeah*

YD: *YEAH! Oh, oh, no,hold the band...*

[Band Stops Playing]

YD: *Now you gonna have to do better than that on the yell. Ol' Yello Dyno just can't get the band motivated with that performance. Let's try the girls. I'll say "Yeah," you say "Yeah" back. OK? Ready? YEAH!*

Girls: *YEAH!*

YD: *Now the boys, YEAH!*

Boys: *YEAH!*

YD: *Now together, YEEAAAH!*

Both: *YEEAAH!*

YD: *That's pretty good. But I just don't think that's gonna get the band started. That right guys?*

[Squeak From Band]

YD: *See what I mean? I tell you what. I'll share with you an ancient dyno secret handed down to me from my family over one million years ago. It's the secret of the Yello Dyno Yell! (laugh) O.K. girls, you first. Take your breath way down, down, ... two inches past the belly button. Take a big breath and let it out. Ready? YEAAAAAH!*

Girls: *YEEAAH!!*

YD: *Wow! Now boys! YEAAAAAH!*

Boys: *YEEAAH!!*

YD: *Yeah! Now you got to help me y'all. You got to get down, you got to give me some help. And as you know, we all need help sometimes. So when you need help ... you got to have it. You got to say "Help, this is not my DAD!" Go!*

Both: *Help! This is not my DAD!*

YD: *Yeah! And you say, "Help! This is not my MOM!"*

Both: *Help! This is not my MOM!*

YD: *Yes! "Help! This is not my BROTHER!"*

Both: *Help! This is not my BROTHER!*

YD: *Yes! You have done it. You have the ancient secret! You have the power! The Power of the Yello Dyno Yell! YEEEAAAAH!*

MUSIC: *Dyno Stomp*

Announcer: *Ladies and Gentlemen. Give it up for that paleontolic personality, that safety maven of soul – Yello Dyno!*

YD: *Hope you enjoy the show ... and remember ... SAFETY RULES!*

"My grandson is a brave little guy who is not afraid of anyone. We didn't want to crush his spirit, but we wanted to give him some wisdom. *Can't Fool Me!'s* eight songs have really empowered him – especially Tricky People."

— D.D. Knoppe, grandmother, San Antonio, Texas

TRICKY PEOPLE

We thought that a cool, classic rock and roll tune was the best way to help children understand a difficult topic – the tricks adults use to lure children. This approach is a far cry from the "big, dark stranger on a corner" concept of "bad" adults that children often conjure up when left to their own imaginations. This song had two main objectives: to help children recognize the tricks used by Tricky People and to instruct them on what to do if they are ever approached by a tricky person. The engaging female singer instructs kids about Tricky People using three typical scenarios (lures) in a completely non-fearful way. She also helps make the safety rules for dealing with Tricky People's lures practical, down-to-earth, and most of all - simple.

Verse 1
What if you see a guy in town
Who wants his puppy found
What do you do when he asks for help
And no one is around

Take three steps back
Take three steps back
That's how you can begin
Take three steps back
Take three steps back
Then run like the wind

Chorus 1
Tricky People
    Tricky, Tricky People
They look like you and me
Tricky People
    Tricky, Tricky People
Are bent where you can't see

Verse 2
What if a guy shows you a badge
And he says he's a cop
Now, what do you do?
How do you check?
Before you go - you stop!

You call 9-1-1
Or you call "O"
That's how you begin
And if they say "NO!"
Take three steps back,
And then run like the wind

[Repeat Chorus 1]

Verse 3
What if a guy gives you some cash
If you'll go with him now
What if the little voice inside of you
Says "No sir," "No way," "No how!"

Take three steps back
Take three steps back
That's how you begin
Take three steps back
Three steps back
Then run like the wind

Chorus 2
Tricky People
    Tricky, Tricky People
Have pain down in their heart
Tricky People
You can't fool me
'Cause I'm too smart

"I firmly believe music can teach children anything. For example, when they have to recall factual information such as their phone numbers, kids can recall it much easier and more quickly – especially in a stressful situation – if they can associate it with a tune."

    – Valerie Gammon, parent, book editor, Austin, Texas

HELP ME OPERATOR

What better way to ensure that children remember their telephone numbers, including their often forgotten or difficult-to-remember area code, than to set them to music? And while we're at it, why not teach them how to dial "0" and "911" for emergencies and tell them what to say when they get the operator on the line? This may at first glance seem like a song only for young children, but many older children do not know their area codes because they never have to use them. Similarly, most children have never had to call an operator for an emergency, so they are unsure of exactly what to do. The pace of this bluesy shuffle not only gives kids the correct tempo for memorization, it will also help calm them down when they sing it to themselves if they are ever in an emergency situation.

If you have an emergency
Pick up the phone and dial "O" (tone)

Verse 1
Help me Operator
Tell me what I should do
I need some help
And I've got to get through
I just dialed "O"
And I'm talkin' to you
And here's another little thing
That you can do

Chorus 1
Dial 9-1-1
Dial 9-1-1
Say your name and problem
Say your address too

Dial 9-1-1
Dial 9-1-1
Say your name and problem
And your address too

Verse 2
Can you say
Your telephone number
My friend
Area Code first

And then you begin
First you dial ONE
First dial ONE
Now we're going to practice
"Ready and ONE" (tone)

[Chorus 1- Sing-along]

Verse 3
Let me hear
Your telephone number again
Area Code first
And then you begin
First you dial ONE
First dial ONE
Now let's sing it
"Ready and ONE" (tone)

[Chorus 1- Sing-along]

Verse 4
It really is so simple
It's actually fun
"O" for Operator
Or dial 9-1-1
Say your name and problem
Say your address too
Sing your phone number
I'm so proud of you

[Chorus 1 - Sing-along]

"Recently, in the mall something scary happened to my daughter. She said, 'Mommy, I want to go home and listen to Yello Dyno, he makes me feel safe.' The music has really impacted her. She loves it."

— Robyn Gross, mom, Pasadena, Maryland

WE TRUST OUR FEELINGS

This charming ballad reawakens children's natural instincts and feelings way down inside. Unfortunately, even when we are very young we start to believe that our natural instincts may not be valid or can't be trusted. The sweet, motherly female singer in this song not only lets children know that their inner feelings really exist and that those feelings deserve respect, she explains to them that these feelings have a tremendous amount of power behind them that can actually help keep them safe. You can almost see her hugging each child as she sings, "When you trust your inner feelings you'll have an ocean on your side."

Verse 1
There's a light up in the sky
It's no bigger than your eye
And it shines upon the earth
It's there at each and every birth

You see it lives way down inside
And it's there for all your life
You know it's really very smart
It's the light of your heart

Chorus 1
And this sweet light acts like an ocean
Warm, whirling, moving deep inside
And this light is our true feelings
We trust our feelings all the time

Verse 2
So when your light says something's wrong
You should act - not wait too long
When you're feeling all alone
You have the power to be strong

You touch the light down in your heart
It's so easy - just a thought
It's the same around the world
For every guy and every girl

Chorus 1
And this sweet light acts like an ocean
Warm, whirling, moving deep inside
And this light is our true feelings
We trust our feelings all the time

Chorus 2
Can you feel your own heart light?
Like the ocean moving deep inside
When you trust your inner feelings
You'll have an ocean on your side
You'll have an ocean on your side

"My five-year-old daughter is so adorable, everyone wants to hug her and pick her up. Recently, she asked me to help her memorize the words to 'My Body's Mine!' 'I need to sing the words to people so they know that my body is mine,' she told me."

    – Suzanne Ward, mom, Austin, Texas

My Body's Mine!

There are songs that are just meant to be danced to, songs that even if you wanted to you couldn't stop your body from moving to the beat. So it's appropriate that a song, which teaches children that they have rights regarding their bodies, should be a song that you just have to move your body to. This Caribbean dance tune teaches children in a fun way that they can choose the level of physical affection that is comfortable to them. It also approaches the sometimes difficult-to-talk-about-topic of "private parts" in a fun, playful manner – "what my bathing suit covers is private and mine, and that's a safety rule." Also, this song's lyrics are the kind that you just can't get out of your head, especially five little words that will help children keep themselves safer: "My body's mine, mine, mine!"

Chorus
My body's mine
  Mine, mine
My body's mine
  Mine, mine
I can take it to school
I can keep my cool
'Cause you know my body's mine

My body's mine
  Mine, mine
My body's mine
  Mine, mine
I am no fool
I play by the rules
'Cause I know my body's mine

Verse 1
Just the other day
A lady came up to me
She said "This is the cutest little guy
That I have ever seen"
And then she hugged
So tight my air was gone
So I said "NO! That hurts me so"
And sang my body song

[Repeat Chorus]

Verse 2
Well wouldn't you know
I saw this stranger in the mall
He looked real nice
But I thought twice
And you know that I said "NO!"
And then I moved
At least three steps back
In my heart was a bell
So I ran to tell
And I sang my song like that

[Repeat Chorus]

Verse 3
Well we all know
When we go to the pool
What my bathing suit covers
Is private and mine
And that's a safety rule
You don't touch me there
'Cause I will run and tell
It's against the law
And I'll tell what I saw
And sing my body song

[Repeat Chorus]

"While at the theater with my 13-year-old daughter, a man asked her, 'Are you an actress?' and other questions. After several terse 'no's,' he asked 'Are you alone?' She said, 'No, that's my dad and I hope he doesn't go to jail.' 'Why?' he asked. 'If he sees you talking to me he might hurt you!' Then with a smile she asked, 'Do you think I cut the dialogue, Dad?'"

— Gerald Meyerman, dad
Guatemala City, Guatemala

G.O.M.F.

There was only one way to give children the attitude they need to walk away from an adult who might try to strike up an inappropriate conversation, or "lay a rap," on them — a country and western boogie. Most children are polite to adults, but to follow the safety rule of not talking to people they do not know, children may have to "cut the dialogue" with an adult at some point in their life. This song gives them that right. The strong male singer in G.O.M.F. (Get Outta My Face) instructs them how to best do that — "you can do it kinda clumsy or you can do it with grace" — and he gives children the confidence, or attitude, to accomplish what can be a difficult task for a child. This song also talks to kids in a way they can understand so that they can keep themselves safe — and, hey, if an adult ever attempts to cross your child's safety line, your child can just "tell that big turkey, hey, get outta my face."

Verse 1

I'm the kinda kid
Who likes to go to town
I play a little ball
You can say I get around

But here's a little something
You just might want to know
In case

Chorus 1
If a stranger comes to you
And starts to lay a rap
Don't hang around
Don't fall for his trap

Take three steps back
It's a natural fact

You can do it kinda clumsy
You can do it with grace
But you tell that big turkey
"Hey, Get Outta My Face"

Verse 2
You see I'd rather be safe
Than always polite
Your mom or dad will tell you
That night after night

'Cause some apples taste great
Some apples have a worm

[Repeat Chorus 1]

Verse 3
So if after "Hello"
And you say "Hi" back
Cut the conversation
Take three steps back

'Cause even when it rains
You naturally run inside

Chorus 2
Ya got your eyes that can see
Ya got your ears that can hear
Ya got your heart that can feel
Ya got your feet that can get up
And run like the wind

"Hey Jack, Get Outta My Face"

You can do it kinda clumsy
You can do it with grace
But you tell that big turkey
"Hey, Get Outta My Face"

"My seven-year-old daughter danced through the entire cassette with almost reckless abandon. Seeing, first-hand, such a positive response was such a pleasure. I wish I'd had a video camera. My wife, an elementary school teacher, was very impressed with *Can't Fool Me!*. The memory hooks really work."

– T. La Bella, J.D., dad and Child Custody
Attorney, Middletown, New York

IF YOUR PARENTS GET LOST

If a child gets lost in a mall or ball park he has the task of getting himself found. To do that, he needs to do the right thing quickly and do it with confidence. First of all, this song sets up a sweet twist for the child: it's his *parents* who are lost, not him, and he must find them. By instructing children through the use of two specific stories about how children find their parents, this song dispels the two worst things a child can do if he is lost – wander around and look scared. The clear, strong, "walk tall" voice of the female singer and the soothing voice of the male singer do more than just tell children what to do, they evoke the feeling of strength and confidence that a child needs to "be the boss," to find a security guard or a mom with kids, and to find their "lost parents." Moreover, the last verse of this song gives children a strong message of hope: if they are ever lost, they can follow the safety rules "and in no time at all" find their lost parents.

Rhythm Chorus
Where did you go?
Where did you go?
You were right here just a moment ago!

Verse 1
I'm awalkin' through the mall
I'm awalkin' real tall
I'm findin' help right here
I'll betcha mom's real scared

Mom's probably just runnin' behind
She'll do better next time

I find the lady at the counter
And I speak real clear
"I need some HELP!"
I'm gonna stick around here

Mom's probably just runnin' behind
She'll do better next time

[Repeat Rhythm Chorus]

Verse 2
I'm in a ballpark
And it's gettin' kinda dark

I yell for Dad real loud
I might even draw a crowd

Dad's probably just runnin' behind
He'll do better next time

I can find a mom with kids
I'll be glad if I did
Ah! a security guard
That wasn't very hard

Dad's probably just runnin' behind
He'll do better next time

[Repeat Rhythm Chorus]

Verse 3
So if your parents get lost
It's your turn to be the boss
I'll be walkin' real tall
And in no time at all
They'll be laughin' and cryin'
They showed up in no time

They'll be laughin' and cryin'
They showed up in no time

"This is the most beautiful album I have ever heard. This is the most beautiful spirit I have ever heard. You cared enough to make an album for children's safety in such a professional way."

— Sue Ham, grandmother, Tyler, Texas

SAFELY HELD IN YOUR HEART
(LUKE'S SONG)

This is our theme song. It was inspired by real-life feelings and events. "Safely Held In Your Heart" evokes all of the feelings of love and safety for which every person longs, from birth to old-age. In this family love ballad, a man, woman, and child express their deep and tender feelings of love for each other. The emotions beautifully expressed in this song are the very feelings why every parent works so hard to keep their children safe, and the reason why each child believes he or she is worth keeping safe. Love is the most important safety rule, because a child who feels loved is a child who knows they are valued. This is a ballad that every family can make their very own.

Verse 1
Mother, I couldn't tell you
I had no words to say
Love you gave me so freely
I can never repay

Chorus 1
Safely held in your heart
Safely rocked in your arms
Love continues to grow
Today, my child is born

Verse 2
Darling, I have to tell you
I think you're wonderfully strong
You're my sweet inspiration
Oh, how lucky we are

Chorus 2
Safely held in your heart
Safely rocked in your arms
Love continues to grow
Today, our child is born

Verse 3
Father, I can't tell you
I have no words to say
Love you give me so freely
I can never repay

Chorus 3
Safely held in your heart
Safely rocked in your arms
Love continues to grow
And today, I am born

Choral Rounds
Safely held in your heart
  Safely held in your heart
Safely rocked in your arms
  Safely rocked in your arms
Safely held in your heart
  Safely held in your heart
Love continues to grow
Today, our child is born

APPENDIX E

WHAT YOU NEED TO KNOW ABOUT PARENTAL ABDUCTIONS

"Most parental kidnapping is not done out of love for the child. 'The majority of parental kidnapping is due to rage of the other parent – kidnapping is not good for the child. It creates anxiety, fright, depression, difficulty with trust, and fear of new people'."

> – "Abduction by Parents: The Unrecognized Crime", *Parents*

"Parental abduction is not an innocent crime. It is not safe. It is not harmless. The children suffer being uprooted again and again. They lose any sense of security and belonging. Instead, they bleed with guilt and overpowering sadness. And the family behind sits in agony, awaiting a call – the call that will lift the enormous burden of pain from their hearts."

> – "From Visitation to Abduction: A Family's Nightmare," *Missing Children Report*

"Although parental kidnapping may not sound as traumatic as abduction by a complete stranger, the impact is just as devastating. The loneliness and loss I felt were terrible."

> – "Welcome home, Brian," (by Deborah Wilson
>   Runner, mother who was separated from her son
>   by her ex-husband for fifteen years),
>   *Ladies' Home Journal*

Many people are surprised at the prevalence of child abduction by their non-custodial parents. In fact, most parents never suspect that their ex-spouse would literally kidnap their own child. Yet in 1999, The National Center for Missing and Exploited Children released government statistics that approximately 203,900 children were taken by non-custodial parents (family abductions) – often separating the children from their custodial parent for many years. Fortunately, 98% of these children were returned home and none of them were killed. By comparison, that same year, there were approximately 58,200 *non-family abduction* (by strangers) and only approximately 115 of these were considered the long-term, more dangerous type of abduction.

Many of these parental kidnappings occur during the divorce process when the parents' feelings about each other may become hostile. When one parent is feeling rejected or angry, taking the child can be seen as a way to get revenge or to punish the other parent. Sometimes it is about abuse, and the overpowering need to control; not love or goodwill for the child, according to research statistics. Whether based on anger, spite, or misunderstanding, if one parent decides to keep a child from the other parent it can be done, but it is not legal or right for anyone involved, much less, the child. Once he is abducted, the custodial parent spends countless hours and thousands of dollars, not to mention the extreme emotional cost, trying to recover his or her child – a process similar to finding a needle in a haystack. A plan for visitation and compatibility is by far the best route.

Among the thousands of kidnapping cases by non-custodial parents each year are the following three examples:

> "David's birthday was coming up the next week, so I agreed that he [her former husband, Ralph] could see him for the day. We arranged a pickup in a parking lot because I still did not want him to know where we lived. When I arrived with both kids in the car, he punched me and stole them."
>
> > – Geoffrey L. Greif and Rebecca L. Hegar,
> > *"When Parents Kidnap: The Families Behind the Headlines"*

> "On July 9, 1992, the unimaginable became a devastating reality. Heidi H's three children, Hans, Heather, and Laurel , were kidnapped by their non-custodial father, Neil. Neil was blessed with many advantages: intelligence, striking good looks, convincing charm. A man who had all of the ingredients to have the whole world within his grasp. Few would suspect his dark side – the grainy, unpredictable paranoia, his explosive temper and violent obsession for vengeance against his estranged wife." (Note: Neil has been located and the children have been recovered, 1994.)
>
> > – "From Visitation to Abduction: A Family's Nightmare", *Missing Children Report*

> "The judge granted me physical custody of Brian. Mike received liberal visitation rights, yet this still angered him so much that, on several occasions, he threatened to take our son away from me. Concerned, I reported the threats to the judge, but he said that nothing could be done unless Mike actually acted on his threats...A week after the divorce became final, Mike came to pick up Brian for

the weekend. He didn't return on Sunday evening, and no one answered the phone at the rooming house where he was staying."

– "Welcome Home, Brian", Ladies' Home Journal

Because the child is with a parent, people often don't view this form of abduction as destructive. But the seriousness of parental abductions is tragically underestimated and often considered by mental health providers to be as equally disparaging and traumatic as abduction by someone the child doesn't know. For one thing, the kidnapping parent is rarely motivated by concern for the child. More often than not a missing child's caseworker can tell you their case file shows that a non-custodial parental abduction is acted out in revenge committed against the former spouse. There is little love for the child in this situation. Could anyone really think that a balanced, loving parent could or would rip their child away from his other parent, siblings, school chums, close friends and family members? Psychological, emotional, and/or physical abuse are the prices paid by the child in virtually every case. Remember that parental kidnapping is illegal, so the child is basically living a life on the run, always in hiding and never able to establish long-term relationships or roots. For children, the pain of this lifestyle includes:

- suffering the loss of the parent and family members from whom they were taken,

- moving often, changing names, more sexual abuse or battering, being kept out of school, forced to tell lies, and not being allowed to establish normal friendships with other children,

- experiencing anxiety, depression, difficulty with trust, and fear of new people,

- dealing with self-esteem problems due to being told that the other parent doesn't want them (as often happens).

Steps To Prevent Parental Abduction

"As a former private investigator, I have worked closely with hundreds of families involved in domestic and custody disputes, and criminal child abduction. I remain convinced of one fundamental truth: the majority of acts of child abduction are preventable. In particular, with non-custodial parental abduction I was continually shocked at how many signs there were before the abduction actually took place. And yet, the parents took no steps to educate their children and protect them from this occurring. Without question, parents who educate themselves and their children with the basic safety knowledge are empowered to act responsively rather than react helplessly to child abduction."

> — Dr. George R. Jones, a crisis intervention
> specialist, minister, and former private
> investigator, Lynchburg, Virginia

If a parent is ever in a situation that could even remotely lead to a parental abduction, he or she must become vigilant. Protecting your child from an ex-spouse who is intent on abduction is extremely difficult. Recognizing this up front should encourage you to maintain at least a civil, if not friendly, relationship with your ex-spouse.

To protect your children, your first step should be to create a family plan that would help you be reunited with your child if you ever become separated. One important aspect of this plan is to gently, but thoroughly, prepare your child for the possibility of being taken by their non-custodial parent. You can begin this process by explaining to your child that the anger between you and your ex-spouse is not the child's fault. Tell them an angry parent can make big mistakes. Be sure they know you love them and always want them with you, even if the other parent tells them that you don't. Then let them know that they should always call you, to be sure it is okay with you, for them to go anywhere with the other parent. If the other spouse will not let them call you, then the child should know that something is very wrong. As a backup plan, you can select people whom the children can trust, so that they have a source besides yourself to contact if they are in trouble or if they think their abducting parent is lying to them. If that happens, they must follow your family plan of action.

Here are eight important steps custodial parents should take to help prevent an abduction from occurring and, if an abduction does occur, to help ensure a speedy recovery.

1. Work through custody issues first, before the property settlement, rather than after. This helps prevent any anger over property issues from impacting custody decisions. Also, if you and your ex-spouse are having problems, act quickly to establish legal custody. In some states, where no custody is established, it is not illegal for a parent to take his or her child. (Know the laws that apply to custody and jurisdiction in your state or the state where the divorce occurred.)

2. Include special provisions in the custody decree regarding the beginning and end dates of visits, requiring legal approval to take the child out of state, and requiring written consent to take the child from school.

3. Keep child support and visitations separate. A frustrated parent might take a child in anger if visitation rights are withheld. Do not antagonize him or her by withholding visitations based on support payments alone.

4. Do not ignore any abduction threat. Document the threats with a witness, by keeping a log with the date, time, and a detailed description of the scenario or by tape-recording the event. (Some states require that you tell the other person that you will be recording a phone

call.) Threats about taking your child should also be taken seriously. Notify the police and give them copies of any restraining orders that are in effect against your ex-spouse. You may also request restricted locations for visitation rights if you can prove potential harm to your child. The potential abductor should be advised that taking a child is punishable by imprisonment, a fine, or both. Notify schools, babysitters, child care centers, your church or synagoge, neighbors and friends of your concern; if you have legal custody, make sure your child's teachers and caretakers know and refuse to release your child to your ex-spouse, or anyone other than an authorized person. You may wish to provide pictures and descriptions of those people not to release to for ease in recognition during busy times, such as pick-up time at the day care center or at the school.

5. Be on the alert for sudden changes in your ex-spouse's life. Any changes, such as quitting a job or talk about selling a home, may be preparation to leave. If you notice sudden changes in your ex-spouse's behavior, take appropriate precautions. Trust your intuition.

6. If you haven't already done so, begin collecting important information, such as the year, make and style of the car(s), license plate number(s), and driver's license number; social security number(s); alias(es) and nick name(s); date and place of birth; relative's phone numbers and addresses; hobbies and interests; personal statistics such as weight, height, hair style and color, banking, financial details, and credit or debit card number(s). Photocopy anything you can get your hands on, but don't make threats that you will use the information. Simply squirrel it away in a private place and tell no one its there, except trusted, quiet mouthed persons that could retrieve it in the event something tragic occurs and you cannot retrieve it.

In most custodial kidnappings, a close friend or relative of your ex-spouse knows where the child is.

7. Calmly discuss the potential abduction problem with your child. Discuss parental abduction just as you would any personal safety information. Make sure your children know that if they were ever taken it would be against your will and that you will look for them until you find them. Tell them they can tell a teacher or new friend's parent that your other parent doesn't know where they are, and a call home or to the job, or 911 is needed. Tell them how to dial 1-(the area code) and their important phone number(s).

8. Contact proper authorities. Do not delay if you think your child has been taken by your ex-spouse – begin your search immediately. If your child is abducted make sure the police take the right type of report, and that your child is entered into the FBI's National Crime Information Center (NCIC) system right away (a warrant is not required). Waiting 24 hours is NOT required no matter what you may be told, and this is not just a civil matter, it is illegal to steal and conceal a child. IT IS THE LAW. Call back to confirm that the NCIC posting has been done. Hire a family law attorney to work with you. (An attorney who is not experienced in custody matters will cost you lost time, money, and possibly custody in the long run)

Also, any national missing child non-profit organization can assist you without charge. They can help with custodial interference cases, stranger abductions, and/or runaways. Among the services offered are referral to family law attorneys (some of which may provide services without charge), as well as authorities and social services which you can rely on for guidance. Their caseworkers will guide you past the block walls and seemingly endless dead-ends. They provide missing child posters, as well as tangible customized search and reunification plans. For assistance in finding the missing child center nearest you, contact the Association of Missing & Exploited Children's Organizations (AMECO) at 866-398-2601. This association is the leading resource in America for referring desperate families to hotlines, websites and the free help you may need, throughout the world.

For more information on parental abduction education, the National Center for Missing & Exploited Children (NCMEC) has a 78-page handbook on the subject. Visit their website at www.missingkids.com or call 1-800-843-5678.

This section is based in part on information published by the National Center For Missing and Exploited Children and Melody C. Gibson, Executive Director and CEO of OPERATION LOOKOUT National Center for Missing Youth.

APPENDIX F

WHAT TO DO, STEP-BY-STEP, IF YOUR CHILD IS LOST OR MISSING

What To Do if Your Child is Lost

Turn around for a minute and your child will have crawled between the clothes racks or wandered to look at toys in a department store. Luckily, a child is normally lost for just a few seconds or minutes. Still, in that few minutes the fear you experience is immeasurable.

You can't keep your eye on your children every second (although until children reach an age where they can understand that they must not walk or run away from you, parents have to make every effort not to let them out of their sight). You must plan ahead to make sure you find your child fast if he or she is ever lost at a ball field, an amusement park, the mall, or wherever. Children won't know what to do when they're lost unless you tell them ahead of time. It will be reassuring to all of you to know you have a "lost and found" plan in case you are ever separated. Then you and your children will take the necessary steps and avoid the immobilization that panic can bring about.

If your child is ever lost, you should not assume that he will turn up in just a few minutes. One story from *America's Most Wanted* illustrates this rule: a three-year-old child disappeared from her parents' side in a Walmart store. Once the parents realized that their daughter was lost, the parents told the manager. He immediately implemented the store's "Code Adam" program for lost children. Employees hurried to all the exits to lock the doors. Soon they found a middle-aged man trying to get out one of the back doors of the store with the child. The child turned to the store clerk and said, "Can you take me to my mommy, please?" Without the store's "lost child" program, who knows how far away the man would have gone with the child.

Here are five step-by-step guidelines, recommended by The Yello Dyno Program, that parents should follow if their child is ever lost:

1. Act now – time is crucial. It is important to stay as calm as possible so that you can think and communicate thoroughly.

2. Enlist help. Call a security guard, policeman, store manager, or whomever you can get to help you look for your child. If your child is lost you want as many people looking as possible. If you are in a place with a public-address speaker system, use it to call for your child.

3. Give authorities an accurate description of your child. An Immediate Response Child I.D. card is invaluable in this situation. An incomplete description of your child will slow down the search – imagine how many three-foot high, brown-haired boys dressed in jeans there are in a mall on a Saturday afternoon. In the average mall, 10,000 people could pass through on that day. At the very least, you should have a clear, up-to-date photograph of your child in your wallet to show to the authorities.

4. Check every logical location, then fan out. If you have already taught your child to stay in the area where you were separated, then you can concentrate your search there. Or better yet, if you and your child have agreed on a meeting spot if you are ever separated, be sure you or someone stays in that spot to meet your child if she shows up. If the child is lost at home or in your neighborhood, make sure to check the house from top to bottom. One telling example of this guideline occurred one summer afternoon when a mother couldn't find her six-year-old daughter. She immediately enlisted other parents' and children's help, and they began searching all over the neighborhood. After almost two hours of frantic searching, her older sister found her sleeping under her mother's bed. After searching your own home, check with all of your child's friends and look in or call the places he or she normally spends time.

5. Plan ahead to help prevent trouble in public places. Many parents have a variety of ways they use to help ensure their children stay close to them and to help find their children quickly if they are ever lost. Here are a few:

- Stay on your toes. Children are incredibly fast and naturally curious.

- Dress your children in distinctive clothing so that they will stand out in a crowd. Some parents creatively tie colorful helium balloons to their children's wrist.

- At a crowded beach, one frantic mother looked for her three-year-old child by kneeling on the ground and looking through all of the long adult legs walking around. She found him right away.

- At a stadium or auditorium write down the child's section and seat number on the back of his hand.

- Thoroughly discuss with your child what to do if he is lost and explain to him what you will do to find him. In public places agree to a meeting spot if you are separated.

- When you find your child, remember that this is not the time to reprimand him for getting lost. Instead, let him know you are glad to see him and praise him for being smart and brave.

What To Do if Your Child is Missing

The pooled resources of many good people can make all the difference in the world to you if you have a missing child. In moments, "Code Adam" or the "Amber Alert" will go into effect if it is activated in your area. The media will take up the story and broadcast it to an interested public. The picture you carry in your wallet will suddenly mean more to you than when you showed it to grandma at Christmas. And the missing children's centers will have a vital purpose in your life, where before nobody in your family had reason to care.

The most important point to remember is to take action immediately, even if you think your child may have wandered off voluntarily. Others may need to take over for you, depending on your emotional state. Let them help you get comfortable, calm down and ask you questions. They are compassionate humanitarians who care and want to help.

1. **File a Report.** File a missing child report with your local police or sheriff right away. There is no longer a rule that the police must wait twenty-four hours before they consider looking for your child. Be truthful in reporting family conflicts, troubled relationships, or other unpleasant circumstances. Authorities are critically handicapped if they do not have the facts and circumstances leading up to your child's disappearance. Which is more important – your pride or your child's life?

2. **Register.** In the United States, ask your local police to register your child as "missing" with the National Crime Information Center (NCIC) and your State Bureau of Investigation. Follow up with a call to your nearest FBI office to verify entry in the NCIC computer in Washington, DC. They will enter it for you if the police have not. The FBI is authorized by the Parental Kidnapping Prevention Act of 1980 to search without delay for abducted children taken across state lines. Similar procedures are followed in Canada with the RCMP. In Canada, contact the provincial police and RCMP (the Canadian Missing Persons division) to record the information. There is a strong cooperative effort to thwart abductions between Canada and the United States.

3. **Use a Missing Children's Center.** Most missing children centers, of which there are approximately 40 in the USA and Canada, can be contacted 24 hours a day, 7 days a week through their hotlines or websites. There's never a waiting period, and there's never a fee for service. Some centers can expedite opening your file faster than others, and some will accept the forms you fill out for one center, and use it with theirs. An

investigative caseworker will work with the authorities involved. They will create your child's poster, and provide emotional and tangible support to you throughout your search, regardless of the duration. They can begin mass picture distribution above and beyond what local police are able to do. Their toll-free phone number for "sighting calls" will generate leads for law enforcement to follow up on. Many centers place your child's picture on the Internet and broadcast your child's image via email, fax or mail. To reach a certified missing child center closest to you, refer to the contact information at the end of this section.

4. **Insist on a Follow-Up.** Insist that your local police follow up on all leads. Keep a file with the detective's name, your missing children center's contact names, and phone numbers with area code, case numbers, and record all information concerning the investigation.

5. **Be Thorough.** When searching for your child, don't allow any stone to be unturned. One thing you can do is to retrace the last known steps your child took. Do it at the same time of day as the disappearance, because people who regularly travel that route may be valuable witnesses. Don't assume that police are giving highest priority to the search for your child. Ongoing or new crimes may take precedence. Keep yourself in their awareness by calling regularly.

6. **Use Phone Power Correctly.** Keep a pencil and paper by the telephone to record any information received. Tape record any messages and voices. Use an answering machine message to tell your child that you are looking for him or her and how to reach you, including the area code. If you think your child might try to reach you or someone you know by phone, keep phones manned night and day. Keep a cell phone charged up. Keep your old phone number if you must move, or have it

forwarded to your new number. If you are concerned that your child doesn't know your area code, you may want to call your telephone number in all existing area codes. Explain your situation to people at these numbers and ask for their help if your child calls. And because it is so inexpensive these days to install a toll-free number, you have a greater chance of getting help if you notify everyone you can be reached at a particular 800 number.

7. **Offer a Reward.** Your place of business, friends, or community may be compelled to help with this. Make certain the reward is offered not just for information, but the information that leads to the return of your child. Law enforcement or your missing child center can assist you with the verbiage to go on the posters they create for you.

8. **Distribute Posters.** In some cases posters are actually more dangerous than helpful, because they may cause an abductor to leave the area due to the fear of being apprehended. Law enforcement and your missing children center will help you make this decision. If it is decided that posters are beneficial in your case, give the missing children center and your detective a clear, current photo. Some printing businesses will donate or reduce their fees to help you keep costs down. Your missing child center operates their casework offices, for the most part, 5 days a week, with a manned 24-hour hotline for emergencies and sightings after-hours. They are generally competent and willing to inform you of any reliable leads they forwarded to the police. Post these flyers everywhere that seems worthwhile. A poster will generate sighting calls. An abductor may see the poster and release the victim. (If the child ran-away, the posters will reflect your concern to encourage a call home.)

9. **Contact Runaway Hotlines.** If you believe your child may have run away, in the U.S. call the local runaway

hotline as well as the National Runaway Switchboard at 1-800-621-4000. You can leave a message for your child and find out if your child left one for you. Let your child know that you are willing to listen.

10. **Check Hospitals.** Check for unidentifiable children at hospitals and morgues. Obtain dental records, fingerprints or DNA on your child in the event a person fitting the description of your child is located deceased. Positive identification can come from these items.

11. **Consider a Private Detective.** If you hire a private detective, choose carefully. You may be approached by several private detectives. Be sure to check references and the Better Business Bureau, the police and/or your missing children's center.

12. **Involve the Media.** A victims advocate can help you and tell you what the media needs from you, how to appear in front of the camera, and how to answer interviewer's questions.

13. **Check Credit Card Charges.** Check your credit cards to see if there are purchases that are not yours. This information could help locate your child, a runaway, or the abductor.

14. **Check with State Motor Vehicle Department.** If a car is involved, check with your state's motor vehicle registration department.

15. **Check with Social Security.** If your child is missing, the Social Security Department will send a letter from you to your missing child's last known address. You must give proof that your child is missing, along with specific information required for the records search.

16. **Check with the State Department.** Check on the status of your child's passport at your State Department (or with the Provincial Government in Canada).

17. **Check with Local Military Recruiting Offices.** Check with the local recruiting offices and the national headquarters of each branch of the armed services to see if your child has joined the military. They have a missing person's division.

18. **Contact Team Hope.** Consider contacting Team Hope, a group of parents that have experienced having a missing child. You will receive understanding, help and hope. Team Hope can be reached at 866-305-HOPE.

19. **Financial Assistance.** If you experience the crisis of having a missing child, there are many people and organizations that care about you. This experience will certainly challenge you emotionally, but it can also drain you financially. You should know, therefore, that there is a Victim Compensation Fund to help you cover the expense of counseling for you and your family. Team Hope, law enforcement, or your missing children service center should be able to tell you how to obtain this help.

20. **Locate Help from a Missing Child Organization.** The best way to locate the missing children center nearest you is to contact the Association of Missing & Exploited Children's Organizations (AMECO) at 866-398-2601. You will want to contact more than one missing center to gain the highest level of exposure possible. You may also want to contact the National Center for Missing and Exploited Children at (800)843-5678 or through their website at www.missingkids.org.

This section is based in part on information published by the National Center For Missing and Exploited Children and Melody C. Gibson, Executive Director and CEO of OPERATION LOOKOUT National Center for Missing Youth.

BIBLIOGRAPHY

Books

Brodkin, Margaret and Coleman Advocates for Children & Youth. *Every Kid Counts*. San Francisco: Harper Collins, 1993.

Campbell, Don. *The Mozart Effect - Tapping the Power of Music to Heal the Body, Strengthen the Mind, and Unlock the Creative Spirit*. New York: Avon Books, 1997.

Cooper, Paulette and Paul Noble. *Reward*. New York: Pocket Books/Div. Simon & Schuster Inc., 1994.

Dana, Trudy K. *"Safety Away From Home." Safe and Sound*. Pgs. 165-169 & 180-201. New York: McGraw-Hill, 1988.

Children's Express. *Voices From The Future*. Ed. Susan Goodwillie. New York: Crown Publishers, 1993.

De Becker, Gavin. *The Gift of Fear. Survival Signals that Protect us from Violence*. New York: Little, Brown and Company, 1997.

De Becker, Gavin. *Protecting the Gift. Keeping Children and Teenagers Safe (and Parents Sane)*. New York: Dell Books, 2000.

Douglas, John and Mark Olshaker. *Mind Hunter. Inside the FBI's Elite Serial Crime Unit*. New York: Scribner. 1995

Dziech, Billie Wright and Judge Charles B. Schudson. *On Trial. America's Courts and Their Treatment of Sexually Abused Children*. Boston: Beacon Press, 1991.

Eyre, Linda and Richard. *3 Steps to a Strong Family*. New York: Simon & Schuster, 1994.

Faber, Adele and Elaine Mazlish. *How To Talk So Kids Will Listen & Listen So Kids Will Talk*. New York: Avon Books, 1982.

Fancher, Vivian Kramer. *Safe Kids: A Complete Child-Safety Handbook & Resource Guide for Parents*. New York: John Wiley & Sons, Inc., 1991.

Ferguson, Donna. *The Someday Kid. A True Story of Sexual Abuse and its Relationship to Pornography*. Summerland: Harbor House (West), Inc., 1993.

Ferguson, Donna. *The Assault on America's Children. Safeguarding Your Child from Becoming a Victim of Sexual Abuse*. Summerland: Harbor House (West), Inc., 1994.

Freeman-Longo, Robert E. and Geral T. Blanchard. *Sexual Abuse in America: Epidemic of the 21st Century*. Brandon: The Safer Society Press, 1998.

Garbarino, James, Ph. D. *Lost Boys. Why Our Sons Turn Violent and How We Can Save Them*. New York: The Free Press/Div. Simon & Schuster, Inc., 1999.

Golant, Susan. *"Part III. In The World." Fifty Ways to Keep Your Child Safe*. Los Angeles: Lowell House, 1992.

Goldstein, Seth L. *The Sexual Exploitation of Children*. Boca Raton: CRC Press, 1987.

Greif, Geoffrey L. and Rebecca L. Hegar. *When Parents Kidnap: The Families Behind the Headlines*. New York: The Free Press, 1993.

Hare, Dr. Robert D. *Without Conscience. The Disturbing World of the Psychopaths Among Us*. New York: Pocket Books, 1993.

Hollingsworth, Jan. *Unspeakable Acts*. New York: Congdon & Weed, 1986.

Hughes, Donna Rice with Pamela T. Campbell. *Kids Online. Protecting Your Children in Cyberspace*. Grand Rapids: Fleming H. Revell/Div. Baker Book House, 1998.

Kirwin, Barbara R., Ph. D. *The Mad, The Bad, and the Innocent. The Criminal Mind on Trial – Tales of a Forensic Psychologist*. New York: Little, Brown and Company, 1997.

Klepsch, Marvin and Laura Logie. *Children Draw and Tell. An Introduction to the Projective Uses of Children's Human Figure Drawings*. Bristol; Brunner/Mazel, 1982.

Koplewicz, Harold S. and Robin F. Goodman; editors. Forward by Katie Couric. *Childhood Revealed. Art Expressing Pain, Discovery and Hope*. New York: Harry N. Abrams, Inc., 1999.

Korem, Dan. Suburban Gangs. *The Affluent Rebels*. Richardson: International Focus Press, 1994.

Korem, Dan. *The Art of Profiling. Reading People Right the First Time.* Richardson: International Focus Press, 1997.

Kraizer, Sherryll Kerns. *The Safe Child Book.* New York: Dell Publishing Co., 1985.

Kyte, Kathy S. *Play It Safe: The Kids Guide to Personal Safety and Crime Prevention.* New York: Alfred A. Knopf, Inc., 1983.

McGee, James P., Ph. D., and Caren R. Debernardo, Psy. D. *The Classroom Avenger.* Baltimore: James P. McGee, 1999.

McNamara, Joseph D. *Safe & Sane.* New York: Perigee Books, 1984.

Magid, Dr. Ken and Carole A. McKelvey. *High Risk. Children Without A Conscience.* New York: Bantam Books, 1989.

Malchiodi, Cathy A. *Breaking the Silence. Art Therapy with Children from Violent Homes.* Levittown; Brunner/Mazel, 1997.

Marshall, W. L. and D. R. Laws, and H. E. Barbaree. *Handbook of Sexual Assault.* New York: Plenum Press, 1990.

Martin, Kimbra. *Snapshots.* Irving: Authorlink Press, 1999.

Megan Nicole Kanka Foundation, Inc. *Who Is Watching Our Children? A Parent's Guide to Awareness Through Education.* Trenton: 1995.

Novelli, Norma and Mike Walker; as told to Judith Spreckels; editor. Peirce O'Donnell; conclusion.*The Private Diary of Lyle Menendez.* Beverley Hills; Dove Books, 1995.

Miller, Alice. *Thou Shalt Not Be Aware. Society's Betrayal of the Child.* New York: Meridian/Penguin Books, USA, 1990.

Miller, Alice. *For Your Own Good. Hidden Cruelty in Child-Rearing and the Roots of Violence.* New York: The Noonday Press, 1990.

Mintle, Linda, Ph. D. *Kids Killing Kids.* Creation House, 1999.

Niehoff, Debra, Ph. D. *The Biology of Violence. How Understanding the Brain, Behavior, and Environment Can Break the Vicious Circle of Aggression.* New York: The Free Press, 1999.

Pipher, Mary, Ph. D. *Reviving Ophelia. Saving the Selves of Adolescent Girls.* New York: Ballantine Books/Div. Of Random House, Inc., 1994.

Pollack, William, Ph. D. *Real Boys. Rescuing Our Sons from the Myths of Boyhood.* New York: Owl Books/Henry Holt and Company, Inc., 1999.

Pollack, William S. Ph. D. with Todd Shuster. *Real Boys' Voices.* New York: Random House, 2000.

Rossi, Jani Hart. *Protect Your Child From Sexual Abuse.* Seattle: Parenting Press, 1984.

Samenow, Stanton E. Ph. D. *Inside the Criminal Mind.* New York: Times Books/Div. Of Random House, Inc., 1984.

Shore, Dr. Kenneth. *Keeping Kids Safe. A Guide for Parents of Toddlers and Teens – and all the Years in Between.* Paramus: Prentice Hall Press, 2001.

Siegler, Ava L. Ph. D. *What Should I Tell The Kids? A Parent's Guide to Real Problems in the Real World.* New York: Penguin Books USA, 1993.

Steinberg, Shirley R. and Joe L. Kincheloe, editors. *Kinderculture. The Corporate Construction of Childhood.* Boulder: Westview Press, 1997.

Steinhorst, Lori with John Rose. *When the Monster Comes Out of the Closet. Westley Allan Dodd In His Own Words.* Salem: Rose Publishing, 1994.

Strasburger, Victor M.D. *Getting Your Kids to Say "No" In the '90s When You Said "Yes" in the 60's.* New York: Fireside Simon & Schuster, 1993.

Van Der Zande, Irene. *Kidpower: Guide for Parents and Teachers.* Santa Cruz: Kidpower, 1991.

Walsh, John with Susan Schindehette. *Tears of Rage. From Grieving Father to Crusader for Justice: The Untold Story of the Adam Walsh Case.* New York: Pocket Books/Div. Of Simon & Schuster, Inc., 1997.

Wooden, Kenneth. Child Lures. *What Every Parent and Child Should Know About Preventing Sexual Abuse and Abduction.* Arlington; The Summit Publishing Group, 1995.

Magazine Articles & Papers

Checklist of Characteristics of Youth Who Have Caused School-Associated Violent Deaths. *The National School Safety Center.*

"The Tragedy of America's Missing Children." *U.S. News & World Report*, October 24, 1983, pp. 63õ64.

"Protecting Kids: A Matter of Growing Concern." *Time*, November 18, 1985, pp. 47.

"How Not to Have a Missing Child." *Good Housekeeping*, February 1986, pp. 230.

"Keeping Hope Alive." *Newsweek*, November 27, 1989, pp. 95-96.

"Zachary Scott Comes Home." *Missing Children Report*, 1993, pp. 6-8.

Adler, Jerry. "Kids Growing Up Scared." *Newsweek*, January 10, 1994, pp. 43-50.

Anderson, C.A., & Bushman, B.J.(2002) "Media Violence and Societal Violence". *Science*, 295, 2377-2378.

Andrews, Lori B. "Terrified Generation?" *Parents*, December, 1986, pp. 139-232.

Baumeister, R.F., Bushman, B.J., & Campbell, W.K. (2000). Self-esteem, Narcissism, and Aggression: Does Violence Result from Low Self-esteem or from Threatened Egotism? *Current Directions in Psychological Science*,9,26-29.

Bawden, Jim. "Better Safe Than Sorry." *Starweek*, March 21-28, 1992, pp. 4-5.

Burden, Ordway P. "John Walsh and the Most Wanted." *Texas Police Journal*, 1994, pp. 8-9.

Bushman, B.J., & Bonacci, A.M.(2002) Violence and Sex Impair Memory for Television Ads. *Journal of Applied Psychology*, 87,557-564.

Bushman, B.J., & Bonacci, A.M.(2001) Media Violence and the American Public: Scientific Facts Versus Media Misinformation. *American Psychologist*, 56,477-489.

Bushman, B.J.,& Baumeister, R.F. (1998). Threatened Egotism, Narcissism, Self-esteem, and Direct and Displaced Aggression: Does Self-Love or Self-Hate Lead to Violence? *Journal of Personality and Social Psychology*, 75,219-229.

Cerra, Frances. "Missing Children: New Facts About Fingerprinting, Videotaping, and the Milk Carton Search." *Ms.*, January, 1986, pp. 14-16.

Dwyer, K.D. and C. Warger. Early Warning,Timely Response: A Guide to Safe Schools. (1998) *U.S. Department of Education*.

Gleick, Elizabeth. "America's Child." *People*, December 20, 1993, pp. 84-90.

Hodges, Heidi and Bonnie White. "From Visitation to Abduction: A Family's Nightmare." *Missing Children Report*, 1993, pp. 9-11.

Hoyt, Carolyn. "Child Abductions: What a Mom Must Know." *McCall's*, March, 1994, pp. 60-67.

Kantrowitz, Barbara. "Stalking The Children." *Newsweek*, December 20, 1993, pp. 28-29.

Lems, Kristin. "For a Song: Music Across the ESL Curriculum." *Paper presented at the annual convention of Teachers of English to Speakers of Other Languages*, Chicago,IL., March 1996. (ED No. 396 524).

Levine, Mark and Deirdre Martin. "Have You Seen Me?: Aging the Images of Missing Children." *Law Enforcement Technology*, July, 1991, pp. 34-40.

McCarty, Frank. "The Electronic Trail of Robert Lewis Smith." *Missing Children Report*, 1993, pp. 12-13.

O'Connell, Diana and Paula Mielke. "Careful, Not Fearful." *Sesame Street Parents' Guide*, May, 1991, pp. 12-15.

Oldham-O'Hara, Carol. "Could You Please Take Me Home Now?" *Missing Children Report*, 1993, pp. 14-16.

Perry, Bruce D., M.D.,Ph.D., Memories of Fear: How the Brain Stores and Retrieves Physiologic States, Feelings, Behaviors and Thoughts from Traumatic Events. *Images of the Body in Trauma* edited by J. Goodwin & R. Attias. Basic Books, 1999.

Perry, Bruce D., M.D.,Ph.D.,et al, Childhood Trauma, the Neurobiology of Adaptation, and "Use-dependent" Development of the Brain: How "States" Become "Traits". *Infant Mental Health Journal, Vol. 16, No. 4*, Winter 1995.

Perry, Bruce D., M.D.,PhD., Neurodevelopmental Adaptations to Violence: How Children Survive the Intragenerational Vortex of Violence. *"Violence and Childhood Trauma: Understanding and Responding to the Effects of Violence on Young Children"*. Cleveland, Gund Foundation, 1996.

Perry, Bruce D., M.D.,PhD., G. Michael Gomez, M.D. Role of the EMS Provider in Crisis Intervention: Neurophysiological Aspects of Acute Trauma in Children. *Instructor Resource for Teaching Prehospital Pediatrics: EMT Training Manual*. Houston, Baylor College of Medicine, 1995.

Perry, Bruce D., M.D.,PhD., Neurodevelopmental Aspects of Childhood Anxiety Disorders: Neurobiological Responses to Threat. *Textbook of Pediatric Neuropsychiatry.* American Psychiatric press, Inc., Brumback.

Perry, Bruce D., M.D.,PhD., Memories of Fear: How the Brain Stores and Retrieves Physiologic States, Feelings, Behaviors and Thoughts from Traumatic Events. *"Images of the Body in Trauma"*, Basic Books, 1997.

Raab, Jamie. "Every Mother's Fear." *Family Circle,* March 25, 1986, pp. 24-130.

Runner, Deborah Wilson. "Welcome home, Brian." *Ladies' Home Journal,* September 1993, pp. 22-29.

Smolowe, Jill. "A High-Tech Dragnet." *Time,* November 1, 1993, p. 43.

Stepp, Laura Sessions. "Missing Children: The Ultimate Nightmare." *Parents,* April, 1994, pp. 47-52.

Thad, Martin. "Who's Stealing Our Children."? *Ebony,* February, 1986, pp. 139-144.

Thuman, Michiela. "Missing Children." *American Baby,* October, 1985, pp. 54-60.

Van Biema, David. "Robbing The Innocents." *Time,* December 27, 1993, pp. 31-32.

Walsh, John. "The Story Behind the Picture." *Guideposts,* September, 1984, pp. 2-6.

Wright, Rosalind. "Where Are Our Children?" *Ladies' Home Journal,* March, 1994, pp. 118-196.

Newspaper Articles

"Quick Action Credited in Abducted Girl's Return." *Austin-American Statesman,* July 5, 1994.

Barden, J.C. "Amid Rising Divorce, Parents Are Abducting Thousands of Children." *The New York Times,* May 6, 1990.

Caldwell, Jean. "Rebecca Knew She Was in Danger When She Saw the Truck." *The Boston Globe,* January 17, 1994, p. 13.

Dreyfous, Leslie. "Awareness, Education Help Fight Abductions." *Austin American-Statesman,* Saturday, January 29, 1994.

Elliot, David. "When Stealing Children Is Legal." *Austin American-Statesman,* May 14, 1994.

Granados, Christine. "Child Pornography Arrest Shocks Neighbors." *Austin American-Statesman,* 1994.

Murphy, Sean P. "Beware of Kidnapper, Police Say." *The Boston Globe,* February 17, 1994.

Robertson, Alonza. "Parents Warned To Be Prepared." *Las Vegas Review-Journal/Sun,* April 10, 1994.

Santoli, Al. "A Better Way To Protect Our Children." *Parade,* July 24, 1994, pp. 12-13.

Wright, Scott W. and Miguel M. Salinas. "Eash Missing Person Case is Different, Police Say." *Austin American-Statesman,* July, 1994.

Television Programs

ABC. *20/20.* "The Lures of Death." 1984.

ABC. *20/20.* "Can They Be Caught." 1984.

ABC. *20/20.* "They're Murdering Our Children." 1984.

ABC. *20/20.* "The Best Kept Secret." 1984.

ABC. *20/20.* "Why The Silence." 1985.

ABC. *20/20.* "Making Him Pay." 1994.

ABC. *ABC News.* "How To Be Safe In America." 1993.

ABC. *Good Morning America.* "Kids View the Future." 1993.

ABC. *The Home Show.* (Six shows) 1993.

ABC. *Good Morning America.* "Child Abduction." 1994.

ABC. *The Oprah Winfrey Show.* (Two shows) 1993.

CBS. *48 Hours.* "Missing Without a Trace."' 1993.

CBS. *48 Hours.* "Child Hunter." 1994.

Channel 5. *Spectrum.* 1993.

CNN. *Daybreak.* "Two Girls in New Jersey Claim Sexual Abuse by Sex Ring." 1993.

CNN. *Larry King Live.* "The National Crisis of Child Abductions." 1993.

CNN. *Morning News.* "Mother Tries to Make Sense of Daughter's Killing." 1993.

CNN. *Newsnight.* "Chicago Woman Reunited With Seven-Week Old Daughter." 1993.

CNN. *Prime News.* "Southern California Authorities Search for Child Abuser." 1993.

CNN. *Prime News.* "Father Dedicates His Life to Searching for Missing Kids." 1993.

CNN. *Sonya Live.* "Stolen By Strangers." 1993.

CNN. *The World Today.* "Ernie Allen Interviewed About Child Protection Act." 1993.

CNN. *The World Today.* "Parents Express Fear for Their Children's Safety." 1993.

CNN. *The World Today.* "President Clinton Signs Child Protection Act Into Law." 1993.

CNN. *Morning News.* "Dad Lobbies For Polly Klaas Bill Against Repeat Felons." 1994.

CNN. *Morning News.* "Mothers Discuss Their Search for Their Missing Children." 1994.

CNN. *Newsday.* "Linda Ellerbee Teaches Kids How to Respond to Strangers." 1994.

CNN. *News hour.* "McMartin Molestation Case Leaves Legacy for Preschools." 1994.

CNN. *The World Today.* "Neighborhood Up in Arms With Police Over Child Killer." 1994.

FOX. *America's Most Wanted.* 1993.

HBO. *How to Raise a Street Smart Kid.*

NBC. *Donahue.* 1993.

NBC. *The Crusaders.* 1994.

NBC. *NOW with Tom Brokaw and Katie Couric.* 1994.

NBC. *Today Show.* 1994.

PBS. *Street Smarts: Straight Talk for Kids, Teens, & Parents.* 1992.

Viacom International. *Montel Williams.* "Can You Rehabilitate a Child Molester?" 1994.

WKRC, Cincinnati, Ohio, *Kids and Strangers.*

Video Cassettes

Kantz, Will. *Child Obsession. Pedophiles Talk To Parents.* Fort Worth; JN Productions, 1996.

Salter, Anna C. Ph. D. *Truth, Lies, and Sex Offenders.* Thousand Oaks; Sage Publications, Inc.

Office of the Attorney General, Dan Morales. *Child Abuse. What Can We Do?* Sponsored by the Crime Victim's Compensation Division, the Texas Medical Association and Texas CASA, Inc.

Audio Cassette

Assessing and Treating Sex Offenders, 1999. Gene Abel, Fred Berlin, Anna Salter.

The Sound of Knowledge, Inc. Specialized Training Services. Public & Private Violence. San Diego; The Sound of Knowledge, 1999.

Sources for Part 4: *Protecting Your Child From Violent Kids*

Dwyer, K.D. and C. Warger, "*A Guide to Safe Schools: Early Warning, Timely Response,*" U.S. Department of Education (1998)

Gavin de Becker Emergency Conference on School Shootings

Garbarino, James, Ph.D., *Lost Boys: "Why Our Sons Turn Violent and How We Can Save Them"*

McGee, James P., Ph.D. and Caren R. Debernardo, Psy. D., *"The Classroom Avenger"*

Mintle, Linda, Ph.D. *"Kids Killing Kids"*

National School Safety Center, *"Checklist of Characteristics of Youth Who Have Caused School-Associated Violent Deaths"* www.nssc1.org

Niehoff, Debra, Ph.D. *"The Biology of Violence"*

Steinberg, Shirley R., and Joe L. Kincheloe *Kinder-Culture: "The Corporate Construction of Childhood"*

Note: This bibliography represents the majority of the research sources for this book (other than personal interviews). While every effort has been made to properly credit sources, it may not be a complete listing. Please contact the author for corrections or revisions.

NCMEC

For general information the National Center for Missing and Exploited Children provides a wealth of information in print and on their website. They also offer a Cyber Tipline that handles leads from individuals reporting the sexual exploitation of children online. Call 1-800-843-5678 or visit their website at www.missingkids.com.

AMECO

The Association of Missing & Exploited Children's Organizations is the leading resource for referring desperate families of missing and abused children to hotlines, websites and the free help you may need throughout the world. Contact them at (866) 398-2601.

Child Abuse Forensic Institute

Child abuse forensic referral services are available to parents and their children through this non-profit organization. It was created as a resource and referral organization for parents or litigants in need of expert advice or assistance in civil litigation involving child abuse allegations. Contact Seth Goldstein, Esq., Executive Director, at (831) 655-6331, or visit the website at childabuseforensics.org.

American Academy of Child & Adolescent Psychiatry

Learn about the emotional, behavioral and cognitive development from early adolescence through the teen years, and find a child or adolescent psychiatrist in your area. Call (202) 966-7300 or visit their web site at www.aacap.org.

OPERATION LOOKOUT
National Center for Missing Youth

For family and non-family abduction and runaways, contact Melody C. Gibson, Executive Director & CEO, at 1-800-LOOKOUT (566-5688) or through the website at www.operationlookout.org.

Computer Crime Investigations

Help for computer-related crimes dealing with children. Under certain conditions Officer Jones is available to arrange speaking engagements, training, lectures, or assist in cyber related investigations. Verified, immediate threats to a child will be given priority. Contact Detective Harold Jones, MCSE, at the Riverside Ohio Police Department at 937-233-1820 or Email to hjones@cops.org or datacop992@aol.com.

Gavin de Becker is a nationally recognized expert on predicting and managing violent behavior. He is the author of *The Gift of Fear*, which spent four months on the New York Times Bestseller List. *Protecting the Gift: Keeping Children and Teenagers Safe (And Parents Sane)* was a Number One parenting bestseller. His books are published in fourteen languages. This three-time Presidential appointee is a Senior Fellow at UCLA's School of Public Policy and Social Research.

gavindebecker.com

Dear Friend,

In the many years I have been on the front lines of child safety education, there are only two books that I always recommend: *The Gift of Fear* and *Protecting The Gift*. Why? Because we have become a voyeur society of worriers instead of warriors, consumed by dramatic tragedies that are constantly paraded before us by the media. In the same breath we ignore acting on the signals that would prevent our own tragedies from occurring in our own neighborhoods – even in our own homes. Both prophetic and profound, yet in language that is disarmingly simple and direct, these books remove the blinders of denial, while reconnecting adults and children to their instinct for self-preservation and giving them the guts to act in their own self-defense. Gavin de Becker, by sharing his gift of awareness and amazing insights into human behavior, will undoubtedly save many lives. Quite possibly it will be your own or your child's.

Now that you have read this book on behalf of the children in your care, if you read only one other book in your life on personal safety, it has to be Gavin de Becker's *The Gift of Fear*. If you decide to read a second, it should be *Protecting the Gift*.

AWARD-WINNING VIDEOS

Help Children Build Survival Skills and Conquer Fear

"Though no video can replace effective parental protection (of course), I've reviewed many programs aimed at kids. I was most impressed with a series called "Yello Dyno." It is a musically-based educational system that helps children remember important safety information."

- Gavin de Becker

Ages 9-12   Ages 4-8

Tricky People! is a spell-binding music video that teaches kids how to recognize, avoid, and escape the deceptive behavior of those who would seek to harm them. This award-winning safety tool is especially empowering for pre-teen girls. Includes *Parent Guide*.

Can't Fool Me! is "Yello Dyno Lite," a simpler and lighter music video that teaches the younger children in your life how to stay safe.

BENEFITS

REINFORCES INSTINCTS & INTUITION which have often been buried or forgotten due to social conditioning.

EMPOWERS KIDS to recognize dangerous behavior and not be fooled by pleasant appearances or "Tricky People."

BUILDS SELF-CONFIDENCE which is a cornerstone of personal safety.

ESTABLISHES A COMMUNICATION LINK so your children will come to you throughout their lives for advice and counsel.

EDUCATES WITHOUT FEAR through music and entertaining stories that assure easy learning and high recall.

CORRECTS "Stranger Danger" education with vital new information.

GIVES YOU PEACE OF MIND knowing they have the personal safety skills to protect themselves.

NON-FEARFUL • MUSICALLY-DRIVEN • AWARD-WINNING

ORDER FORM

Your Name and Address:

Name

Street   Apt.

City   State   Zip

Daytime Phone Number (Including Area Code)

Save on Combos! See Other Side.	Quan.	Price Each	TOTAL
Raising Safe Kids in an Unsafe World (Paperback)		17.95	
6 Heroes! Teaching with Music & Real Stories (Cassette)		9.95	
Can't Fool Me! (Cassette with 8 Songs)		11.95	
Can't Fool Me! (CD with 8 Songs)		15.95	
The Fun Way To Safe Kids! (Song & Activity Book)		9.95	
Can't Fool Me! (Music Video, Ages 4-8)		16.95	
Tricky People! (Music Video, Ages 9-12, with Parent Guide)		19.95	
"At-Home" I.D. Card Kit (Makes 2 Laminated Cards)		6.95	
"At-Home" DNA I.D. Kit (One Child Per Kit)		14.95	
Safety Rules! Poster for Kids (17x22, Color)		6.95	
Special Reports (Hard Hitting "Insider" Info – Set of 6)		11.95	
STARTER KIT Save $13.85 ($53.80 Value)		39.95	
POWER PACK Save $23.70 ($83.65 Value)		59.95	
SUPER POWER PACK Save $29.65 ($109.60 Value)		79.95	

Description of all COMBOS on other side. All prices subject to change.

Add for Shipping & Handling
< $25 add $7
$25 - $75 add $9
> $75 add $11

Prices in U.S. $. Canadians add $5 extra for customs handling.

Subtotal	
Shipping & Handling	
TX Residents add 7% Sales Tax	
TOTAL	

☐ **Check or M.O.** (Make payable to YELLO DYNO)

☐ **VISA**   ☐ **MasterCard**   ☐ **DISCOVER NOVUS**   ☐ **AMERICAN EXPRESS**

Enter Credit Card Number (No Dashes)

Expiration

Month   Year

Signature

✍

ORDER TOLL FREE AT 888-954-KIDS
Mail orders to:
Yello Dyno • 203 Barsana Avenue • Austin, TX 78737

ORDER ONLINE AT WWW.YELLODYNO.COM

SAVINGS ON COMBOS

Big savings on powerful combinations for child safety education.

Yello Dyno's **STARTER KIT**	*Raising Safe Kids in an Unsafe World* *Can't Fool Me!* CD *The Fun Way to Safe Kids* (Song & Activity Book) FREE GIFT with Combo - 6 Heroes ($9.95 Value)	**$39.95** A $53.80 Value *Save $13.85*
Yello Dyno's **POWER PACK**	*Raising Safe Kids in an Unsafe World* *Can't Fool Me!* CD *The Fun Way to Safe Kids* (Song & Activity Book) *Safety Rules!* Poster *Can't Fool Me!* Video (Ages 4-8) 3 Special Reports (1, 2 & 3 in Print Version) FREE GIFT with Combo - 6 Heroes ($9.95 Value)	**$59.95** A $83.65 Value *Save $23.70*
Yello Dyno's **SUPER POWER PACK**	*Raising Safe Kids in an Unsafe World* *Can't Fool Me!* CD *The Fun Way to Safe Kids* (Song & Activity Book) *Safety Rules!* Poster *Can't Fool Me!* Video (Ages 4-8) *Tricky People!* Video (with Parent Guide • Ages 9-12) 6 Special Reports (1-6 in Print Version) FREE GIFT with Combo - 6 Heroes ($9.95 Value)	**$79.95** A $109.60 Value *Save $29.65*

SPECIAL REPORTS OFFERED IN ABOVE COMBOS

1 - *The 11 Methods and Styles of Seduction Used by Child Abductors*
2 - *Seven Secrets from the Pros on Keeping Your Child Safe*
3 - *Consumer Report on Children's Personal Safety Products*
4 - *Recognizing the Secret Language of Child Predators*
5 - *Yello Dyno's Guide to Internet Safety*
6 - *Yello Dyno's Guide to Protecting Your Child from Violent Kids*

Non-Fearful • Musically-Driven • Award-Winning

Give the gift that cares
when you're not there.

Order Form Other Side

To Order Call Toll Free!
888-954-KIDS

Complete description of products & curricula online.

ORDER ONLINE AT WWW.YELLODYNO.COM

ANTI-VICTIMIZATION
YELLO DYNO PRO
CURRICULA

For well over a decade, Yello Dyno's entertainment-driven programs have been offered in thousands of North American schools to help educate, empower and protect more than two million children. The new professional Anti-Victimization Curricula are an important solution to the dangers of modern childhood. Age appropriate, they incorporate music, videos and scripts to minimize teacher preparation time and insure maximum success. Topics taught include protecting children from abuse (physical and emotional), sexual abuse, abduction, bullies, internet stalking, date rape, violent kids and school violence. Yello Dyno's non-fearful, musically-based approach to these difficult subjects has made teaching easy and fun for students and teachers alike.

(Inquire about our Spanish Programs.)

- **Safety Party!** (PreK-1)
- **Yello Dyno Sez!** (PreK-3)
- **Can't Fool Me!** (2-4)
- **Tricky People!** (5-6)
- **Internet Safety** (5-6)

EDUCATOR WORKSHOP
- **Yello Dyno Pro Staff Development**

PARENT WORKSHOP
- **Raising Safe Kids in an Unsafe World**

Complete Description of Curricula and Ordering Online

CURRICULA TESTIMONIALS

"As the Director of Special Services and grant writer I have chosen to work with Yello Dyno to deliver our elementary school Child Abduction and Safety portion of our Health Curriculum following the New York State Standards. My expereince is that the instructional work is superb. The lessons delivered to the children were both relevant and exciting. The children gained a better understanding of how to protect themselves. I felt the children were comfortable with the material and when they left the assembly, many were singing the Yello Dyno songs. Many of the teachers have implemented the Yello Dyno Curriculum with easy-to-use lessons and musical CD into their classroom programs. If you have the opportunity to use their services, I would highly recommend them."

> – Jack P. Weisenborn
> Grant Writer and NY State Certified S.A.V.E. Trainer
> Grand Island, NY

"I am happy to recommend Yello Dyno materials to anyone who is doing Prevention Education in a classroom setting. We have successfully adapted the materials for short presentations that educate children on who Tricky People are and what they can do to keep themselves safe. We have given over 120 presentations reaching 1500 students. What we have found is that this material is visually appealing to children, and they love the music components. These two things, along with the scripts, aid us in keeping their attention, and allow us to present difficult subject matter in a way that the children can easily absorb. The age group of the majority of our audiences has been between 4 and 10, but we have found that children as old as 12 enjoy it as well. I think that what is most gratifying is that upon our follow-up visit so many of the children have retained the information from our first trip."

> – Corey Hale
> Project Sanctuary
> Ukiah, CA

Jan, I received the Yello Dyno music, *Can't Fool Me!*. I have been using it with Pre-Kinder, Kinder and First Grade. The children are wanting to hear it over and over again. The music motivates them to want to pattern their self-made responses on the Yello Dyno album. They dearly love Yello Dyno. He is like a hero for them. Almost on a weekly basis I hear stories from the children telling me how they have used the Safety Rules of Yello Dyno to be safe from Tricky People.

> – Judith Pfeifer
> Gilbert Elementary
> San Antonio, TX

FROM PROFESSIONAL EDUCATORS

. "Most safety and prevention products are uninteresting and dull to children, so when they need them most, they don't remember how to use them. Yello Dyno is 100% on the mark! The curricula are well scripted, wonderfully musical and full of energy - enough to fill any kid's head with all the right stuff - critical knowledge when needed most. Finally! Here's a WINNING program children shouldn't live without."

> – Melody C. Gibson, Executive Director & Cofounder
> OPERATION LOOKOUT/National Center for Missing Youth
> Everett, WA

"Our students' overwhelmingly positive response to the Yello Dyno character and his infectious songs and lyrics that have penetrated our school for the last year have made this program a 'must have' to meet our curricular requirements for this subject matter that in the past has made some teachers uncomfortable presenting. As we prepare for Yello Dyno's return visit, we are inviting you to extend an open invitation to anyone in our area who may be interested in bringing this program to their school so that they may experience personally the excitement and sustaining effect Yello Dyno has with our students."

> – Frank J, Cannata, Principal
> Grand Island Central School District
> Grand Island, NY

"We have used the Yello Dyno Program in Community School District 20 for the past three years and are consistently satisfied with it. Their approach is entertainment driven and completely non-fearful. The easy-to-use materials and concepts, along with the teacher/parent workshops and children's assemblies about child abuse prevention, give us the tools and the knowledge to help our staff educate our students about personal safety as well as reinforce this information for life-long retention. We would highly recommend the Yello Dyno Program to any school who is looking for a proactive plan to protect their children from people meaning them harm."

> – Vincent Grippo, Senior Superintendent
> Community School District 20
> Board of Education, City of New York

"The Yello Dyno Program is one that I believe in and use with my own son. I highly recommend it to any elementary school that is concerned about the safety of its children. Thank you for your help."

> – Dr. Laird P. Warner, Superintendent,
> Rose Tree media School District, Media, PA

About The Author

Jan Wagner is a respected expert on the anti-victimization of children. As creator of the *The Yello Dyno Method*™, Jan has pioneered the non-fearful, musically-driven approach to child safety education. She has also authored many other award-winning educational tools including two ground-breaking videos, *Can't Fool Me!* and *Tricky People!*. Since 1987, Yello Dyno's award-winning products and curricula have helped over 2 million children live safer and happier lives.

Raising Safe Kids has become a parenting classic. This completely updated New Edition additionally contains over 110 pages of new and timely information.

RATE YOUR CHILD'S STREET SMARTS IN **3 MINUTES**

INSTRUCTIONS:

For each of the questions below, rate your child's knowledge and safety skills from 1 to 5. After you are done, add your answers together and place the total in the box at the end of the form.

1 = Very Weak   2 = Weak   3 = Average   4 = Strong   5 = Very Strong

___ Does your child know how to recognize the lures used by Tricky People?

___ Does your child know HOW and WHEN to say "NO!" to an older person?

___ Does your child know HOW and WHEN to "cut the conversation"?

___ Does your child know what to do if someone attempts to take them using a weapon?

___ Does your child know which "strangers" to ask for help if they are lost?

___ Does your child know that an adult asking for directions is usually a sign of danger?

___ Does your child know HOW and WHAT to yell in a dangerous situation?

___ Does your child know to tell you if an older person asks him/her to keep a secret?

___ Does your child know the proper way to ask for help when making a 911 call?

___ Does your child know what to do if confronted by someone with a badge?

_____ **Total**

1 - 25 = High Risk - Homework time!
26 - 40 = Moderate Risk - Surprised?
41 - 50 = Low Risk - Good parenting!

ANSWERS AND ACTION STEPS ARE IN THE BOOK!